BK 822.33 W748
ON THE DESIGN OF SHAKESPEARIAN T
1957
D1274452

ON THE DESIGN OF SHAKESPEARIAN TRAGEDY

UNIVERSITY OF TORONTO DEPARTMENT OF ENGLISH

Studies and Texts, No. 5

ON THE DESIGN OF SHAKESPEARIAN TRAGEDY

UNIVERSITY OF TORONTO PRESS

REPRINTED, 1958
REPRINTED, 1963, IN THE
UNITED STATES OF AMERICA

PREFACE

THE ATTEMPT IN THE PRESENT STUDY of ten of Shakespeare's tragedies has been to see them as parts of an organic whole with certain significant interrelations and dynamic connections representing the movement and rhythm of Shakespeare's tragic vision as well as its form. The triadic scheme employed—"thesis," "antithesis," and "synthesis," the scheme which constitutes the larger divisions of the critical analysis—is offered as a heuristic device for whatever it may be worth on its own merits, and without implying any further reference to the system of Hegel or of any other philosopher than the actual analysis of the plays here considered may afford. It may be that there is yet room for another attempt to consider the major tragedies of Shakespeare as constituting an organic unity, if, as in the present case, a selective simplicity and economy of treatment is aimed at, rather than more extended divagation over the now all but limitless expanse of Shakespearian commentary. Such, at least, must be the apology for the modest limits of the present essay, which has no definitive pretensions. It is, like any other hypothesis, subject to the kind of experimental verification contingent upon the circumstances that the hypothesis should cover an important group of phenomena, that it should offer the simplest explanation of those phenomena, and that it should be contradicted by no known evidence. This verification the friendly reader is invited to make for himself.

This study was begun under the pleasantest auspices during a year's tenancy of a research fellowship at the Henry E. Huntington Library in San Marino, California, and was carried further towards completion with the help of a summer grant from the Committee for Research in the Humanities of the University of Toronto. For these, and many other kinds of assistance from readers of the manuscript, and for the painstaking efforts of the staff of the University of Toronto Press, I am deeply grateful; and for a generous grant from the Humanities Research Council of Canada which has contributed towards publication. My colleagues of the

University of Toronto, Northrop Frye, A. S. P. Woodhouse, and R. S. Knox, have had the kindness to read a draft of this book in the earlier stages of its preparation and have helped me with many valuable suggestions. The editorial criticism of Miss Francess Halpenny has proved of the greatest help in the final stages. For the book's remaining deficiencies, I alone am responsible.

All references to the text of Shakespeare in the present study are to the *Complete Works*, ed. G. L. Kittredge (Boston, Ginn & Co., 1936).

H. S. W.

University College, Toronto

CONTENTS

ON THE DESIGN OF SHAKESPEARIAN TRAGEDY

TO

L. L. W., J. S. W., L. S. W.

INTRODUCTION

IN THE FOLLOWING PAGES, Shakespeare's first tragedy, *Titus Andronicus*, has been excluded from consideration, perhaps arbitrarily, as too specialized in its effect as a tragedy of blood to have much bearing upon the inquiry here proposed. Likewise, it has seemed best to exclude *Richard II* and *Richard III*, which need to be studied in relation to Shakespeare's other plays dealing with English history. We have then a group of ten tragedies, if we include *Troilus and Cressida* in this kind, as the bibliographical evidence of the First Folio indicates that we should.[1]

The point of departure for this attempt to trace a unifying principle in a representative group of Shakespeare's tragedies is the observation that, among the ten tragedies to be considered, four of them—*Romeo and Juliet*, *Hamlet*, *Othello*, *Macbeth*—invoke Christian assumptions; indeed, they can hardly be discussed without some reference to a specifically Christian way of thought. In the remaining six tragedies—*Julius Caesar*, *Coriolanus*, *Troilus and Cressida*, *Timon of Athens*, *Antony and Cleopatra*, *King Lear*—references to a Christian way of thought do not appear. This is an important difference, for it affects decisively the mood and significance of each particular play. If we wish to study this difference closely and in orderly fashion, the commonly accepted chronological arrangement of the plays will not serve.

Probably no great sacrifice is involved in disregarding the chronological order. Though it seems likely that Shakespeare improved his art as he gained more experience (it is suggested, in the next chapter, that in *Romeo and Juliet* he made a serious mistake in method, a mistake which might be attributed to his comparative lack of experience at the time he wrote the play), it is far beyond the ambition of the present study to distinguish the degrees of skill in Shakespeare's later tragedies; and it is hardly to be supposed that his art improved in a regular chronological progression. The whole question of Shakespeare's "improvement" as a writer of tragedy, if it is a question that can be answered at all, is one that cannot be examined here. Rather, it will be assumed that the conceptions and designs of his tragedies were all potentialities of his imagination which particular demands brought to fulfilment at particular times. Shakespeare's versatility and creative power were enormous throughout his dramatic career. At the turn of the sixteenth century, for instance, he seems to have been engaged upon plays as different in form and mood as *Twelfth Night*, *Hamlet*, and *Troilus and Cressida*, within a period of a year or two. It is equally clear that he wrote plays to order and catered to changing theatrical fashions. This was his professional duty, his special and indispensable contribution to the company of the Globe. But he wrote also to please himself. The taste of the audience might determine the kind of play he provided at a particular time, but it never controlled or seriously limited what matters most, the art with which the kind of play—whether history, comedy, or tragedy—is executed. We may conclude that, in general, we should be more concerned with *how* Shakespeare wrote each of his plays than with *when* he wrote them. And it follows that to study a group of plays in an order more convenient for our purposes than the chronological order is a legitimate and sensible procedure.

The purpose here, then, is to group the tragedies so as to facilitate comparisons among them according to a twofold and a threefold division. The twofold division concerns the distinction already referred to—according to the presence or absence of references to a Christian order of things. The threefold division indicates a triadic synthesis issuing from the twofold division. First, it will be well to explain the twofold division in some detail; then, we may turn to the discussion of the triadic synthesis.

The two primary divisions are called, respectively, "the order of faith" and "the order of nature."[2] "The order of faith" signifies that in all four plays of this group a Christian conception of the significance of human actions in this world is an ordering principle of the drama. "The order of nature" signifies that in the plays of this group the governing principle is a conception of the natural order of this world in which man's nature is a part, without overt reference to a divine control of that order or to a system of rewards or punishments after death.

Here it will be appropriate to consider the bearing which Shakespeare's treatment of religious issues in the plays has upon our study of them. This is a very difficult matter. Shakespeare's dramatic medium does not permit him to express personal views, and there is no evidence that he might have wished to do so. There is no real equivalent of the Greek tragic chorus in his plays. Everything that is said—or almost everything; the opening prologue of *Romeo and Julet* is an exception, and there are a few others—is said in and through a dramatic character. As Professor Kittredge has so well remarked, Shakespeare could put himself in anyone else's place and when he had done so he could make that person speak as he would speak if he had been gifted with Shakespeare's power to express.[3] We have no ground, accordingly, for speaking of Shakespeare's opinions or beliefs as expressed in his plays. That is not the issue.

A. C. Bradley states the issue for us precisely:

> In this tragic world [i.e., of Shakespeare], then, where individuals, however great they may be and however decisive their actions may appear, are so evidently not the ultimate power, what is this power? What account can we give of it which will correspond with the imaginative impressions we receive?

After a salutary but rather dismaying warning that anything we may say in answer to this question will probably reflect our personal bias which we "read into" the plays, he proceeds:

> It will be agreed, however, first, that this question must not be answered in "religious" language. For although this or that *dramatis persona* may speak of gods or of God, of evil spirits or of Satan, of heaven and of hell, and although the poet may show us ghosts from another world, these ideas do not materially influence his representation of life, nor are they used to throw light on the mystery of its tragedy. The Elizabethan drama was almost wholly secular; and while Shakespeare was writing he practically confined his view to the world of non-theological observation and thought, so that he represents it substantially in one and the same way whether the period of the story is pre-Christian or Christian. He looked at this "secular" world most intently and seriously; and he painted it,

we cannot but conclude, with entire fidelity, without the wish to enforce an opinion of his own, and, in essentials, without regard to anyone's hopes, fears, or beliefs. His greatness is largely due to this fidelity in a mind of extraordinary power; and if, as a private person, he had a religious faith, his tragic view can hardly have been in contradiction with this faith, but must have been included in it, and supplemented, not abolished, by additional ideas.[4]

Bradley's opinion is always weighty, and we differ from him at our peril; but here his argument does not seem altogether cogent.

That the Elizabethan drama was almost wholly secular may be readily granted. Theatricals were generally suspect and frowned upon throughout the Middle Ages, and, though they gained a popular footing and even the support of the later mediaeval church through their association with a religious or moral purpose in the mystery and morality plays, after the Reformation, especially in England, they maintained their claim to toleration precariously, despite the enemies of the older religion and all its ways, the pulpit censors and puritans who suspected all shows and spectacles as instruments of Satan. The players in the professional theatres needed the protection of powerful nobles and—what counted most of all—the known indulgence of the Queen herself. The practising Elizabethan dramatist—a Marlowe, Greene, or Peele—was often scarcely a cut above the players, save in his own estimation as a university man or through the patronage of some influential person. It would have seemed impudence in such a man to set up as a religious teacher in a meeting-house of Satan like the Curtain or the Rose. The theatre of the Elizabethans was, according to the descriptions thundered from London pulpits and by the tacit admission of a great many of the laity, for the diversion of the ungodly.

This is not to say that it was in any way opposed to the church or its teaching, save very exceptionally, perhaps, in the tentative ironies of Marlowe. The remorseful Greene, with his alternating bouts of wickedness and penitence, is a far better representative of the university wits and of the orthodoxy of playwrights and audience alike. The Elizabethans were accustomed to keep their mirth and their piety in different compartments. The church was the place for religious instruction and worship, and it was the office of the clergy to direct in such matters. The theatre was the place for more worldly indulgence—if one allowed oneself that indulgence.

There can be hardly any question, then, of Shakespeare's regarding himself as a religious teacher in his plays; such a pretension would have been highly improper, perhaps irreverent; and it seems a more than doubtful proceeding to look for religious allegories in his plays, as some have done. Yet Shakespeare's characteristic way of thought was Christian, and this Bradley seems disposed to grant at the end of the passage quoted above; the conclusion seems inescapable that his Christian point of view *does* materially influence his representation of life in some of his plays, though not overtly in all of them. There is an important distinction to be made, among the tragedies, especially, between those plays in which a Christian scheme of things is clearly seen to be relevant and indeed regulative, and those in which such a Christian scheme is not overtly relevant and in which any normative reference to such a scheme is avoided.

When Prince Escalus says, at the end of *Romeo and Juliet*,

> See what a scourge is laid upon your hate,
> That heaven finds means to kill your joys with love!

the reference to "love" is equivocal: it includes both the love of Romeo and Juliet and that greater, over-ruling Love which is divine providence; and the reference further looks forward to the turning of the hatred of the two families to love—all of which is argued more at length in the next chapter. The Prince's speech sets the significance of the whole play in perspective, draws it together into a meaningful pattern, sums it up. Its Christian conception seems intended to control and unify the whole. Likewise, Hamlet's terrible design of sending Claudius's soul to hell is not intelligible apart from a context of Christian thought; and this situation is fundamental to the whole play. As Hamlet exhorts Gertrude for the sake of her soul's salvation in another world, so Othello wakens Desdemona that she may repent before she faces eternal judgment: this is the most terrible irony of *Othello*. And Macbeth bitterly reflects that he has given his "eternal jewel" to "the common enemy of man" to make the seed of Banquo kings. All of these references and situations are fundamental in the plays in which they occur, and all of them have but a single significant context: a context of Christian thought. This Christian point of view profoundly influences the representation of life in these plays: it is of the essence of their purport and effect.

On the other hand, in the tragedies based upon Plutarch's accounts of Julius Caesar, Brutus and Cassius, Antony and Cleopatra, and Coriolanus, it is apparent that Christian references would be inappropriate, that Shakespeare is making some effort of historical imagination in treating these themes, thinking himself back into the *milieu* of thought and belief to which the characters and events belong;[5] at least, he is careful to avoid the absurdity of attributing Christian ideas or sentiments to the characters of the Roman plays—that is, in any significant context[6]—and the author makes no comments of his own. Now, we might conclude that the avoidance of all Christian allusions in these plays is a condition imposed simply by the subject-matter rather than an evidence of Shakespeare's desire to avoid Christian references in some of his tragedies. It is likewise to be observed that in the remaining tragedies—*Troilus and Cressida*, *Timon of Athens*, and *King Lear*—though the sources can hardly be called "historical" in any strict sense, the setting of all three plays is imagined as pre-Christian and any overt Christian references would therefore be out of place.

Yet we may be reluctant to conclude that the avoidance of Christian allusions in these tragedies is simply a condition imposed by the subject-matter. We may prefer to put it another way: among the reasons that led Shakespeare to choose these particular themes for treatment was the fact that he could treat them as tragedy without overt reference to a Christian scheme of things. Two considerations support this view; neither is in itself decisive, but together they indicate a balance of probability: (1) Shakespeare could have chosen themes with settings in Christian times had he wished to extend his consideration of the specifically Christian implications of tragedy beyond the four plays already thus characterized; (2) in *The Winter's Tale*, where the setting is ostensibly pre-Christian, there are Christian references and important Christian implications.[7] The matter of this play is romance, but hardly more so than the matter of *Troilus and Cressida* and *King Lear.* If Shakespeare could, for his own purposes, import Christian references into *The Winter's Tale,* we may infer that he could and would have done the same thing in *King Lear,* had he thought it fitting. He is scrupulous in avoiding Christian references in *King Lear,*[8] even where they could have been used with great dramatic effect for his audience, as in the reconciliation of Lear and Cordelia; and we may conclude that the difference in this respect between *King Lear* and *The Winter's Tale* is that *King Lear* is a tragedy and *The Winter's Tale* is not.

Thus far it has been argued that the arrangement of the ten tragedies here studied in two groups according to the presence or absence of significant Christian references is in agreement with Shakespeare's deliberate purpose. It remains to show the ground for considering (1) that the relationships we can thus perceive are critically important; (2) that Shakespeare achieves his greatest success in the second group.

If we examine the group of four tragedies together—*Romeo and Juliet, Hamlet, Othello, Macbeth*—we may observe reasons for regrouping them in two pairs. The most obvious difference, perhaps, is that the mood of *Romeo and Juliet* and *Hamlet* is less sombre than that of *Othello* and *Macbeth.* Then, too, the role of accident is much more prominent in *Romeo and Juliet* and *Hamlet*: *Romeo and Juliet* is a chain of accidents, and Horatio sums up the action of *Hamlet* as a succession of

> carnal, bloody and unnatural acts;
> Of accidental judgments, casual slaughters;
> Of deaths put on by cunning and forc'd cause;
> And, in the upshot, purposes mistook
> Fall'n on th' inventors' heads.

And in both plays, correspondingly, the directing hand of Providence is plainly discernible: the "greater power than we can contradict"[9] that "shapes our ends."[10] In *Romeo and Juliet,* the agents are wholly unaware of this shaping purpose in the action, until the Prince points it out at last; in *Hamlet,* the protagonist gradually becomes aware of the directing power and submits himself to it. "If your mind dislike anything," says Horatio, just before the duel with Laertes, "obey it. I will forestall their repair hither and say you are not fit." And Hamlet's reply comes decisively:

> Not a whit, we defy augury; there's a special providence in the fall of a sparrow. If it be now, 'tis not to come; if it be not to come, it will be now; if it be not now, yet it will come; the readiness is all. Since no man knows aught of what he leaves, what is it to leave betimes? Let be.

In *Othello* and *Macbeth* there is no significant chain of accidents: the agents are wilful and self-consciously deliberate. Iago plots the downfall of Othello step by step (Othello is the victim of evil, though he shares responsibility for the evil that befalls him); Iago wills the evil, and Othello, in his blindness, with him. Macbeth plans the murder of Duncan, chooses his subsequent course of tyranny; and if the witches influence him, and his wife as well, the witches are in some sort a projection of his own ambitions and his fears, his wife a part of himself. But the essential point is that Macbeth chooses to do wrong knowing that what he does is evil, that it imperils his eternal salvation; so with Iago, whose evil purpose infects Othello. In both these plays, then, we may trace the theme of deliberate wickedness and its consequences. In *Othello*, the protagonist, though greatly at fault himself, is also the victim of an evil power; in *Macbeth*, the protagonist *is* the evil power. The chief actors, whether knowingly or unknowingly, pay a terrible price for the evil that is done. There is a fulfilment of more than human justice in the end. We feel that the wages of sin is death, though we are sorrier for Othello than for Macbeth.

In *Romeo and Juliet* and *Hamlet* we see human beings and human events as subject to Christian providence; in *Othello* and *Macbeth*, to a divine order of justice which is part of the providential order. In each play, the significant relation between the human and the divine is seen through the loss of something which humanity values—the love of Romeo and Juliet, the genius of Hamlet, the nobility of Othello, the courage and imagination of Macbeth. In this way, Shakespeare makes us feel the tragic aspects of a Christian point of view, the different tragic potentialities of a

Christian order of things—for each tragedy deals with a different aspect of that order, and with contrasting emphases. It would seem that Shakespeare is here exploring the tragic quality of human life when we understand it in the light of Christian faith, the faith in divine providence and divine justice.

Now it looks as if Shakespeare with these four plays had all but exhausted the possibilities of tragedy within an overtly Christian frame of reference[11]—unless he wished to repeat himself; and presumably he did not. It may be granted that Shakespearian tragedy produces a sense of some great loss to humanity: there is no need to recapitulate the terms of Bradley's argument.[12] This is the sadness of tragedy, the "tears of things." If there is a reward for human beings in this world or the next, that is no concern of the tragedian; at most, he can but imply this—and *Romeo and Juliet* and *Hamlet* come as near to doing so as tragedy permits, with the reconciliation of the families in the one, and Horatio's

> Goodnight, sweet prince,
> And flights of angels sing thee to thy rest!

in the other. To carry this implication farther would be to achieve comedy, or "tragicomedy," as Shakespeare did indeed in other plays. But in the tragic medium, he was properly concerned only with the tragic effect; there can be no fully "happy" ending for mortals in tragedy proper—and that form, as Shakespeare treated it, is here our only concern.

It was logical, then, that he should turn from the more positive and hopeful aspect of tragedy as seen through the faith in Christian providence that turns all things to good, to the sterner, more uncompromising tragedy of individuals implicit in the Christian scheme of sin and punishment, the Christian faith in divine justice. But there is another and different realm of tragic experience, the realm of purely human events, of what happens in this world without overt reference to a supernatural ordering principle—what the Elizabethans would call "the order of nature" as distinct from the order of Christian faith.[13] And this realm offered Shakespeare a richer, fuller range of tragic effects than he could achieve within a specifically Christian context while still maintaining the effect proper to tragedy—unless, conceivably, he had chosen to write a tragedy on a specifically religious theme; but this he did not do. The Christian view, as Shakespeare represents it in the tragedies of the "order of faith," affords no *tragic reconciliation* but rather yields, if carried to its conclusion, a resolution of tragedy into comedy. According to the Christian idea of providence, all life, all human experience, ultimately turns to good; it is part of the "Divine Comedy"; and what we call "tragedy" is but a partial and imperfectly comprehended stage or aspect of the divine plan or harmony or whole. Unquestionably, Shakespeare was mindful of this consideration and devoted his major, and, for the most part, his later efforts in tragedy to the more strictly tragic realm of the "natural" order.

The expression "tragic reconciliation" as it has here been used requires definition; but it will be convenient to proceed with the next point before returning to it. If we follow the clue of moods in the remaining plays, it is apparent that *Julius Caesar* and *Coriolanus* have in common certain positive values. Brutus and Coriolanus are great and admirable men, and although both plays have a pervasive irony, their catastrophes are not harrowing; they are meditative studies of the tragic inadequacy of human nobility; they interest and satisfy without disturbing us; they leave us in a serene mood of contemplation. The contrast offered by *Troilus and Cressida* and *Timon of Athens* is indeed violent. Here everything is bitter, negative, passionately denunciatory of human vileness—though there are significant differences between the two modes of invective which we need not now pause to examine. The contrasting "movement" between the two groups, so to designate it, is plainly marked and affords an analogy with the contrasting movements already distinguished under the "order of faith." But no one of the four plays mentioned thus far—*Julius Caesar, Coriolanus, Troilus and Cressida, Timon*—is comprehensive in its tragic scope; no one of them is a very great tragedy; they are all extremely interesting in different ways, but the effects they leave with us are the effects of something stated from only one tragic point of view, a one-sided experience of the tragic pathos, though it is concentrated, even violent, in *Troilus and Cressida* and *Timon of Athens*.

Few, perhaps, would deny that *Antony and Cleopatra* and *King Lear* are the two most comprehensive of Shakespeare's tragedies. Here is all of human life that matters, if we view it tragically: the high political destiny of empires and the love of man and woman; the whole world as the setting of this love; the luxury and mystery of the East pitted against the disciplined power of the West; the story of a great commander and a great queen—in *Lear*, the duty of children to parents; the sense of universal nature's outrage at the ingratitude of Goneril and Regan in the setting of the storm, and the calm that follows with the love of Cordelia for her father; the tragic sacrifice of that love; and the parallel story of Gloucester and his two sons to make the theme still further comprehensive. It is no paradox to say that these two plays comprehend and reconcile the tragic significances of the others. There is all the fury and invective of *Timon of Athens* in *King Lear*, and more; and yet there is also the representation of the devotion of children to parents, far more movingly depicted in *King Lear* than in *Coriolanus*. The cause of the state is represented on a larger canvas in *Antony and Cleopatra* than in *Julius Caesar*; and the love of man and woman, so bitterly vilified and exposed as base in *Troilus and Cressida*, in *Antony and Cleopatra* is vindicated, ennobled, rendered beautiful. That is what is here meant by "tragic reconciliation": the loss is inherent in the story and inevitable, but we are left with the sense that human life has been ennobled in and through the tragic experience. The greatest tragedy pays the highest tribute to the human spirit; *Antony and Cleopatra* and *King Lear* represent Shakespeare's greatest achievements in tragedy.

Technically, likewise, these two tragedies, written towards the end of Shakespeare's practice in this kind, comprehend the full range of the means he used to achieve a tragic effect. *Antony and Cleopatra* interprets a sequence of historical events with close fidelity to its Plutarchan source, presents to us what we may take to be the dramatist's imaginative conception of what the historical persons involved in the action were actually like. The principals of the action become for us indeed much more than dramatic projections of actual persons; they become poetic symbols of earthly love, far grander than either one may seem if regarded simply as an individual, through the tragic pattern of their love which the dramatist builds for us. Yet the Antony and Cleopatra of the play create a remarkable impression of history revivified and enacted before our eyes, of actual people and actual events, remote from us in time yet essentially contemporaneous, and, but for the heroic roles of the participants in some of the greatest events of human history, man and woman as they are found in every time and place, loving and fighting and suffering.

Technically, *King Lear* is at the other pole of Shakespeare's dramatic and poetic virtuosity. Here, the actual is obscured or disregarded in the overwhelming effect of the poetic symbols the play projects—in the action, in the characters, above all in the sweeping grandeur of the lines. The story of Lear and his three daughters, and Gloucester with his two sons, has nothing of historical actuality, of the *tranche de vie*; it is a symbolic projection of poetic truth, of what is universal in human experience and thus transcends the particulars of everyday reality. The art with which this effect is achieved is boldly arbitrary, much less careful of concealment than the art of *Antony and Cleopatra*. Yet the effect of *King Lear* is even grander than that of the historical tragedy, with an awe-inspiring grandeur that warrants the technique, that exists and imposes itself through the technique rather than in spite of it. It is the consummate wedding of drama and poetry, the crown of Shakespeare's achievement in tragedy.

To describe succinctly the movements and the interrelations among the various plays that we have been discussing, the terms of the Hegelian triad—thesis, antithesis, synthesis—have seemed useful. These terms are sufficiently general and devoid of moral or emotional connotations to indicate the rhythmic patterns of Shakespearian tragedy here described without begging too many questions. They suggest, too, that the mood, the thought and movement here called "thesis," in some way beget the movement of thought and mood called "antithesis," that *Othello* and *Macbeth* "grow out of" Shakespeare's experience in writing *Romeo and Juliet* and *Hamlet*; that the mood and thought of *Julius Caesar* and *Coriolanus* provoke the mood and thought of *Troilus and Cressida* and *Timon of Athens*; or it may work the other way; or indeed the movement may be seen in still more complicated fashion as playing back and forth between the two divisions of the plays we have considered. But it is unnecessary to complicate unduly our study of these cross-currents. It would be impractical, for the present purposes, at least, to try to study the interrelations of four plays at once; two at a time are enough. My chief concern has been to show that the two movements called "thesis" and "antithesis" balance each other without achieving a union or reconcilement of opposites. That reconcilement is achieved only in the last movement, called "synthesis," where the tragic implications of all the preceding tragedies here examined are comprehended and rendered into a mighty harmony—a harmony, that is, which is strictly tragic, concerned with the things of this world, with the natural order of man in which there is the mystery of human wickedness and suffering, and the equal mystery of human magnanimity and love.

THE ORDER OF FAITH

THESIS: *ROMEO AND JULIET* AND *HAMLET*

1. *Romeo and Juliet*

THE TRAGIC CONCEPTION of *Romeo and Juliet* is simply stated for us in the opening sonnet-prologue.[1] By thus announcing his theme and describing the central action, Shakespeare prepares us for the method he will follow throughout the play. We are to watch a sequence of events as they move towards the catastrophe in the full knowledge that they are tragic, that the tragic culmination is somehow inevitable. The tragic effect is to be one of anticipation and its realization. The Greek tragedians, and their imitator Seneca whom Shakespeare knew better, could count on their audiences' familiarity with the story of the play. Shakespeare uses his opening prologue in *Romeo and Juliet* to establish the same condition.

The action concerns not simply two lovers but two families.[2] An ancient feud breaks forth anew, involving in its course two lovers whose destiny it is to be sacrificed to the healing of their families' strife, "which, but their children's end, naught could remove." The pathos is that the lovers' sacrifice is inescapable; their love is "death-mark'd"; they are "star-cross'd," fated to die in the fifth act. But the tragic outcome is not quite unrelieved. There is to be a kind of reconciliation at the end, though we are not to expect a "happy" ending. Thus carefully are we prepared to understand and anticipate the ensuing action.

This method of foreshadowing the outcome is carried through the play, in the premonitions and misgivings of the two lovers. "I dreamt a dream tonight," says Romeo, as he goes with Benvolio and Mercutio towards the Capulet party. Mercutio at once takes him up, rallies him, makes his melancholy remark the occasion of his elaborate fancy of Queen Mab. Yet as Benvolio tries to hurry them on: "Supper is done, and we shall come too late!" Romeo reflects,

> I fear, too early; for my mind misgives
> Some consequence, yet hanging in the stars,
> Shall bitterly begin his fearful date
> With this night's revels and expire the term
> Of a despised life, clos'd in my breast,
> By some vile forfeit of untimely death.
> But he that hath the steerage of my course
> Direct my sail! On, lusty gentlemen!

As we are later to realize, Romeo's foreboding is all too well justified. Ere another day passes, Romeo will have loved another maiden than the lady Rosaline who now has all his thoughts; he will have married Juliet, anticipating only happiness; but Mercutio will be slain by Tybalt, Tybalt slain by Romeo, Romeo banished from Verona; and the lives of Romeo and Juliet will be eventually sacrificed.

Again, as Juliet looks down upon Romeo at their parting in the second balcony scene, she says:

> O God, I have an ill-divining soul!
> Methinks I see thee, now thou art below,
> As one dead in the bottom of a tomb.
> Either my eyesight fails, or thou look'st pale.

Romeo comforts her, dismissing her fear. In his own second dream, recounted in the opening of Act V:

> I dreamt my lady came and found me dead
> (Strange dream that gives a dead man leave to think!) . . .;

ironically, he here takes the dream as a good omen: for Juliet came,

> And breath'd such life with kisses in my lips
> That I reviv'd and was an emperor;

but in the tomb of the Capulets, Juliet kisses Romeo's lips and he does not awake.

Finally, Juliet pleads with her mother, after her father's fierce ultimatum that she marry Paris:

> O sweet my mother, cast me not away!
> Delay this marriage for a month, a week;
> Or if you do not, make the bridal bed
> In that dim monument where Tybalt lies.

And this last is what actually happens.

These ironic foreshadowings and their fulfilment bear out the sombre emphasis of the opening prologue:

> From forth the *fatal* loins of these two foes
> A pair of *star-cross'd* lovers take their life . . .

and this note of the fatality of it all similarly echoes through the play—Romeo's "consequence, yet hanging in the stars" and his bitter cry, after he has slain Tybalt:

> O, I am fortune's fool!;

Juliet's piteous protest, when she thinks Romeo dead: "Can heaven be so envious?" and her appeal to Fortune after Romeo leaves for Mantua:

> O Fortune, Fortune! all men call thee fickle.
> If thou art fickle, what dost thou with him
> That is renowm'd for faith? Be fickle, Fortune,
> For then I hope thou wilt not keep him long
> But send him back;

then her agonized farewell before she drinks Friar Laurence's potion:

> Farewell, God knows when we shall meet again . . . ;

Friar Laurence's own prophetic warning to the parents, sorrowing for the supposed death of Juliet:

> The heavens do low'r upon you for some ill;
> Move them no more by crossing their high will;

Romeo's resolute

> Then I defy you, stars!

when he learns of Juliet's burial in the Capulet tomb, and his final

> O here
> Will I set up my everlasting rest
> And shake the yoke of inauspicious stars
> From this world-wearied flesh;

Friar Laurence's solemn assurance to Juliet,

> A greater power than we can contradict
> Hath thwarted our intents;

and the Prince's final word:

> Capulet, Montague,
> See what a scourge is laid upon your hate,
> That heaven finds means to kill your joys with love!
> And I, for winking at your discords too,
> Have lost a brace of kinsmen.

All of these echoes and foreshadowings emphasize and re-emphasize a single theme, a single conception: the seemingly inscrutable necessity of the whole action, a necessity imposed by some power greater than men. Romeo and Juliet may cry out against Fortune and the inauspicious stars; the prologue, indeed, prepares us for their cry; but we all know that to cry out upon Fortune or the stars or Fate explains nothing: it is simply a way of naming what we do not understand. There is more to it than this. But let us look first at the way the play is built.

Structurally, the action unfolds in a schematic progression that steadily enforces the same conception. The admirable expository opening centres our attention upon the strife of the two houses. It begins with the servants, is aggravated by the intervention of Tybalt, brings the heads of both families upon the scene breathing impotent vindictiveness, and then the Prince of Verona enters with his stern reproof:

> Three civil brawls, bred of an airy word
> By thee, old Capulet, and Montague,
> Have thrice disturb'd the quiet of our streets
> And made Verona's ancient citizens
> Cast by their grave beseeming ornaments
> To wield old partisans, in hands as old,
> Cank'red with peace, to part your cank'red hate.
> If ever you disturb our streets again,
> Your lives shall pay the forfeit of the peace.

After his departure, the pacific Benvolio recapitulates and prepares us for the entrance of the lovesick Romeo, whose absence from the opening quarrel is not without significance: the family feud is none of his making; his thoughts are all for the fair but indifferent Rosaline.

The ensuing exposition shows us Romeo's change of heart as he falls genuinely in love with Juliet at the Capulets', and their lyrical encounter in the first balcony scene; parallel with this, though but lightly stressed, is the tentative acceptance by old Capulet of the County Paris as his daughter's suitor. The action approaches its crisis with the secret marriage of Romeo and Juliet at Friar Laurence's cell, and hard upon this the second quarrel of the two houses which precipitates the lovers' ruin. The turning point of the action (III, i) carefully parallels the opening quarrel, with the added irony of Romeo's innocent involvement.[3] The strife is provoked again by Tybalt, to vent his frustrated resentment of Romeo's presence at the Capulet party the night before. Encountering first Mercutio and Benvolio, Tybalt rouses Mercutio's wrath by his swaggering airs but turns from him to challenge Romeo as he enters fresh from his marriage to Juliet. Courteously and with unwonted restraint, Romeo tries to turn Tybalt's insult aside, but this spiritless submission is too much for the uncomprehending Mercutio, who draws upon Tybalt and receives his death wound under Romeo's arm as Romeo tries to part them. Honour leaves Romeo no recourse but to avenge his friend's death. The Prince enters with his train a second time, to pronounce Romeo's banishment in the presence of the assembled families, a sentence mitigated from death in view of Benvolio's second explanation but a sentence which foreshadows the end for Romeo and Juliet.

Romeo's involvement in the quarrel has been precisely the opposite of his intention. He sought only to enjoy his love in peace, and, when challenged, to preserve the peace at all costs; "I thought all for the best," he sadly protests to the wounded Mercutio. Nor can we blame him for turning upon the still furious Tybalt as he re-enters upon the scene of Mercutio's death: to have done otherwise would be to betray the spirit that has made him Juliet's lover, and he acts as much in self-defence as in the necessary vindication of his honour. In the first quarrel of the two houses he had no part; in this one, circumstances effectively take the decision out of his hands and against his will he becomes the instrument of perpetuating the quarrel and the immediate victim of it. He is indeed "fortune's fool," and with him the unwitting Juliet.

The irony of Juliet's rapturous

> Gallop apace, ye fiery-footed steeds, toward
> Phoebus' lodging . . .

as she awaits Romeo's coming, innocent of the turn of events, is re-emphasized for us by the swift reversal of her interview with the Nurse in which Juliet first denounces her lover in violent antitheses keyed to the rhetorical ornateness of the play, then, realizing more fully their position, rings the changes upon "banished" as Romeo does with cumulative lyric intensity in the following scene with Friar Laurence.[4] The complications now swiftly multiply. Juliet's supposed inconsolability for Tybalt's death prompts her father to propose her marriage to the County Paris "a Thursday." The poignant farewell of the lovers (ignorant of old Capulet's purposes for Juliet) from Juliet's balcony with its recurring lyrical reminiscences of their two previous meetings introduces the descending movement of the tragedy. Juliet attempts to resist her father's plans for her marriage to Paris, provoking old Capulet's rage and his ultimatum. The consultation at Friar Laurence's cell prepares the too ingenious expedient of the sleeping potion. The proposed marriage with Paris is hastened forward another day, and Juliet drinks the potion. Following Juliet's supposed death and her placing in the Capulet tomb, circumstance again intervenes. Friar John is prevented from delivering Friar Laurence's letter to Romeo explaining the device of preventing Juliet's marriage to Paris. Romeo's man Balthazar, innocently supposing Juliet dead, *does* bring this news to Romeo in Mantua. Friar Laurence learns that his message has not been delivered; ignorant of Balthazar's role, he arrives at the tomb in time for Juliet's awakening yet too late to anticipate Romeo's duel with Paris or Romeo's taking his own life; and he is frightened from the tomb by the approaching watch before he can anticipate or attempt to prevent Juliet's death.[5]

Upon this catastrophe, Prince Escalus enters, for the third time, to pronounce judgment. The cast has already been assembled twice, for the inception of the action and for its crisis or turning point; and we are not to suppose that this final entrance is added as a more or less dispensable recapitulation of the preceding action, familiar though we are with Friar Laurence's explanations; rather, this is the critical point, the "deciding point" of the tragedy, the point at which the meaning of the whole becomes explicit. The action of the tragedy is not complete until the survivors have been influenced by the events, and the explanations are necessary that we may witness their effect. Only thus is the threefold structural pattern complete.

The play culminates with the reconciliation of the rival houses, as the prologue states. Old Capulet and Montague, confronted by the terrible results of their hatred in the deaths of their children, are at length brought to recognize their responsibility. The Prince sums it up:

> See what a scourge is laid upon your hate,
> That heaven finds means to kill your joys with love;
> And I, for winking at your discords too,
> Have lost a brace of kinsmen; all are punish'd.

The parents are truly penitent, and from this time forth, we are to understand, their hatred was turned to love.

The importance of this ending in Shakespeare's design may be seen by contrasting the culmination of the story in his principal source, Arthur Brooke's poem called *Romeus and Juliet.*[6] In Brooke's version, the various instruments of the outcome—the apothecary who sold Romeo the poison, the Nurse, the Friar—are punished or pardoned, but neither the parents nor the enmity of the two houses is even mentioned in censure. Shakespeare's revision of Brooke's ending and his different emphasis are eloquent of his different conception of the point of the tale.

From another point of view, we may test the importance Shakespeare must have attached to the idea the play is designed to express by observing the very arbitrariness with which he manipulates not merely the plot but the characterization as well, in the interest of working out his total design. The arbitrary insistence upon ironic coincidence in the successive stages of the action is evident. But equally arbitrary is the lack of coherent motivation in Friar Laurence's crucial role. Granted that Friar Laurence is timid and unworldly, and proud of his herbalist's resources, besides; he is still an odd kind of spiritual adviser, without confidence in his authority with the two families, and, we must surely add, without elementary common sense. In real life, any man of sense in Friar Laurence's position would have reflected that the proposed marriage of Juliet with Paris was impossible. Juliet was already married to Romeo. And he would have used this circumstance to force a reconciliation upon the two families—a motive which he professed in marrying the young people in the first place. It is evident that he could count upon the Prince's support in thus seeking to reconcile the feud, and Romeo's pardon, and his own, would easily follow upon the achieving of this worthy end.

This sort of speculation is obviously not relevant to the play as we have it; for such a solution would have given comedy, and Shakespeare was here intent upon tragedy. We must allow the author such arbitrary means; the tragic idea, and the tragic effect, are more important than any mere question of psychological verisimilitude. In observing the arbitrariness of the contrivance, however, we are able to gauge the more accurately the author's central concern. It is with the idea of the play, and the artificial means are an index of the length he is prepared to go in expressing it. Shakespeare neither blames Friar Laurence for his romantic folly, nor allows the common sense solution of the lovers' difficulties to occur to him or to them; and we must not consider that any such point is worth making in our criticism of the play except in so far as our consideration of it may help us the better to understand what the play is about.

If the cumulatively parallel episodes of *Romeo and Juliet* may be called the warp of the play's structural design, the woof is a series of contrasts. It is a drama of youth pitted against age, as Granville Barker has noted.[7] Correspondingly, youth stands for love, and age for continuing hate. Most fundamental of all is the contrast, which is not fully revealed until the end, of accident and design.

Arthur Brooke's *Romeus and Juliet* is a translated version of a familiar folk-tale rather clumsily worked up as a popular romance in Pierre Boaistuau's *Histoires tragiques*; in Brooke's version, as in Boaistuau's, the ironic succession of reversals is attributed casually to "Fortune"—the customary resource of the romancer intent only upon the turns of his plot.[8] Shakespeare more ambitiously undertook to comprehend the relations of chance and destiny in his tragic design.

Carefully, then, the responsibility of the lovers for their catastrophe, in Shakespeare's play, is minimized, as it is not in Brooke's version. The fact of the feud is emphasized at the outset, and the involvement of Romeo and Juliet is not only innocent but against their will. Even in the catastrophe itself, their self-destruction is hardly more than their assent to compelling circumstance. Romeo, it is true, buys poison to unite himself with Juliet in the grave; but before he reaches the tomb, Paris intervenes to seal with his death the one chance of Romeo's pausing in his resolve. Granville Barker oddly remarks that Paris's death "is wanton and serves little purpose."[9] Actually, it is calculated to enhance our sense of the pressure of circumstance upon Romeo. He was distraught before he met Paris at the tomb of Juliet, but not utterly desperate, perhaps. Now, with the blood of Paris upon his hands (again contrary to his will and his anguished protest), he has no remaining ground of hope, no reason to delay his purpose. The death of Paris at Romeo's hands is Shakespeare's own addition to the story and hence an especially significant clue to his conception. It is another irony that prepares us for the most poignant irony of all, as Romeo, in his rapt intentness upon joining Juliet in the grave, fails to interpret aright the signs of returning animation in the sleeping girl:

> O, my love! my wife!
> Death, that hath suck'd the honey of thy breath,
> Hath had no power yet upon thy beauty.
> Thou art not conquer'd. Beauty's ensign yet
> Is crimson in thy lips and in thy cheeks,
> And death's pale flag is not advanced there . . . .

Juliet, as she plunges the knife in her breast, thinks only of joining her lover. Shakespeare, of course, is not excusing their self-destruction; but it is no part of his design to blame them. Their deaths are a *donnée* of the story; the point of it lies elsewhere than in their responsibility.

The blame lies with the families, with the elders. But what of the role of chance, of the fate which so evidently has crossed the love of Romeo and Juliet from beginning to end? They fell in love by accident. Romeo went to the Capulet party expecting to indulge his unrequited passion for Rosaline; Juliet came for the express purpose of seeing and learning to love the County Paris. Amid their later difficulties, if Friar John had been able to deliver Friar Laurence's letter; if Friar Laurence had thought to use Balthazar as his messenger, as he first proposed to do (III, iii, 168–70), or if Balthazar too had been delayed; if Friar Laurence, even, had been a little quicker in getting to Juliet's tomb—if any one of these possibilities had occurred, the outcome might have been very different. We are meant to reflect upon this chain of seeming accidents, for they are prominently displayed.

Here, then, in the play as we have it, is the design—an arbitrary one, to be sure—of "a greater power than we can contradict," that finds means to humble the rival houses "with love." It is a stern conception of Providence, to the working of whose purposes human beings are blind, which fulfils the moral law that the hatred of the elders shall be visited upon the children—"poor sacrifices of our enmity," as Capulet describes them—yet whose power turns hatred in the end to love. The design of the tragedy has been a Christian moral, implicit but still sufficiently manifest to the thoughtful. Herein lies the rationale of the play's structure. The three entrances of the Prince mark the three stages of the action intended to show a chain of seeming accidents issuing in a moral design adumbrated in the sonnet-prologue, implicit from the beginning. The final entrance of the Prince marks the logical climax of a tightly built narrative scheme. This concluding stage of the action reveals, in recapitulation, the significance of the whole design, a design in which the catastrophic deaths of the lovers contribute but a part; the punishment of the elders, and still more their reconciliation, complete the pattern.

But if the logical climax of the play's conception lies in this denouement, the emotional climax comes before, with the deaths of Romeo and Juliet. In this, the world's favourite love story, Shakespeare has endowed his young lovers with all the riches of his earlier lyrical style, with the music of his sonnets which echoes through the play; and he has given them a grace and a purity of motive, in keeping with his larger design, that ensures our complete sympathy from beginning to end. As we follow their story, we cannot help taking sides with them against the elders—against the blind selfishness and perversity of their parents, against the stupid animality, however amusing, of the Nurse, against the absurd ineptitude of Friar Laurence; and as we see them hasten unwittingly to their destruction, we can only pity their youth, their innocence, and their ill luck. They themselves have no awareness of a tragic misstep, of a price justly exacted for human pride or folly, and neither have we: their story is full of pathos, but it has in itself little or nothing of tragic grandeur.

The tragic irony of the story, as Shakespeare tells it, lies in the blindness of the elders to the consequences of their hatred until it is too late, in the reversal brought about by the power greater than they. Yet despite the dramatist's efforts to direct our attention to this larger significance of the action—through the prologue and the structural foreshadowing of his whole scheme; through the chain of unlucky coincidences and arbitrary motives; through the reiteration of the theme of fortune and ill chance and fate—our feelings remain linked with the story of the lovers throughout the play; and audiences and actors alike notoriously feel that with the deaths of Romeo and Juliet the interest of the play is at an end, that the subsequent explanations are prolix and anticlimactic and may well be abridged. This feeling is manifestly contrary to what the dramatist aimed at, but he himself is chiefly responsible for our feeling, in having made his young lovers the centre of our regard.

Thus the play misses its full unity of effect because our sympathies are exhausted before the tragic design is complete. The story of a young and idealistic love thwarted is not enough to make a great tragedy; but Shakespeare, trying to place it within a grander conception, has not been able to achieve a larger unity. There is no failure in any detail of execution, and the conception of the play as a whole is worked out with remarkable regularity and precision. But the love story is not quite harmonious with the larger conception; our sympathies do not culminate in this larger conception; they culminate in pity for the lovers. The awe that we should feel as well is not inherent in their story but is indicated (rather than effected) in what seems to us like an epilogue; it is something explained to us at the end rather than rendered immediately dramatic and compelling as the heart of the design. Shakespeare never made this particular mistake again; and we must surely add that, even though he overreaches himself in this play, he yet enchants us with the beauty of what he holds in his grasp.

Even this judgment, perhaps, is too rigorous. If *Romeo and Juliet* is deficient by the severest standard—by the standard of Shakespeare's own later achievements in tragedy—it yet remains one of the loveliest of all his works. And if we consider it not too closely but as we yield ourselves to its lyrical appeal in the theatre, we may find therein a sufficient argument of its unity. The lines from sonnet CXVI, so aptly cited by Sir Edmund Chambers:

> Love's not Time's fool, though rosy lips and cheeks
> Within his bending sickle's compass come;
> Love alters not with his brief hours and weeks,
> But bears it out even to the edge of doom,[10]

commemorate the most lasting impression the play leaves with us, the impression of its imperishable beauty. We distinguish between the transitory life and fortunes of Romeo and Juliet and their love, which remains ideal, and, in a sense, beyond the reach of fortune or death. It is not their love that is blighted, after all, but their lives. The tragic episode of their lives may thus be seen as participating in the "Divine Comedy"; and, fundamentally, this is what we recognize as we are moved by their story. However artificial *Romeo and Juliet* may appear to be in its dramatic form—and it is, indeed, one of the most "artificial" of the tragedies, as Shakespeare's contemporaries understood the term—it has a basic truthfulness in its representation of human feelings and aspirations, and an integrity of pathos that removes it as far as possible from the sentimentalities of artificial tragedy as it was practised by the generation of Shakespeare's successors, from *The Maid's Tragedy*, let us say, or some of the products of the Restoration stage. Or we may think of it in comparison with the pathos of Dickens, which never loses touch with humanity even when it verges upon the grotesque, or with the pathos of Leopold Bloom, which is scarcely diminished by all the Alexandrian ingenuities of his creator.

2. *Hamlet*

The story of Hamlet, Prince of Denmark, contains the most primitive elements of storytelling. In its simplest outlines, it tells of the relations of father, mother, son; of the mingled rivalry and loyalty of father and son in their relations with the mother, as the son becomes the murdered father's surrogate and avenger against the father's supplanter in the mother's love: the theme so memorably represented in the Greek legends of Orestes and Oedipus. Gilbert Murray has traced the affiliations of the Hamlet story with the story of Orestes;[11] and, more recently, Francis Fergusson has studied some of the relationships of Shakespeare's *Hamlet* with the story of Oedipus as interpreted by Sophocles.[12] From still another point of view, the disciples and admirers of Freud keep reminding us that in *Hamlet* Shakespeare adumbrated some of the principal Freudian doctrines concerning the human family.[13] Such studies as these may suggest to us, at the outset, a cardinal point: Shakespeare's *Hamlet* is not merely the story of one man (What would Hamlet be without the Prince of Denmark? as the venerable *cliché* has it) but rather of the human family and its immemorial relationships. The primitive story reflects that early form of human society in which the family is the most stable social unit, the authority of the father in the family absolute, and the blood-revenge of the son against the father's murderer an inviolable obligation.[14] As Shakespeare found the tale in Belleforest's *Histoires tragiques*, and, probably, in the lost play of a predecessor, perhaps Thomas Kyd, it was still such a primitive tale of revenge. In Shakespeare's treatment of it, the story acquires a subtlety and profundity comparable, rather, with the masterpieces of Greek tragedy, a complexity, too, that makes contemporary psychological interpretations of the play seem like over-simplifications.

If the insight and even something of the technique of Shakespeare's *Hamlet* may recall the tragedies of the Greek theatre, and the story in its general outlines a much earlier time, the pervading atmosphere of Shakespeare's play is quite remote from primitive and pagan antiquity. It is prevailingly Christian in thought and feeling. Structurally, the action develops through the intricate intertwining and paralleling of the fortunes of the Hamlet family and the Polonius family; the further parallel of Prince Fortinbras, in a sense external to the main action involving Hamlet and Laertes, adds another dimension to their story. In the closely woven texture of incident, Claudius is the foil and opposite of the elder Hamlet as represented by his son, and each has his confidant and supporter—Polonius for Claudius and Horatio for Hamlet as proxy for his father. Ophelia is a foil for Gertrude, each in a sense a provocative cause of the developing action. In the comprehensive design, there are three sons seeking to vindicate the claims of a father; and, as Caroline Spurgeon has shown,[15] according to the pervasive symbolism of the imagery—a sickness that must be purged from the state—the revenge of Laertes takes the form of sickness and Hamlet's that of purgation, while Fortinbras in retrieving his father's defeat succeeds to the throne of a Denmark restored to health. The ever-present suggestion of the sickness that afflicts all Denmark, emphasized and reiterated in the imagery of the play, of the human guilt of Claudius and Gertrude, of Polonius and Laertes, of Hamlet's father and of Hamlet himself, of the blind striving and repeated frustration of their human wills and purposes, is countered by the emergent theme of an over-ruling Providence which shapes the action towards a climax none of the actors foresees, a climax in which justice at length prevails, the land is purged of its sickness, the kingdom of Denmark restored to pristine health.

If we read the play in this way—and admittedly there are other ways of reading it—we may regard it as a subtler, richer, grander elaboration of the tragic conception we have just been tracing in *Romeo and Juliet*. Like the latter, *Hamlet* is a story of two families involved in feud; and though *Hamlet* is much more intricate in design, richer in texture and more profound than the earlier play, it too traces the process whereby the human passion of hatred is purified and directed to a beneficent outcome by a power "greater than we can contradict" that shapes our ends. It would be impractical in these pages, according to the scheme of analysis here followed, to try to take any comprehensive or detailed account of the unending variety of interpretations that Shakespeare's *Hamlet* has prompted, and continues to call forth.[16] The following discussion will attempt chiefly to trace in *Hamlet* the themes analogous with those of *Romeo and Juliet*, and to show grounds for regarding these themes as central in the play's design.

Our impression of the complexity of *Hamlet* arises especially from the ambiguous and even contradictory suggestions we receive from what the hero says about himself in soliloquy and the action he takes—or fails to take—as the plot unfolds. The method, in marked contrast with that of *Romeo and Juliet*, is one of suspense and increasing puzzlement for the audience, and of great dramatic effectiveness as it builds its seeming paradoxes and contradictions concerning Hamlet's motives. Is Hamlet a procrastinator, the victim of a consuming melancholy that prevents him from following any consistent or effective plan of action? Or is he rather to be regarded as a heroic revenger of the type of Hieronimo in *The*

Spanish Tragedy, rendered much more complex, intellectual, and sensitive, yet prevented from taking his revenge not by any temperamental weakness but rather because his antagonist is so formidable?

These time-honoured questions assume that the central issue of the play concerns Hamlet's delay in taking his revenge upon Claudius. But the very question: Why does Hamlet delay? may be considered an irrelevance in the critical interpretation of the play, a question for which Shakespeare has not provided an answer. Robert Bridges argued, years ago, that Shakespeare purposely drew the character of Hamlet with an artful ambiguity calculated to elude analysis, on the principle that "Shakespeare sometimes judged conduct to be dramatically more effective when not adequately motived";[17] and Dover Wilson makes essentially the same point. He allows that the impossibility of determining the precise degree of Hamlet's responsibility for his acts may be a matter of what Keats called Shakespeare's "negative capability"—the art whereby the dramatist instinctively leaves conflicts unresolved and unexplained—but he dwells upon the balance perfectly maintained throughout the play between Hamlet's "sore distraction," what he himself calls "his madness" (V, ii, 248), and his anguished and always rational self-questionings:

> Thus the soliloquies, which confirm us in our belief that there is something wrong with him because he tells us it is so, prove to us at the same time that he is fundamentally sane.... Hamlet can draw a line between "himself" and "his madness," a thing impossible for Ophelia, and so we gain the impression that he is usually normal but subject to occasional fits of madness. That Shakespeare never allows us to perceive exactly where the line falls is part of the artful balance.[18]

And he concludes that we were never meant to discover the heart of Hamlet's mystery:

> That it has a heart is an illusion; Hamlet is an illusion. The secret that lies behind it all is not Hamlet's but Shakespeare's: the technical devices he employed to create this supreme illusion of a great and mysterious character, who is at once a procrastinator and a vigorous man of action, at once a miserable failure and the most adorable of heroes. The character of Hamlet, like the appearance of his successive impersonators on the stage, is a matter of "make-up."[19]

The ambiguous suggestions are undeniable, though the consideration of what Hamlet's "madness" consists in is not so important, perhaps, as Dover Wilson supposes; nobody seriously maintains that Hamlet is ever out of his wits. But the doubts raised by Hamlet's ponderings on the effects of his melancholy sharpen the contrast between Hamlet's acts and his own reflections upon them in a way that Dover Wilson has not fully perceived.

> As many critics have noted [he writes], Hamlet often acts, but never upon deliberation. The assumption of the "antic disposition," the decision to test his uncle by means of the play, the murder of Polonius, the substitution of the "changeling" letter, the scene with Laertes in the graveyard, and the killing of the King at the last are all actions taken on the spur of the moment. . . . Everything that Hamlet does, he does too readily by far at the suggestion of others; Fortune sounds the stop. Nor does he greatly care, so long as he can be *doing*.[20]

This way of regarding Hamlet's behaviour overlooks an important difference between Hamlet's conduct before he unmasks Claudius's guilt in the play of "The Mousetrap," and afterwards. The assumption of the "antic disposition" is a plan that Hamlet carries into effect deliberately over a considerable period of time, and its usefulness in concealing his thoughts and purposes from his enemies we may observe in the repeated failures of Polonius, Rosencrantz and Guildenstern, and especially the astute Claudius, to discover what they would like to know about Hamlet's real state of mind or his intentions. We watch Hamlet himself creating this doubtful and misleading impression of his sanity in his encounters with Polonius (II, ii, 173 ff.); his ambiguous concealment of his motives from Rosencrantz and Guildenstern, to whom he hints that his melancholy derives from disappointed ambition (II, ii, 258 ff.); and the uneasy puzzlement of Claudius after he has overheard Hamlet's meeting with Ophelia (III, i, 170 ff.). The playing of "The Murder of Gonzago" is another plan carefully devised by Hamlet and carried through under his direction with complete success. According to Dover Wilson, the play-within-the-play does not go at all as Hamlet had planned;[21] but however much or little of Dover Wilson's ingenious interpretation of this episode we may be willing to allow, on his own showing Hamlet proves more than equal to the players' bungling; he acts with the coolest readiness and effectiveness. In all of this, there is no lack of deliberation or of efficient execution. Hamlet has shown himself capable of taking thought to meet the most difficult of situations, of elaborate, even cunning, planning, and of resolution in carrying out his plans. He is himself an actor of no mean capacity within his own play.

Up to the playing of "The Mousetrap," then, Hamlet has acted to confirm the Ghost's charges against Claudius; his actions have been counter-balanced, however, by the bitter self-reproaches of his second soliloquy and the melancholy brooding of "To be or not to be. . . ." So impressive are the soliloquies that we may neglect to notice how successfully Hamlet has pressed the attack upon his enemies. Yet if we consider the corresponding ill success of Claudius's attempts to fathom Hamlet's motives and intentions, the failure of Rosencrantz and Guildenstern to gain Hamlet's confidence, and the blundering folly of Polonius, we must surely conclude that the initiative rests with Hamlet in the first half of the play.

With the established proof of Claudius's guilt confronting him, however, Hamlet ceases to follow any concerted plan of action. It is as if his course were clear enough and relatively unimpeded up to the point at which he confirms Claudius's guilt; thereafter he loses the initiative. He goes to attend his mother's summons, after the play, and, quite unexpectedly, in passing the King's apartment, comes upon Claudius kneeling in prayer, the victim ready offered for his revenge. His fierce resolve to send Claudius's soul to hell influences Hamlet to hold his hand. In the interview with his mother, Hamlet impulsively stabs at the figure concealed behind the arras, who turns out to be Polonius. Here Hamlet puts himself, seemingly, in Claudius's power. He has revealed to Claudius, in "The Mousetrap," his knowledge of Claudius's guilt, made abundantly clear his own purpose of revenge; and Claudius, his earlier misgivings fully confirmed, now has the perfect pretext for sending Hamlet to England, under the thinly veiled guard of Rosencrantz and Guildenstern, there to be delivered to his death. Yet it is at this point, on the eve of his departure, that Hamlet chooses to make his remarkable declaration,

> I do not know
> Why yet I live to say "This thing's to do,"
> Sith I have cause, and will, and strength, and means
> To do't.

Unless we suppose that Hamlet is here reproaching himself for reserving his revenge upon the kneeling Claudius—and this seems most unlikely—the evidence of the play does not show any other opportunity for Hamlet's revenge from the time Hamlet has conclusively established Claudius's guilt. We can only suppose that Hamlet's self-reproach is here excessive (as it has been all along), that he feels bewildered and frustrated by the course of events, and, in his angry frustration, describes for us his state of mind rather than what manifestly appears to be his present check-mated position.

On the voyage to England, an impulse moves Hamlet to examine the despatches of Rosencrantz and Guildenstern while they are asleep; the chance of his having his father's signet with him enables Hamlet to turn the tables upon Claudius and his time-serving representatives; the unforeseen encounter with the pirates rescues Hamlet from his captors, while Rosencrantz and Guildenstern sail on to the death intended for him in England. This has all been not merely a matter of Hamlet's acting impulsively; it has been a series of lucky accidents from beginning to end. As Hamlet later describes these happenings to Horatio, they seem to him providential:

> Our indiscretion sometime serves us well
> When our deep plots do pall; and that should learn us
> There's a divinity that shapes our ends,
> Rough-hew them how we will—

Certainly, these happenings have been no part of Hamlet's own devising, nor, by the same token, an evasion of responsibility, conscious or unconscious.

When Hamlet returns to Denmark, his mood and attitude have undergone a remarkable change. He seems calmer, more self-possessed, despite the outburst against Laertes at Ophelia's grave. In this spurt of anger, to be sure, we recognize the same fierce impetuosity that has been a part of Hamlet's complex make-up from the beginning; yet the growing ascendancy of the other side of his temperament—the meditative, melancholy, sober constraint—is unmistakably emphasized too from the opening of Act V. It is almost the whole purport of the scene with the grave-diggers—a scene which cannot be sacrificed in a production without reducing the end of the play to melodrama—as it is of Hamlet's later interview with Horatio (V, ii) and of his apology to Laertes just before the duel. Hamlet is now easier in his mind, more master of himself. We hear no more of his self-reproaches. He no longer doubts that he will act to punish Claudius:

> Does it not, thinks't thee, stand me now upon—
> He that hath kill'd my king, and whor'd my mother;
> Popp'd in between th' election and my hopes;
> Thrown out his angle for my proper life,
> And with such cozenage—is't not perfect conscience
> To quit him with this arm? And is't not to be damn'd
> To let this canker of our nature come
> In further evil?

But he has now ceased to think of himself as executing his own plan of revenge, of resolving upon a course of action and following it. Now he simply holds himself in readiness to act as circumstances shall direct: "There's a special providence in the fall of a sparrow. If it be now, 'tis not to come; if it be not to come, it will be now; if it be not now, yet it will come: the readiness is all."

The question of Hamlet's delay in revenging himself upon Claudius is not different, essentially, from the question of Claudius's lack of success in coping with Hamlet. Claudius becomes fully aware of Hamlet's deadly antagonism at the same point at which Hamlet becomes completely convinced of Claudius's guilt; from that point in the action, the conflict between them is mortally joined. Claudius, certainly, acts with resolution and despatch and is quite undeterred by scruples. Yet he is subject, even more than Hamlet, to the ironic reversals of circumstance. He sends Hamlet to certain death in England, as he thinks; and Hamlet returns to Denmark not merely unscathed but freed from his burden of self-questioning, stronger and more menacing than ever. Claudius plots with Laertes the triple means of killing Hamlet in the fencing-match—by the unbated foil and the poisoned drink: Claudius's suggestion; by the anointing of the foil with poison: Laertes' contribution. The poisoned drink intended for Hamlet kills Gertrude and exposes Claudius's treachery; both Laertes' foil and the poison serve for the killing of Claudius; and Hamlet dies, not by Claudius's contrivings but as the result of a scratch from Laertes' poisoned weapon.

Thus we may see, at length, how neither antagonist has really directed or controlled the outcome. It has been, as Horatio at last describes it, a tissue of accidents,

> Of accidental judgments, casual slaughters;
> Of deaths put on by cunning and forc'd cause;
> And, in the upshot, purposes mistook
> Fall'n on th' inventors' heads.

We may leave it at that, if we choose. There is no more explicit commentary upon the outcome, as there is in the final scene of *Romeo and Juliet*. But the same design is apparent in the pattern that events have followed. We have watched the blind striving of both antagonists, of Claudius intent only upon keeping the fruits of his ambition and his lust, of Hamlet intent upon his own revenge. Claudius's intentions remain unchanged throughout the play, despite the reproaches of his conscience; his efforts have but a single aim, his self-preservation. Hamlet, at length, through the agony of his frustration, comes to recognize his true role as the instrument of justice rather than the dispenser of it; and he learns how to accept what comes, quietly, humbly, with manly resolution rather than with the assortment of heroic poses that had earlier beguiled him, and that beguile Laertes, in his callowness, to the end. And finally, all unforeseen both by the unsuspecting plotters and by their intended victim, justice is fulfilled—upon Gertrude, upon Laertes, upon Claudius, upon Hamlet himself; and in the holocaust, motives and merits are weighed and adjusted, not overtly, but definitely nonetheless. The intervention of a stern Providence is foreshadowed ("There's a divinity that shapes our ends . . .") and in the outcome it is too manifest to require a didactic epilogue in the manner of *Romeo and Juliet*. Laertes is penitent; so is Gertrude, as far as we can judge. Hamlet has paid his penalty, fulfilled his task; and flights of angels sing him to his rest. Only Claudius seems lost.

If we read the play in this way, the question of Hamlet's motivation necessarily appears to be a very minor point. Since we do not assume that he could have had his revenge upon Claudius at a time or in a manner of his own choosing, the soliloquies may be taken to reflect not Hamlet's procrastination but his bafflement and melancholy as he labours under a mistaken notion of the role he is destined to fulfil. Ambiguous suggestions are bound to arise from his self-examinations because he himself does not understand how or why he is withheld from his revenge. From

> O, that this too too solid flesh would melt, . . .

to

> How all occasions do inform against me, . . .

the soliloquies are masterly studies of Hamlet's self-absorption, of the half-conscious dramatization of himself by a young man entangled in a serious dilemma, a young man possessed of the highest intellectual gifts, but egotistical and self-centred with the single-minded concentration, the innocent intensity that is possible only in youth, and that, in its customary unawareness of itself, is hardly ever offensive. This is why Hamlet is so hard upon Ophelia; youth is quite merciless in its judgments when labouring under a sense of wrong; it is not Hamlet's attachment to his mother and his sense of outrage at Gertrude's betrayal of his ideal, great though this is, that he vents upon Ophelia; it is his sense of outrage at *Ophelia*, that she could place obedience to her father before her love for him. Hell hath no fury like a young man scorned; and Shakespeare shows us this trait of his hero, among many others, if we will but see it, in the Nunnery scene and elsewhere.

It is a sign of Hamlet's genius that he can be half-ashamed of the glimpses he catches of himself, as he unpacks his heart with words; yet he cannot quite help himself; and we must not expect him, in his agitation, to tell us what really ails him. The soliloquies are dramatic and ironical, with an irony that is implicit and eloquent in the very extravagances of Hamlet's rhetoric. Shakespeare has fully learned, by this time, how to avoid all comment in his tragedies, not simply the overt comment of a prologue but also the comment of a choral character like the Prince in *Romeo and Juliet.* We must puzzle out Hamlet's predicament for ourselves; and we must have our wits about us as we do so, for he is not a simple character. But if we follow him closely through the play, we may see how he grows up; how at length he abandons all his rhetorical posturings, his operatic arias; how he changes from a youth—a youth of genius, but still a youth—into a man.

Hamlet's experience and his state of mind, in his soliloquies, in his feverish plans, his sudden bursts of action, and his reactions of melancholy and frustration and self-loathing, then, may all be seen as psychologically sound and logical; the study of Hamlet is, indeed, as many a reader has remarked, perhaps the subtlest and most careful of all Shakespeare's probing at the roots of human behaviour. Certainly, there is no good ground for suspecting Shakespeare of playing a trick upon us in his representation of Hamlet, of making his motivation deliberately incoherent and inexplicable. To be sure, Shakespeare must have calculated the immense dramatic advantage to be gained by representing Hamlet's uncertainties; but this is itself a profound psychological insight, a legitimate dramatic effect; and the best testimony to its success lies perhaps in the fact that many a commentator has assumed that Hamlet's uncertainty about his predicament reflects Shakespeare's uncertainty, as well as his own.

We may observe the same dramatic irony in Shakespeare's treatment of the Ghost of Hamlet's father. Is the Ghost to be regarded as a Protestant or a Catholic, or as neither? Is the duty of revenge that he enjoins upon his son really an act of justice divinely warranted, in the fulfilling of which the Ghost acts as an intermediary? Or is it rather a purely human vengeance, the perpetrating of which by Hamlet in the spirit intended by the Ghost would imperil Hamlet's eternal salvation? These are questions about the Ghost and his relations with his son which can hardly be said to be settled, though a great deal of learning has gone into the attempt to answer them.

We must, indeed, try to see the Ghost with the eyes of Shakespeare's audience: it was contrived and addressed to their point of view and understanding; but we may deal with it satisfactorily enough, perhaps, without going into fine theological distinctions. Shakespeare was not writing for an audience of theologians but for an assemblage of ordinary Elizabethan folk, for the most part rather more worldly minded than pious, and, though better instructed in the tenets of the Christian faith, but little more concerned with theological refinements than theatre audiences are nowadays.

When the Ghost of Hamlet's father first appears, we do not know what to make of it, any more than do Bernardo, Marcellus, and Horatio. Though we may know well enough, somewhere in our consciousness, that it is only an actor walking up and down in a suit of property armour, the sight is dramatically thrilling; still more so its effect upon the appalled trio to whom the Ghost first appears. Even today, with our sceptical understanding as we sit in a modern theatre in a comfortable plush seat, it can give us gooseflesh, if the business is at all skilfully managed. Our imaginative effort in the theatre will, of course, be the easier for the learned researches of Lily B. Campbell,[22] Dover Wilson,[23] and others; and we have read the contemporary treatise of Lewes Lavater, *Of Ghostes and Spirites Walking by Nyght*.[24] A contemporary spectator would probably not be quite so well informed. For it seems unlikely that ordinary members of Shakespeare's audience came to the theatre primed with such lore, any more than we go to see a film about General Rommel, let us say, primed with a precise knowledge of the details of his campaign in Africa and his subsequent relations with Hitler and the German High Command. We learn about these matters from what we see happening upon the screen. We have a general impression of the events with which the picture deals and no more. We take it on faith that everything did happen as the screen-story represents it; and, if the film is a good one—as it was—we are quite content with the interpretation that the script writers have supplied. We may suppose this to be a fair approximation of the uncritical attitude of a hypothetical theatregoer of Shakespeare's day towards the Ghost in *Hamlet* at the beginning of the play. Let us try, then, to imagine the feelings of a spectator in Shakespeare's theatre, seeing and hearing the play for the first time.

This theatregoer is, shall we say, a Protestant, and believes that ghosts are some *thing* and that they do sometimes appear to people under alarming circumstances. His parents, perhaps, who were brought up in the older faith, believed that a ghost might be the authentic spirit of a departed father; but he has been taught to look upon such beliefs as popish superstition, and he suspects that when people talk of seeing ghosts, either they have been the willing or unwilling victims of an illusion, or, just possibly, they have been beguiled by a demon come from hell. But he has no certainty about any of this; and there is enough of the faith, or superstition, of his fathers in him to give him gooseflesh indeed when the Ghost of Hamlet's father stalks onto the stage even in broad daylight. His further impressions of the Ghost will be guided by what he sees and hears in the play itself.

The crucial point regarding the Ghost, for our spectator, will be the interview of the Ghost with Hamlet (I, v); here, he receives virtually all the data he has to go upon. When the Ghost says,

> My hour is almost come,
> When I to sulph'rous and tormenting flames
> Must render up myself,

the hearer might suspect that he came from hell; and when the Ghost charges Hamlet,

> So art thou to revenge . . .

he knows that the Ghost is enjoining upon his son an act expressly forbidden by Scripture: "Recompense to no man evil for evil. . . . Dearly beloved, avenge not yourselves, but rather give place unto wrath; for it is written, Vengeance is mine, I will repay, saith the Lord" (Rom. 12 : 17, 19; Deut. 32 : 35). But when the Ghost goes on to speak of being

> confined to fast in fires,
> Till the foul crimes done in my days of nature
> Are burnt and *purg'd* away . . .

his words suggest an abode more like the Catholic purgatory.[25] In the Ghost's later references to his sufferings in the mysterious place from whence he comes,

> a tale . . . whose lightest word
> Would harrow up thy soul . . .

the significant point is that he avoids actually describing his torments so that there is no further clue to their provenance. His account of his murder at the hands of Claudius,

> Cut off even in the blossom of my sin,
> Unhous'led, disappointed, unanel'd,
> No reck'ning made, but sent to my account
> With all my imperfections on my head,

sounds as if it came from a Catholic; but his harping upon the "unnaturalness" of his murder (I, v, 25, 28), and, by implication, at least, upon Hamlet's "natural" duty of revenge (I, v, 31-34), and above all, his failure to invoke any religious sanction throughout his charge to Hamlet—all this seems far indeed from Christian sentiment. Finally, when Hamlet in his supercharged excitement plays a fantastic game of "Adam, where art thou?" with the Ghost under the stage (I, v, 148 ff.), neither our imaginary spectator nor we can make anything more of this than a bewildering puzzle. We would gladly think that the Ghost is whatever Hamlet thinks it is, for we are on Hamlet's side. But it becomes increasingly plain that Hamlet cannot make up his mind about the status of the Ghost; and neither can we.

We may conclude that Shakespeare does not wish to make explicit the status of the Ghost (carefully avoids doing so, in fact, by beclouding the issue) further than to suggest (1) that the Ghost functions in a context of Christian significance, coming from a realm of the after-life that Christians believe in, whether hell or purgatory; (2) that the Ghost enjoins upon his son a "duty" which a professing Christian must regard as a grave sin, the sin of personal vengeance forbidden by Scripture;[26] (3) that Hamlet, in his overwrought excitement and for the moment, accepts the obligation imposed by the Ghost without trying to understand what warrant he has for so doing.

Later on, Hamlet will try to understand that warrant, passionately, searchingly. This is an essential part of the play's design and of its perennial fascination: the nightmarish uncertainty of Hamlet's predicament, an uncertainty for which he is hardly to be blamed. It is his very scrupulousness of conscience that makes him uncertain of the apparition he has seen. He loathes his uncle with single-minded intensity and is all but convinced of his guilt; he is completely fearless of him, reckless indeed of consequences, if only he can do his duty and act justly—with piety towards his father's spirit, with justice towards his father's murderer; and he longs to be delivered of his agony of delay through action. Yet the very integrity of his purpose requires him to hold off until he *is* certain of Claudius's guilt. At length, he will conclude, through the test of "The Mousetrap," that the Ghost's accusation was a true one; and he will bitterly accuse himself of that "almost blunted purpose" of which the Ghost reminds him in Gertrude's closet; but through it all, the Ghost's precise status will never be cleared up, and in the end we may notice that Hamlet has practically forgotten that mysterious figure.

If we take it that the revenge the Ghost urges upon Hamlet and that Hamlet tries his best to fulfil is actually a sin that imperils Hamlet's own soul, the irony of the action and its outcome, the unified effect of the whole, is manifest and harmonious in all its parts. We observe the tragic irony of Hamlet's attempts to do wrong from the strongest of merely human motives, and the suffering he inflicts upon himself, and others, as a result; how his very scrupulousness only contributes to his melancholy, and yet is connected in some way, we may think, with the providential grace that prevents him from murdering the kneeling Claudius, while the murderer, who fain would pray for grace, cannot find the grace to pray. Hamlet's purpose, frustrated he knows not how, at last becomes simply a submission of his will to divine ordinance, as his frustration leads him to brood upon the vanity and transitoriness of all things human—Alexander's dust stopping a bunghole of a beer barrel; imperious Caesar plugging a crack to keep the wind out of a hovel—"A man's life's no more than to say 'one.' . . . The readiness is all." Yet in the act of submission he triumphs and frees Denmark from its curse.

The catastrophe of *Hamlet* is clearly Christian in its implications. Denmark has been purged of its rottenness, justice has been done, and the peace that crowns the end represents the purification of the hero's motives through his submission to the will of heaven quite as much as the freeing of the state from guilt. The tragic price that it has cost is not so much in the "waste" that Bradley speaks of[27]—for Hamlet died as nobly as a man could wish; even Laertes and Gertrude were touched to finer issues in their deaths than in their lives—as in the suffering incident upon human wilfulness and human blindness. Claudius is not solely the villain of the piece; he comes very near remorse, in his eloquent attempt to pray; and we gather that he would have been quite content to keep the state of affairs in the opening of the play, at peace with men, governing wisely—for he was able to rule—and succeeded by Hamlet. Gertrude, in her easy-going sensuality and natural affectionateness, knows no disquiet until her son awakens her conscience; and she is without malice, only self-indulgent. Her charm is sufficiently witnessed by Claudius's affection, the Ghost's solicitude for her, and Hamlet's horror at her gentle moral indifference which he had never realized until after the death of his father. She is, or has been, the idol of all three; and we cannot fail to recognize, in Shakespeare's masterly touching in of her character, the sweetness and lovingness of her disposition. It is a wonderful stroke of nature thus to embody for us the fact, which we may easily verify in our own experience, that the most attractive people are sometimes the frailest morally. Polonius suffers more through stupidity and ingenuous pride than anything else; he is a harmless old busybody who would be merely amusing, if also at times a bore, under ordinary circumstances. Laertes is "a very noble youth," but for his ambition to play the heroic revenger and his readiness for treachery as he plays into Claudius's hands in the duel with Hamlet. Hamlet himself, for all his genius, is self-centred and wilful, and the deaths of Polonius, of Rosencrantz and Guildenstern, of Ophelia, are all consequences of his determination for revenge. The needless sacrifice of Ophelia is, perhaps, most poignant of all, as we recognize her utter ignorance of the meaning of the events in which she becomes a victim; for she must have supposed that the terrible calamities of Hamlet's madness and her father's murder at his hands were owing to her having rejected Hamlet, and this thought overwhelms her reason. Her whole world comes toppling upon her, and, so she thinks, she has been the unwitting and unwilling cause of it all.

But no one has acted quite wittingly in this play, not even Claudius, whose will to evil is rather the desperate man's striving to keep what he has got than deliberate malice; he is more like Macbeth than Iago. And we realize increasingly, as the theme develops, the rottenness at the core of the whole society of the play. We see how it afflicts each person of the cast in his or her degree of guilt, and not least Hamlet himself. It is not the worst kind of evil. It is rather the natural and inadvertent evil of everyday experience, issuing from human traits that we recognize, apart from the tragic context, as commonplace—ambition, the passions of the flesh, the self-regarding that goes most often by the innocent-sounding name of self-respect. These are the worst traits of human nature that the play reveals; and it is as if we were given a glimpse, through an apparently accidental contrivance of circumstances, of the swamp of evil desires, of lusts and fears and vanities through which we walk in this world, for the most part carelessly enough. In Claudius, in Gertrude, in Polonius or Laertes, Rosencrantz and Guildenstern, in Ophelia and the elegant Osric, even in Hamlet—though he is, to be sure, exceptional—there, but for the grace of God, go I.

There are countless ways of estimating Hamlet's sickness: the sickness of all Denmark, of human society in every time, is mirrored in it; and we must not shut our eyes to it, however wonderful we may think he is. We may remind ourselves of D. H. Lawrence's disenchanted lines:

> And Hamlet, how boring, how boring to live with,
> So mean and self-conscious, blowing and snoring
> His wonderful speeches, full of other folk's whoring!

Or, if we prefer, we may recall Goethe's judgment:

> A lovely, pure, noble, and most moral nature, without the strength of nerve which forms a hero, sinks beneath a burden it cannot bear and must not cast away.

If either view causes us a shudder of dissent—and Goethe's certainly causes me one—we can hardly deny the grain of truth that each contains: the sickness of Hamlet and of mankind.

Shakespeare's contemporaries would have called this evil "original sin." That is the sickness that afflicts Hamlet's Denmark, that destroys the innocent Ophelia and the guilty Claudius, that includes in its toll Rosencrantz and Guildenstern, Polonius and Laertes, Gertrude and Hamlet's father, and Hamlet himself. The play is built upon the theme of human guilt, of *hybris* and *nemesis*, we might say, except that there is no providence in the theodicy of the ancients. That is precisely the measure of the Christian bias and reference of *Hamlet*, which some commentators would ignore. Without that reference, the play resolves into its primitive elements, another tragedy of blood revenge. *Hamlet*, indeed, contains this theme; but it also transcends it, and that is the token of its profundity.

3. *Romeo and Juliet* and *Hamlet*

It remains to speak in summary of the relations between the two plays which we have been discussing in this chapter. It has already been suggested that the two have marked affiliations of mood, though that of *Hamlet* is darker. Both are plays in which our sympathies are drawn particularly to youth, and to youth suffering tragically through the greater responsibility of the elders—the elder Capulets and Montagues against their children, the children against Friar Laurence and the Nurse; Claudius and Gertrude, the grim Ghost of the elder Hamlet, and Polonius in his stupidity, against the young world of Hamlet,[28] Ophelia, Horatio, Laertes, and Fortinbras. As we remember Romeo and Juliet, Mercutio and Paris, we remember a world full of hope and gaiety, the wit and grace of youth; the catastrophe, for each of them, brings chiefly a deeper sense of their beauty and the pity of their loss, of a brightness that goes out of life with them. In *Hamlet*, the mood is sterner, more agitated, more intense; yet Hamlet is never nobler than when he dies; Laertes' end is not very different in its effect from that of Paris; and Ophelia, though she is no Juliet, and treads upon the verge of insipidity and bathos—she is, after all, her father's daughter—never quite forfeits our sympathy.

The directing and shaping power of Providence is central and paramount in both plays, though there is the difference that in *Romeo and Juliet* the persons of the drama are unaware of this directing power until the end, whereas Hamlet becomes aware of it and accepts its direction. In each play, striving humanity acts blindly and quite unavailingly in the effort to control the course of events, moved by hatred, by lust, or by ambition; and these human passions are purified, or rendered harmless, though at a tragic cost. The ending of each play might evoke as its commentary the closing chorus of *Samson Agonistes*:

> All is best, though oft we doubt,
> What th' unsearchable dispose
> Of highest wisdom brings about,
> And ever best found in the close . . . ;

though it is not Shakespeare's way to provide any such comment himself.

Technically, the two plays are in the most marked contrast, a sufficient indication of Shakespeare's great advance in mastery of his craft between the writing of *Romeo and Juliet* and of *Hamlet*. The method of *Romeo and Juliet* is that of anticipatory irony; from the opening sonnet-prologue to the end, everything is foreshadowed, each development of the action carefully prepared for; the inescapable doom of the tragic victims closes in upon them with increasing ironic emphasis and reiteration enforced by the parallel and balanced development of the plot structure. There is no question of divided motive in the protagonists, or of their power to escape their tragic destiny; and as the tissue of accidents which beset the love of Romeo and Juliet unfolds, there is little suspense about the outcome. We await "the fearful passage of their death-mark'd love" with the anticipation that every suggestion of the play has prepared, and that anticipation is at length fulfilled. In *Hamlet,* there is no prologue, no evident foreshadowing of the tragic pattern of the action; the apparently divided motives of the protagonist puzzle critical ingenuity to interpret, and the turns of the plot reveal an increasing complexity and ambiguity. As we compare the two plays, indeed, we recognize that the formal simplicity of *Romeo and Juliet* is best suited to its lyrical matter of youthful love, just as the ambiguities and suspense of *Hamlet* are best suited to its darker theme of inherited blood-feud, of incest and murder, and of the hero's tormented and divided purposes.

Romeo and Juliet is the more firmly knit of the two in its rigidly unified structure; yet it is a patently arbitrary design, almost archaic in its simple conventional pattern, compared with the later tragedies. *Hamlet* is looser, more discursive, subtler, one might almost say, more digressive and prolix. Corinna is said to have counselled the young Pindar to sow with the hand rather than the whole sack; and the opposite opinion was expressed in Keats's criticism of Shelley and in George Meredith's criticism of Hardy. Some such technical alternatives may have engaged Shakespeare's attention between the writing of *Romeo and Juliet* and *Hamlet.* At any rate, the composite text of *Hamlet,* as we customarily read it, gives the impression of a theme so rich that the artist, in his opulent genius, could hardly bear to have done with it; though the discursive amplitude is more observable in the elaborate exposition than in the study of the central conflict itself. The play is at the opposite pole from *Romeo and Juliet* in this respect.

There is a difference, too, in the symbolic effect of *Hamlet* which the comparison with *Romeo and Juliet* renders more apparent. The Hamlet of the fifth act, after his return to Denmark, as we see him in his great meditation upon mortality by the grave of Ophelia, the Hamlet also of the following interview with Horatio, provides a most impressive emblem of the way in which we may become dimly and wonderingly aware of our human situation as agents in a drama whose unfolding is utterly beyond our direction or our knowing. It is irony within irony—Hamlet's ignorance, and his eventual recognition of that ignorance; it is the irony of Socrates, the deepest irony of all. Nothing of this deeper irony—the irony that pervades the whole of *Hamlet*, but which becomes most manifest in the last act—touches the action or the actors of *Romeo and Juliet*. This is a good measure, if any were needed, of the depth of *Hamlet* in comparison with the smoother, thinner texture of the earlier play.

The two plays, finally, are comparable in that they achieve the same emotional design, though with greatly varying intensity. Neither play leaves us with the impression of human suffering and wickedness utterly unrelieved or unredeemed. The providential resolution that is worked out is tragic but ultimately beneficent. In *Romeo and Juliet,* it is the reconciliation of the two families, though at the cost of the children's lives; in *Hamlet,* it is the purging of the state of Denmark from sickness to health, though at the cost of all the lives we value save those of Horatio and Fortinbras. The loss, in both plays, is tragic; but in both there is also some compensating gain, an upward turn at the end, a quiet and tranquillizing close.

ANTITHESIS: *OTHELLO* AND *MACBETH*

1. *Othello*

WE HAVE SEEN, in the two preceding tragedies, something of the evil in man—the natural and unthinking evil of an inherited hatred in *Romeo and Juliet*; the equally natural evil of selfishness, of lust and ambition, in *Hamlet*. In the pattern which these plays trace, the evil is transcended or obliterated at a cost, and the directing force is seen to come from without; the total action fulfils a design apparently controlled by Providence. But the role of Providence in human affairs is not always evident; if so, there would be little scope for tragedy. What little there might be, *Romeo and Juliet* and *Hamlet* make use of. *Hamlet* is not deeply tragic, and *Romeo and Juliet* even less so. The logic of these plays indeed implies a stage beyond tragedy, a form which is not tragedy but tragi-comedy. The sense of tragedy in human life remains, however, even in the Christian perspective of secular man. The awareness of providential direction is not a matter of understanding but of faith. Somewhat better understood, though still within the realm of faith and subject to providential control in the sense that it is all part of the divine plan, something more terrible to human imagining, is man's will to evil and the conviction of sin; and this is matter for tragedy, indeed. In this direction it was necessary that Shakespeare should turn, if he continued to write tragedies in a context of Christian feeling.

Othello is the saddest of the tragedies, the most painful. Its power is easily demonstrable, wherever the play is well played. We can all sympathize with the young girl's cry to the actor playing Othello, "You fool! Can't you *see* she's innocent!" Othello's blindness, and Iago's wickedness, are almost too much for us to bear. And yet, while we are in the theatre, and after we come away from it, we have no doubt that the intense feelings we have been experiencing are fine, in some way very valuable. What it all signifies, however, is matter for considerable difference of opinion.

Mr. T. S. Eliot has discovered ironic implications in the role of Othello, and more recently it has been argued that *Othello* has no specifically Christian implications.[1] If we are to continue to trace the design of Shakespearian tragedy here suggested, it must be made clear that *Othello* implies a definitely Christian attitude and point of view, that the play, like *Romeo and Juliet* and *Hamlet*, is based upon Christian assumptions. If this design is apparent in the play, the emphasis will not be upon the benevolent role of Christian providence in directing human affairs. The prevailing mood is sterner in Othello than in the earlier tragedies. *Othello* is concerned with the Christian belief in sin and punishment.[2]

Mr. Eliot somewhere reminds us that pure malice is a rare thing. Most of us mean well enough, provided we can get along comfortably. Consistent malice is seldom to be met with in the people we judge to be sane; at most, it is briefly glimpsed as a potentiality in people otherwise no more savage or heartless than ourselves. And yet we can all readily imagine such a being, one who is consistent in malice if in nothing else. How much more readily could the Elizabethans, who believed in the literal embodiment of Satan, and in his power to take possession of men. This is the context in which Iago belongs. Whether Shakespeare asked himself what a man would be like if Satan had taken full possession of him we need not speculate. Such a conception both he and his audience would readily take for granted without needing to formulate it, as we perhaps need to do to remind ourselves that it was once soberly held by people as sane and thoughtful as we are. Coleridge's phrase about Iago—"the motive-hunting of a motiveless malignity"—is a real insight; how else can we regard Iago's self-revelations? His soliloquies are like Hamlet's perplexed self-questionings in this, that neither one gives us a final answer to the questions he raises. Iago begins with his explanation to Roderigo: he resents being passed over for promotion. A little later, he tells us that he suspects Othello with his wife; later still, that he lusts after Desdemona and fears Cassio with his nightcap too. We might almost say that he is puzzled to explain to himself the intensity of his own malice and is continually trying to find excuses for it. And yet "puzzled" is not quite the right word, for through all his explanations runs his delight in the artistry of his plans and deceptions, his immeasurable egotism. After all, his malice *is* inexplicable; Iago himself cannot explain it; that is what makes it terrible; it is accountable to nothing and to no one. It is simply the nature of the man:

> Such men as he be never at heart's ease
> Whiles they behold a greater than themselves;

but there is a pettiness about Iago that never shows in the Cassius of *Julius Caesar*. Iago hates Othello because Othello is the better man, and as he hates Cassio:

> He hath a daily beauty in his life
> That makes me ugly.

With such a man everything is food for his malice. There is no appeasing him. His ego feeds upon the misfortunes he contrives for others, and what he feeds on only makes him hungrier. He is proof against pity and remorse alike, as his last interview with Desdemona and his sullen defiance of his captors at the end only too painfully show us. In short, he is the demi-devil that Othello finally calls him, half a devil and half a man; yet the littleness in each of his components is formidable, spider-like, and appallingly human besides.[3]

The play begins and ends with Iago, and he is the moving force until the catastrophe is reached. Though the action moves in a single line, with none of the intricate interweaving of parallels displayed in *Hamlet*, the emotional pattern has, as it were, two poles of concentration: mounting horror at the insatiable malice of Iago, pity for the suffering helplessness of his victims. These effects are securely attained at the expense of a good deal of arbitrariness in the manipulation of the plot and even inconsistency of character, as E. E. Stoll has most thoroughly demonstrated.[4]

Such considerations as Desdemona's lack of opportunity for the unfaithfulness of which she is accused, or Emilia's failure to put two and two together earlier, do not matter to us, as we are caught up and swept along by the intense interest of Iago's designs, by feelings of sympathy, dismay, and dread, by the irresistible poetic power of the whole.

Still, the play is Othello's story: he is central throughout. It is hard to sympathize with him very much if we consider him dispassionately, if we stop to reflect. He is such a simpleton, so easily hoodwinked, so childishly carried away by passion, so utterly incapable of taking thought. But in the theatre, under the spell of a fine actor—even in reading, under the spell of Shakespeare's poetry, if we let ourselves be carried along by it—we do not feel any of this reluctance. And we should not. It is utterly irrelevant, or worse. If we cannot sympathize with Othello, we might as well miss the play altogether; indeed, we have missed it.

Othello is great by virtue of his suffering. He is great in himself, no doubt, and we see enough of this earlier in the play—his perfect self-command and command over others, epitomized in a single speech: "Keep up your bright swords, for the dew will rust them . . ."; his courteous dignity, the natural, unaffected poetry of the man, displayed so finely in his speech to the Venetian senators; his frank and deep love for Desdemona.

Under the deft ministrations of Iago, we witness a remarkable transformation in him. The man of judgment, the commander "whom passion could not shake," becomes a credulous fool, transported with jealous fury, so infatuated that while he demands evidence of Desdemona's guilt he never sees anything save through Iago's suggestion, so beguiled that he keeps echoing, like a refrain to his folly, "honest, honest Iago." If this were all, it would be merely shocking. But throughout, and equally a part of the man's simplicity, we feel the cry, "But yet the pity of it, Iago! O Iago, the pity of it, Iago!" And when he comes to execute justice upon Desdemona, as he thinks, he has subdued his passion so that he is a compound of explosive tenderness. Utterly convinced of Desdemona's guilt and of the necessity of killing her ("Yet she must die, else she'll betray more men"), he yet loves her:

> This sorrow's heavenly;
> It strikes where it doth love.

He kisses her awake, and wakens her that she may repent and so find mercy in heaven:

> If you bethink yourself of any crime
> Unreconcil'd as yet to heaven and grace,
> Solicit for it straight . . . .
> I will walk by.
> I would not kill thy unprepared spirit.
> No, heaven forfend! I would not kill thy soul.

He pleads with her lack of comprehension: "Confess thee freely of thy sin"; and when Desdemona pleads in return

> And have you mercy too! I never did
> Offend you in my life; never lov'd Cassio
> But with such general warranty of heaven
> As I might love. I never gave him token,

Othello's anger mounts:

> O perjur'd woman! thou dost stone my heart,
> And mak'st me call what I intend to do
> A murther, which I thought a sacrifice.

Her death would be a sacrifice if she repented, a sacrifice that would keep her from further sin, a sacrifice of her life to save her soul. And she obstinately refuses to confess. It will be murder, then. He tries once more to save her. Cassio has confessed, he assures her, and Iago has stopped his mouth. And with Desdemona's tragically ambiguous cry,

> Alas, he is betray'd, and I undone!

he smothers her. When Othello realizes his terrible mistake, he judges himself with the same simple directness that he has judged Desdemona:

> O ill-starr'd wench!
> Pale as thy smock! When we shall meet at compt,
> This look of thine will hurl my soul from heaven,
> And fiends will snatch at it.

Mr. Eliot, in a notable passage, has written of Othello's valediction ("Soft you! a word before you go . . ."):

> What Othello seems to me to be doing in making this speech is *cheering himself up*. He is endeavoring to escape reality, he has ceased to think about Desdemona, and is thinking about himself. Humility is the most difficult of all the virtues to achieve; nothing dies harder than the desire to think well of oneself. Othello succeeds in turning himself into a pathetic figure, by adopting an *aesthetic* rather than a moral attitude, dramatising himself against his environment. He takes in the spectator, but the human motive is primarily to take in himself. I do not believe that any writer has ever exposed this *bovarysme,* the human will to see things as they are not, more clearly than Shakespeare.[5]

This opinion raises a fine critical issue. Othello's speech seems to serve as a concluding comment, like that of Prince Escalus at the end of *Romeo and Juliet,* though it is dramatically integrated in the design of the whole as the Prince of Verona's is not. Some such comment could have been supplied by Cassio (who says, indeed, after Othello has stabbed himself, "This I did fear, but thought he had no weapon; For he was great of heart"—a speech which hardly sounds ironical), or by Lodovico, who also speaks after Othello's death, but only concerning Iago. Clearly, Shakespeare wished to leave the summary and crowning comment to Othello. If his speech is unconsciously ironical, then the whole play must be a tissue of irony, and the irony must extend through the total characterization of Othello. Othello, on this view, is not merely the dupe of Iago; he too is an egotist who deceives himself, and the superfine irony lies in watching one egotist deceive another. But this surely cannot be right. This would be to interpret the mood of *Othello* as we might that of *Julius Caesar* or *Coriolanus,* to see in it a detached contemplation of human vanities and false pretensions.[6] Presumably, Mr. Eliot does not mean anything like this.

A better case can be made for a mixed effect. It may be thought that Shakespeare, with his penetration into human motives and human character, never loses sight of the core of selfishness, of self-regarding that is in all of us, that is one aspect of "original sin"—the putting of oneself before God and one's fellow man, the putting oneself first. In the final scene of *Othello*, the hero, with that utter lack of self-consciousness or self-criticism which is the height of human vanity, strikes a heroic attitude, makes an eloquent plea for himself, at the height of his eloquence stabs himself—and the innocent spectator feels a lump in his throat or dissolves in tears; but Shakespeare, even while he renders Othello eloquent and moving, contemplates with quiet irony the spectacle of human self-deception and secretly smiles.

This is certainly a possible reading of the scene. The trouble is that it weakens the dramatic effect of the play's climax. Most people respond with intense feeling to *Othello*—why should we not, unless *we* feel superior to the hero (not a very humble attitude, surely)—and intense feelings are not likely to mix well with a keen perception of irony; we cannot weep and feel critically detached at one and the same time. Or if we do let ourselves experience this diminished effect at the end and say that the emotional climax of the play comes with Desdemona's death rather than with the death of Othello, we must surely consider that the dramatist has partly missed his aim: for the death of Othello is evidently offered as the culmination of the tragedy.

The implications of Mr. Eliot's comment appear to be either (1) that the treatment of Othello is ironical throughout the whole play, in which case he is a less serious and imposing tragic figure than generations of audiences have taken him to be: for self-deception may be comic or pathetic, but is seldom dignified; or (2) that the final scene of *Othello* is at least a partial failure to achieve a tragic climax: Shakespeare provided Othello with what looks like a crowning moment of tragic dignity in his last speech, but it turns out, on closer inspection, to be mainly an ironic comment on human vanity. Either view seems utterly unsatisfactory.

Let us consider how we might justify our inclination to take Othello at his face value, so to speak, at the end. And it need not be merely an aesthetic consideration but a moral consideration too, as Mr. Eliot properly insists. The important issue is not whether Othello thinks of himself in his final speech. No one takes him for a saint; and it is natural and human for anyone but a saint to think of himself, among other things, in his final moments—Hamlet thinks of himself in his final charge to Horatio, and no one blames him for it; and Othello *does* think of Desdemona, too, of the pearl "richer than all his tribe." The important issue is this: whether what Othello says of himself is just, and whether his suicide is tragically fitting, affecting us with the sense of more than individual dignity, with the sense of some important truth about human nature made clear—for great tragedy requires this as its final note.

For the first point, Othello's justness, quotation should be enough:

> Soft you! a word or two before you go.
> I have done the state some service, and they know't—
> No more of that. I pray you, in your letters,
> When you shall these unlucky deeds relate,
> Speak of me as I am. Nothing extenuate,
> Nor set down aught in malice. Then must you speak
> Of one that lov'd not wisely, but too well;
> Of one not easily jealous, but, being wrought,
> Perplex'd in the extreme; of one whose hand
> (Like the base Indian) threw a pearl away
> Richer than all his tribe; of one whose subdu'd eyes,
> Albeit unused to the melting mood,
> Drop tears as fast as the Arabian trees
> Their med'cinable gum. Set you down this;
> And say besides that in Aleppo once,
> Where a malignant and a turban'd Turk
> Beat a Venetian and traduc'd the state,
> I took by th' throat the circumcised dog
> And smote him—thus.

The second point, which is crucial, is not so easily answered. Perhaps it cannot be answered, only felt. But since it must be answered, let us try putting the matter like this. For every man, even for the strongest, the wisest, the most magnanimous, there is a breaking point. For many of us, this point is reached pitifully soon. We cannot stand to be deprived of something—money, prestige, or simply a woman's regard. We cannot stand the prospect of abject failure, or of disgrace. And when some such misfortune comes upon us, as sooner or later it is apt to come, we either seek support in a strength that is greater than ours, or compensate ourselves by some rationalization and go on living as comfortably as we can, or, a few of us, take our own lives. This is common, and there is nothing particularly tragic about it. But if a man is betrayed into destroying what he loves most, if he ruins himself through his own folly without understanding what he is doing or being able to help himself, and then is forced to look at just what he has done and acknowledge his fault, his misfortune is harder than most. There is nothing necessarily tragic about the misfortune itself, hard though it is. Terrible misfortunes happen to people every day. We read about them in the newspaper, and turn over the page. The tragic quality lies not in the happening alone, but chiefly in the human attitude to it. In Shakespeare's play, everything depends upon Othello's attitude, as Mr. Eliot has said, upon how events affect him and how he subsequently acts. If he tries to blame his misfortune upon someone or something else—and Othello could have put the major blame upon Iago, or upon "fate"—he is pitiful but not tragic. But if he sees his conduct for what it truly is and blames only himself, he is heroically honest, even humble, perhaps. And if he is a man whose heart is truly great, and whose attitude moreover is Christian, he may feel that his sin is so black that no punishment is too great for him. If he is a *thinking* Christian, he may further reflect upon God's mercy, and he may remember that the Almighty has "fix'd his canon 'gainst self-slaughter." But Othello is not Hamlet. He is a man of sudden resolves and vehement feelings, to the very end. He does not reflect; he acts. If, then, he truly feels this overwhelming sense of guilt, in his passionate self-accusation he might take his own life. This would be proof, at least, of his sincerity. And, being a great man, he would do it in a grand manner—not brokenly or hesitantly, but with a grave and impassioned calmness and a military sense of justice: justice upon himself, as he had measured justice to Desdemona. We Christian spectators—for we may try to imagine how Shakespeare's audience might respond to this—will feel that his action is wrong, as Othello's conduct has been wrong almost from the beginning. Othello was wrong to trust Iago, wrong to accuse Desdemona and slay her, wrong to forget God's mercy and take his own life. But he was greatly wrong. And if heaven has compassion upon human limitations, upon human blindness and misguided passion, it may perhaps find some pity for a man honest enough to recognize his own fault and judge it, brave enough to face perdition in punishing it, loving enough to feel—even though he cannot endure it—an agony of remorse such as few of us are called upon to bear.

If we experience this as the final effect of the tragedy, everything that goes before falls into place in relation to it. Othello's earlier obtuseness no longer matters; he typifies for us a rare kind of human greatness. And Iago's machinations matter even less. Iago prepares the catastrophe but he does not participate in it. He is caught at last, and to be punished; but after he has served his purpose, we would rather forget him, as Shakespeare all but allows us to.

Yet while the play is going forward, Iago exercises a powerful fascination. His evil purposes are an important part of the design. Iago admirably symbolizes the negativeness of evil. His is the moving power until the climax is reached; but he does not participate in the positive value of the play's effect in any way, and Shakespeare quite properly allows him to fade from our consideration as that positive value emerges and becomes paramount. We may contrast the interestingly parallel method of *Measure for Measure*, the play upon which Shakespeare is thought to have been engaged about the same time as *Othello* (1604–5). In *Measure for Measure*, the Duke is like a beneficent power working out his designs among the guilty, while Iago is a maleficent power working out his designs among the innocent.[7] But whereas the evil that Iago represents fades from our notice, and Iago himself along with that evil, as we feel the pathos of Desdemona and the tragic grandeur of Othello, in *Measure for Measure*, the Duke, from having been almost like the puppet-master who pulls the strings, in the developing action of the play emerges in the end as the central symbol of the triumph of goodness, the adjudicating and unifying power of the whole design.

One major point in our argument remains to be established. A. C. Bradley has emphasized the role of accident in *Othello*, though he does not consider it in this respect comparable with *Hamlet*, and does not mention *Romeo and Juliet*. According to the present argument, these latter are the two tragedies in which accidents are important, whereas in *Othello* they are not. But let us recall Bradley's statement:

> In reading *Othello* the mind . . . is more bound down to the spectacle of noble beings caught in the toils from which there is no escape; while the prominence of the intrigue diminishes the sense of the dependence of the catastrophe on character, and the part played by accident in this catastrophe accentuates the feeling of fate. . . . In *Othello*, after the temptation has begun, it is incessant and terrible. The skill of Iago was extraordinary, but so was his good fortune. Again and again a chance word from Desdemona, a chance meeting of Othello and Cassio, a question which starts to our lips and which anyone but Othello would have asked, would have destroyed Iago's plot and ended his life. In their stead, Desdemona drops her handkerchief at the moment most favourable to him, Cassio blunders into the presence of Othello only to find him in a swoon, Bianca arrives precisely when she is wanted to complete Othello's deception and incense his anger to fury. All this and much more seems to us quite natural, so potent is the art of the dramatist; but it confounds us with a feeling, such as we experience in the *Oedipus Tyrannus*, that for these star-crossed mortals—both δυσδαίμονες—there is no escape from fate, and even with a feeling, absent from that play, that fate has taken sides with villainy.[8]

We may notice, first, that Bradley here specifies only three accidents, properly so called, in the play: (1) Desdemona drops her handkerchief at the moment which suits Iago; (2) Cassio, coming upon the suspicious Othello, finds him in a swoon; (3) Bianca arrives at just the right moment for Iago. These accidents do not constitute a pattern running through the play—such as there is in *Romeo and Juliet*—but happen so close together as almost to constitute a single event, a single stroke of "the devil's luck" for Iago; and we may prefer to call them coincidences, signifying a deliberate contrivance of the plot at this point. But it cannot be granted that "a chance word from Desdemona, a chance meeting of Othello and Cassio, a question which starts to *our* lips"—none of which occur in the text of the play—constitute "accidents" in the above sense. This is to confuse the events of the play, which are critically relevant, with possible events in real life, which are not. The unintentional ambiguity in Bradley's statement is concealed in the inclusion of both sorts of happening under the designation of "accident."

Against the authentic accidents of the play which Bradley cites, let us recall the circumstances that are not accidents but the result of Iago's careful and deliberate contriving:

1. Brabantio is summoned, in the beginning, to learn of Desdemona's deception of him, and thus to embarrass Othello with his outcry and provide a principal ground of Othello's later distrust of her with his

   > Look to her, Moor, if thou hast eyes to see.
   > She has deceived her father, and may thee.

2. Othello is summoned to learn of Cassio's lapse from his office of trust on the watch, and hence develops, by Iago's skilful prompting, the whole situation of Desdemona's pleas for Cassio's reinstatement and Iago's counter-insinuations that Cassio is Desdemona's lover.

3. Most of the business of the handkerchief. Desdemona drops it by accident and Emilia picks it up and offers it to Iago; but from then on, Iago guides the ensuing events: leaves the handkerchief in Cassio's chamber; uses it as evidence with which to convince Othello; supplies the construction Othello places upon the subsequent history of the handkerchief, which is what really signifies.

Thus we come to perceive that Iago is quite capable of beguiling Othello to construe any circumstance which may occur as confirmation of his suspicions. What matters tragically is not the circumstance but the fact that Iago can make Othello see the circumstance through his eyes, through his suggestion. Othello, in his passion, has no more power of independent judgment regarding the "evidence" Iago offers him than has the victim of a trance in the hands of the hypnotist.[9]

This is not to absolve Othello of responsibility. No such sentimentality could have occurred to Shakespeare and his contemporaries, who never tire of affirming that the human reason can and should control the passions and the will. Rather, what we see is the terrible infectious power of evil, how the deliberate malice of Iago infects Othello, corrupts his reason, renders him "passion's slave," so that without understanding what he is doing he commits a tragic wrong. He is fully responsible for the wrong he does, as he himself most justly recognizes in the end. But the remorse he feels for the wrong he committed destroys him; that is why he is fully tragic.

There is another sense in which we might speak of "accidents" in *Othello*. The plots of *Romeo and Juliet*, *Hamlet*, and *Othello* are all of the dramatist's contriving, and all of them contain "accidents" or, better, "coincidences" in the sense of arbitrary or unexpected turns in the development of the action. There is, however, an essential difference within this group of three: in *Romeo and Juliet* and *Hamlet* no one is able to comprehend or turn to his advantage the developing pattern of events, not Friar Laurence or the young lovers or the parents in their blindness; not Claudius or Polonius, or, least of all, Hamlet; but in *Othello*, Iago—up to the catastrophic turning point—plans most of the events, calculates the motives and responses of his victims, and profits with diabolical cleverness from the chances which do occur and which he makes serve his purposes. Thus the tragic effect of *Othello* turns upon the inevitability inherent in the malice of Iago and the character of Othello which Iago knows so well how to influence.

Othello is a soldier, resolute, prompt to act, frankly trustful of his friends and especially of such an officer as Iago, whose "honesty" and loyalty had, as he thought, been tested again and again. He is a Moor and a foreigner, much older than Desdemona, married, for the first time, to a young and fair Venetian, whose youth might prove fickle, for all he knew—Venice was proverbial for light women, and Desdemona had deceived her father. Othello had been expressly warned against her deviousness; yet, if we were to try to represent the impression we receive of her character, this indirectness, together with her courage, her gentleness, and her purity, would indeed go to constitute her charm. But Othello had not known Desdemona long; he had little knowledge of women in any case; his military life had left scant time for cultivating their society or studying them, before he met Desdemona;

and there was a bitter modesty in the man, who thought it quite possible that, for all his greatness and his romantic past, a young girl like Desdemona might hold him but a passing fancy. Obviously, he was no student of human character, witness his faith in Iago; but principally, he was a man, in the grip of jealousy, subject to uncontrollable passion, passion that blinded him, made him mouth and fall down in a trance, be utterly unlike his normal self. That such a man should become the victim of the malice and demonic artistry of Iago—this is the tragic circumstance of the play. And it is not presented to us as an accident. Iago spends much of his time, in his soliloquies, trying to explain to us how and why it all happened; and if he protests somewhat too much, we have no difficulty in believing in the possibility of his villainy: that is completely persuasive throughout.

In this play especially, as we study it, we are bound to take account of the matter so memorably dealt with by E. E. Stoll, of the interval between the dramatic artifice and the intense emotional effect as of an actuality vicariously experienced which the play achieves for us.[10] We are obliged to consider the artifice as a means of gauging the author's intentions and of thus confirming, if we can, the relevance of what we feel and understand when we read the play or see it acted. The skill and daring with which the dramatic illusion is created and sustained in *Othello* are of great interest in themselves; but it is even more important to make an attempt to determine whether such an effect as Bradley speaks of, "that fate has taken sides with villainy," is an intended part of the design. The evidences of Iago's deliberate purposes and his large measure of success in carrying them out, especially in his skilful manipulation of Othello, seem ample warrant for dismissing the ideas of "chance" or "fate" as significant elements. Everything in the play, indeed, is dramatic convention or artifice; there are grounds enough for considering the whole play, its action and its characters, a plain absurdity, as Thomas Rymer long ago argued, if we care to be literal-minded. But if we accept the artifices as postulates of the play and argue from the illusion they produce, we must not identify the artifices, the dramatic conventions, with the illusion they are intended to create. If we accept as a convention the idea that Othello is incapable of seeing through Iago's deception until it is too late, as Shakespeare apparently intended that we should, we must not then speculate upon the chance of Othello's finding out Iago's deception in time, after all—or consider the role of accident or fate significant in the design of the whole, which is the same thing. Rather, the intention, as established by the way the conventions of the play work, is that we should feel the deliberateness of Iago's malice and its inevitable success because of Othello's blindness.

We may return to the point with which we began: the tragic effect depends especially upon our recognition of the Christian significance of the action. Othello kills Desdemona, as he supposes, to save her soul; and he punishes himself by inviting the damnation which, in his remorse, he judges to be the just penalty of his offence. Throughout, Othello has misjudged the situation, and his last error is the greatest of all. Yet he would forefeit much of our sympathy, he would cease to seem heroic, if, under the circumstances and being the man he is, he acted in any other way. This is the measure of his tragic nobility and his tragic inadequacy; and, in his inadequacy, he typifies the human situation, as the Christian sees it.

It has indeed been suggested that the logic of events in the play and of Othello's relation to them implies Othello's damnation, and that the implication is pressed home with particular power in the imagery.[11] This last amounts to interpreting the suggestions of the imagery as a means of comment by the author—the analogy would be the choruses of Greek tragedy. It is true that the play contains many references to "heaven and hell and devils," as Wilson Knight has pointed out.[12] But Mr. Knight has wisely refrained from drawing the conclusion that Shakespeare means thus to comment upon Othello's ultimate fate. Othello, indeed, tells us that he is damned; he dies, we must understand, in that belief. But it is most evident that in the tragedies following *Romeo and Juliet* Shakespeare avoids anything that might reasonably be construed as an author's comment. There is no "choral" character in *Othello*—Othello himself least of all, Othello who has been so pitifully deceived about himself and others throughout the play—

or in any of the later tragedies. It is not merely that the dramatic art is by its nature impersonal, that his medium prevented Shakespeare from making personal comments or overt moral judgments on the characters and actions of the tragedies. There are plenty of ways, legitimate ways, in which a dramatist may comment overtly enough—Mr. Eliot, in our time, is a notable example. But Shakespeare's preference for self-effacement is proverbial, even in his sonnets, where it is possible to discern the lineaments of the dramatic "I" but not of the author. The effect of the imagery of *Othello* is dramatic, not choral. The imagery heightens the dramatic effect of the characters in action but it does not interpret the action for us. What we have, then, in the case of *Othello*, is this situation: Othello, the dramatic character, tells us he is damned; the play echoes with similar suggestions; but if we infer that Othello is correct in his opinion, the inference is ours, not Shakespeare's. And, if we are given to drawing inferences from Shakespeare's plays (as most of us are, including the present writer), we may prefer to think that Shakespeare avoided any judgment concerning Othello's ultimate fate remembering the text: "Judge not, that ye be not judged."

Yet *Othello* is a play imbued with Christian feeling, not least, perhaps, the feeling of Christian charity, though it is a dark tale of human sin and suffering and blindness. And it does not leave us altogether desolated, but filled with compassion for the tragic error and the tragic penalty of a great man.

2. *Macbeth*

Macbeth is a play in which the poetic atmosphere is very important; so important, indeed, that some recent commentators give the impression that this atmosphere, as created by the imagery of the play, is its determining quality. For those who pay most attention to these powerful atmospheric suggestions, this is doubtless true. Mr. Kenneth Muir, in his introduction to the play—which does not, by the way, interpret it simply from this point of view—aptly describes the cumulative effect of the imagery:

"The contrast between light and darkness [suggested by the imagery] is part of a general antithesis between good and evil, devils and angels, evil and grace, hell and heaven . . . and the disease images of IV, iii and in the last act clearly reflect both the evil which is a disease, and Macbeth himself who *is* the disease from which his country suffers."[13]

But there are many ways of reading a Shakespearian play, and two of them are here in point. The first is the student's way, or the scholar's, in which we read with a set of notes, paying attention to every reference and every detail of the language, every suggestion of the imagery, every nuance of irony, and to the structure, the narrative method, the consistency of characterization, and so on—or as much of this as we can keep in mind in a single concentrated effort. There was once a student who was learning to read Aeschylus in Greek. After he had been studying this author for some time, he asked his teacher one day, in his growing enthusiasm, when he might hope to be able to read Aeschylus without notes; and the answer was, "You will *never* be able to read Aeschylus without notes!"

Now, we may venture to think that this answer was wrong, without boasting of being able to read Aeschylus with or without notes ourselves. There is, at least, a time for reading Shakespeare in this latter way, though when we do so it is better to have read him in the other way as well. For the second way is the next best thing to seeing and hearing the play well acted in the theatre, while the first way has comparatively little to do with that experience. At most, it enhances our enjoyment in the theatre, or contributes to another order of enjoyment than that of the theatre—to the antiquarian's love of curious and universal learning; to the student's interest in stagecraft (as distinct from the theatregoer's response to its effect); and to the love of poetry as read. This last may seem to be the primary concern of most students of Shakespeare's imagery—and it is a legitimate and important concern, but not the only one, and not always the chief one.

Thus we may not feel satisfied that a further comment of Mr. Muir's upon the effect of the imagery in *Macbeth* has put the matter in the right light:

> It is perfectly legitimate to disagree with Moulton who ... argued that Macbeth's soliloquy in I, vii, shows that he was deterred not by moral scruples but by fear of the consequences; for the imagery of the speech shows that Macbeth is haunted by the horror of the deed, and impresses that horror upon the audience.... But if we go further and pretend that this poetic imagery is a proof that Macbeth had a powerful imagination, that he was in fact a poet, we are confusing real life with drama.... Because Shakespeare makes Macbeth talk as only a great poet could talk, we are not to assume that Macbeth is a great poet: he is merely part of a great poem.... What gives satisfaction to the spectator or reader is not the comprehension of experience by Macbeth but the poet revealing experience through the mouth of his hero. Macbeth, by his own actions, has robbed life of meaning. Shakespeare restores meaning to life by showing that Macbeth's nihilism results from his crimes.[14]

We may think that the "confusion" of Macbeth's poetry with Shakespeare's is precisely the effect Shakespeare aimed at in the theatre. As we listen to Macbeth's eloquence, we forget about Shakespeare the poet, we forget that we are listening to a poem, we think only of the figure imaginatively evoked for us and embodied upon the stage:

> Seyton!—I am sick at heart,
> When I behold—Seyton, I say!—This push
> Will cheer me ever or disseat me now.
> I have liv'd long enough. My way of life
> Is fall'n into the sere, the yellow leaf;
> And that which should accompany old age,
> As honour, love, obedience, troops of friends,
> I must not look to have; but, in their stead,
> Curses, not loud but deep, mouth-honour, breath,
> Which the poor heart would fain deny, and dare not.

If this is to confuse drama with real life, it is also the "willing suspension of disbelief that constitutes poetic faith"; it is the *dramatic* spell of the character as he speaks poetically; and, for the poetic and dramatic moment in which the illusion we value persists, we feel that Macbeth is a poetic person and we value *him* for the poetry of his utterance. An undesirable confusion with "real life" would occur if we felt a difficulty in accepting the convention of Macbeth's poetic utterance as dramatically plausible and moving—

because we found it hard to believe that so bad a man could speak such beautiful lines, or for some other equally extravagant reason.[15] But actually, the poetry ministers to the illusion, enhances it, charges it with emotion. We do not distinguish the actor from the dramatic character he portrays—unless the actor is a very poor one—or the character from the poetry he speaks: they are all parts of a single and unified experience or impression; it is this single impression that moves us, whether we see and hear Macbeth on the stage, or with our inner eye and ear as we read.

Macbeth is the story of a great man who was afraid. What he was afraid of is a nice question. If we consider the soliloquy of I, vii which precedes Macbeth's decisive conversation with Lady Macbeth ("If it were done when 'tis done, then 'twere well It were done quickly . . ."), we must surely conclude, with Moulton,[16] that Macbeth is deterred only by the thought of the immediate, earthly consequences. He himself repeatedly emphasizes the difference between judgment in "the life to come" (which he would "jump," i.e., chance) and "judgment *here*." Duncan, he says, has been

> So clear in his great office, that his virtues
> Will plead like angels, trumpet-tongu'd, against
> The deep damnation of his taking off;
> And pity, like a naked new-born babe,
> Striding the blast, or heaven's cherubin, hors'd
> Upon the sightless couriers of the air,
> Shall blow the horrid deed in every eye,
> That tears shall drown the wind.

The "damnation" of the deed he takes for granted and is not dismayed by; it is the pity he sees in every eye and the thought of the immediate and necessary consequences ("Bloody instructions, which, being taught, return to plague th' inventor") that hold him back. Is it not remarkable that a man of Macbeth's imagination never pictures to himself the pains of hell (as Claudio does in *Measure for Measure*), never entertains the thought of seeking forgiveness (as Claudius does in *Hamlet*), if he is indeed most troubled at the prospect of having given his "eternal jewel" to "the common enemy of man"?[17] He pits himself not merely against the threat of hell but also against the enmity of "Fate" (as represented in the prophecies of the Weird Sisters):

> come, Fate, into the list,
> And champion me to th' utterance.

He brags to his wife,

> But let the frame of things disjoint, both the worlds suffer,
> Ere we will eat our meal in fear and sleep
> In the affliction of these terrible dreams
> That shake us nightly.

He is confident enough, even after the commission of the crime, to put his faith in the Senecan maxim, *per scelera semper sceleribus tutum est iter*, "Things bad begun make strong themselves by ill." After he has been shaken by the appearance of the ghost of Banquo, he reflects,

> For mine own good
> All causes must give way. I am in blood
> Stepp'd in so far that, should I wade no more,
> Returning were as tedious as go o'er;

and this is as near as he ever comes to repentance. The dubious Hecate of III, v, whether she speaks for Shakespeare or not, certainly speaks for Macbeth when she prophesies,

> He shall spurn fate, scorn death, and bear
> His hopes 'bove wisdom, grace, and fear.

And yet Macbeth is terribly afraid, throughout the play. He is so frightened when he first recognizes the possibility of his murdering Duncan that the image of it unfixes his hair and makes his seated heart knock against his ribs; so he tells us. After he has talked the matter over with Lady Macbeth and she has heartened him by virtually assuring him that she will murder Duncan herself:

> and you shall put
> This night's great business into my despatch,
> Which shall to all our nights and days to come
> Give solely sovereign sway and masterdom. . . .
> Only look up clear.
> To alter favour ever is to fear.
> Leave all the rest to me;

even after this assurance, the thought of the immediate consequences still paralyses Macbeth's decision.[18] It requires an extraordinary exertion of will and persuasion from Lady Macbeth to strengthen his wavering purpose. Professor Kittredge used to point out to his classes that Lady Macbeth, in urging Macbeth to act, uses the three arguments that every wife, some time or other, uses to every husband: "You promised me you'd do it!" "You'd do it if you loved me!" "If I were a man, I'd do it myself!"[19] But Macbeth's mind is made up by her assurance that they may do it *safely* by fixing the guilt upon Duncan's chamberlains.

Immediately after the murder, Macbeth is unnerved. He appeals blankly to his wife, describing the symbolic accusation he has just overheard:

> M. One cried "God bless us!" and "Amen!" the other,
> As they had seen me with these hangman's hands,
> List'ning their fear. I could not say "Amen!"
> When they did say "God bless us!"
>
> LADY M. Consider it not so deeply.
>
> M. But wherefore could not I pronounce "Amen"?
> I had most need of blessing, and "Amen"
> Stuck in my throat.

Macbeth knows well why he should not say "Amen," why he should scorn to pronounce it, if he could think clearly; but he is unnerved by fear: "I am afraid to think what I have done."

Macbeth has gambled that he could commit a crime against heaven and against man—for he recognizes it as both—and escape any ill consequences. He has been provoked to gamble on the strength of the prophecy of the Weird Sisters, but he hardly relies upon that; he needs to see in addition how he may do the deed safely—as he thinks. Scholars have been much exercised to determine the status of the Weird Sisters;[20] but again theirs seems to be a case like that of the Ghost of Hamlet's father: the ambiguities concerning these creatures are deliberate and meant to enhance our sense of their mystery without determining just what they are. They are something like the Norse fates in Holinshed, a good deal like ordinary English witches, and suggestive, besides, of a projection of Macbeth's ambition and his consequent fears; but it is clear that, whatever they are, they do not control events or decisively influence Macbeth's conduct; they may know about Macbeth's future and delight to mock him with their paltering in a double sense, but Macbeth chooses to act—to kill Duncan, to arrange Banquo's murder, to murder Lady Macduff and her children, and to persist in his other nameless crimes. Macbeth clings to the seeming support of their later prophetic pageant,

> none of woman born
> Shall harm Macbeth,

and

> Macbeth shall never vanquish'd be until
> Great Birnam Wood to high Dunsinane Hill
> Shall come against him,

because he has nothing else to cling to, in the end; we see him abandon his false hopes, one by one—it is perhaps Shakespeare's most impressive emblem of the vanity of human wishes. But even to the end, he relies most of all upon himself; that is his tragedy, and also the measure of his heroic, if desperate, courage. With his last hope gone, he still fiercely challenges Macduff:

> I will not yield,
> To kiss the ground before young Malcolm's feet
> And to be baited with the rabble's curse.
> Though Birnam Wood be come to Dunsinane,
> And thou oppos'd, being of no woman born,
> Yet will I try the last. . . .
> Lay on, Macduff,
> And damn'd be him that first cries 'Hold, enough!'

Macbeth's fear is a complex thing to understand, or for an actor to interpret adequately. It is not the fear that is cowardice, timidity, or cravenness. Macbeth, in one sense, is a very brave man, or perhaps we should say, a very bold one. His fear is partly self-distrust, partly bewilderment; perhaps, though it is always a dangerous thing to do, we should read between the lines and say, as many commentators would, that despite Macbeth's concentration in words on the immediate consequences he does also fear the ultimate consequences of his crime, his soul's damnation. And yet, it does not seem as if Shakespeare meant precisely this. Surely he would have made it plainer, if he had. It is a subtler thing which constitutes the chief fascination that the play exercises upon us—this fear Macbeth feels, a fear not fully defined, for him or for us, a terrible anxiety that is a sense of guilt without becoming (recognizably, at least) a sense of sin. It is not a sense of sin because he refuses to recognize such a category; and, in his stubbornness, his savage defiance, it drives him on to more and more terrible acts. Macbeth is the sort of man who keeps telling himself he is exceptional, that he can do the impossible. He will not recognize or submit to his own fears, his own scruples. He tries to be entirely self-sufficient and will not face the all but overwhelming evidence of his insufficiency. He is a Faust who denies the ultimate source of his fear, of his despair.

It is indeed noteworthy that Shakespeare has so patently avoided any religious suggestions to speak of, in depicting Macbeth's fear—though the Christian implications of Macbeth's attitude are plainly marked. We do not get the impression that Macbeth is a rationalist —a *rara avis* in Shakespeare's milieu, but in any case, Macbeth is too much a poet to be anything so bloodless and phlegmatic—or that he deliberately sets himself to defy God. It is rather that while he recognizes the Christian implications of his behaviour, he is not particularly concerned on this score. No doubt his very indifference in this respect is meant to appear shocking; but it looks as if Shakespeare wished to avoid raising a religious issue in the representation of Macbeth's inner conflict—perhaps because the topic was a dangerous one to present before such an authority as King James, for whose entertainment the play was particularly designed. With his characteristic genius, he made capital of this very circumstance in representing, with what for us today must seem like a prophetic insight, the agony of guilt and bitterness that a man without religion may suffer.

And so Macbeth becomes lonelier and more hopeless:

> And that which should accompany old age,
> As honour, love, obedience, troops of friends,
> I must not look to have . . . .

> Tomorrow, and tomorrow, and tomorrow
> Creeps in this petty pace from day to day
> To the last syllable of recorded time . . . .

This is his tragedy, this utter and complete disenchantment, this dull disgust with life, this disappointment—this, and his continual fear. He does not fear hell, we might say, because he *is* in hell: "Why, this is hell, nor am I out of it"; though his vitality will not quite let him give up. He keeps trying to delude himself with hopes and defiances he knows to be vain, and the result is that he begins "to be aweary of the sun." He is tied to the stake, by his own hands; he knows he is like the bear that will be baited to death by the dogs. Yet he never submits. And this terrible effort of human will, the more terrible in a man of Macbeth's mighty imagination, is in its way heroic.

There seems to be no hope whatever for Macbeth at the end, for "this dead butcher and his fiend-like queen." If we follow the sharply antithetic suggestions of the conflict between the forces of good and evil reflected in the imagery of the play as our leading clue to its interpretation, we shall reduce it to a very simple moral pattern. We might thus describe the prevailing effect of *Macbeth* as choral, with Macbeth as the choregus singing in beautiful tropes the tragic agony of his doom; and the design of the inevitable justice that follows Macbeth and the freeing of the land from tyranny would be most closely analogous with the design of *Richard III,* though rendered with much greater imaginative power.

There is much to support such a reading, in the political overtones of the play, in the lightly but definitely implied references to the directing power of Providence, and in the solemn moral emphasis of the last scene. Mr. Henry N. Paul has shown all the circumstances which point to the preparation of the play for performance before King James and his royal visitor King Christian of Denmark on August 7, 1606.[21] Shakespeare drew not merely from his favourite Holinshed but from Hector Boece and various other sources of Scottish history, from the extensive lore of witchcraft, and especially from King James's own writings and known biases, in the effort to please his royal patron; and the play, thus enriched by the King's own learning, is at once an adroit compliment to the royal wisdom, and, by implication, a kind of "Mirror for Princes" in which James might see and applaud the downfall of tyranny at the hands of his own supposed royal progenitors. In the background there is the suggestion of primary causation in the role of Providence. Lady Macduff, in her bitterness, exclaims,

> But I remember now
> I am in this earthly world, where to do harm
> Is often laudable, to do good sometime
> Accounted dangerous folly.

And Malcolm, as if in answer, says to her husband, in the following scene (IV, iii, 22–24):

> Angels are bright still, though the brightest fell.
> Though all things foul would wear the brows of grace,
> Yet grace must still look so.

Earlier, the Lord who speaks with Lennox describes Macduff's mission to England:

> That by the help of these [i.e., Malcolm and his allies]
> (with Him above
> To ratify the work) we may again
> Give to our tables meat, sleep to our nights,
> Free from our feasts and banquets bloody knives,
> Do faithful homage and receive free honours—
> All which we pine for now.

And Malcolm sounds the same note at the end:

> What needful else
> That calls upon us, by the grace of Grace
> We will perform in measure, time, and place.

In the conclusion, the foulness has at length been cleansed—the sins against justice, the bloodshed, and the tyranny—and in the succeeding order the divine sanction, the "grace of Grace" of which Macbeth had been so careless, is once more paramount in the new ruler's thought and purpose.

And yet Macbeth himself represents the most sympathetic human value in the play, and we surely are not meant simply to sit in judgment upon him: this is the chief difference between the tragedy of *Macbeth* and the melodrama of *Richard III*. Throughout *Macbeth*, we watch the deterioration of a great man; but we never lose the sense of his greatness. As he becomes more desperate, Macbeth acquires something of the savagery of Euripides' Medea, though we cannot feel that he has been wronged. Yet if Macbeth is solely responsible, he himself pays the cost. Our repugnance for his savagery is qualified by the spectacle of his suffering; he himself suffers more than anybody else. In this universal pattern, we may recognize the common burden we share with Macbeth, those of us who pay some part of the price for our sins in this world. Macbeth is not the type of the successful man. He is not like Octavius Caesar in *Antony and Cleopatra*, who never knows any scruple of regret or meets with any check; or like Henry IV, whose remorse never interferes, or conceivably could interfere, with the success of his policy. Macbeth is constantly tormented by scruples—humane scruples rather than religious; there is too much of the milk of human kindness in him to make him thoroughly successful. He is gradually transformed into a monster, after the murder of Duncan; and yet we can still catch glimpses of the different man he might have been—a man greatly loved, a courteous man, born to command:

> Now good digestion wait on appetite,
> And health on both,

he says to his guests, a most genial and characteristically profane grace. He is capable of gentleness and generosity: there is a tender human love between him and his wife, though they are both abandoned to evil; we may recall the relation between Claudius and Gertrude, and Shakespeare's capacity for seeing some goodness even in wicked people. Above all, he is a poetic person, a man of great and imaginative sensitiveness, one of those rare persons we sometimes meet, if we are lucky, whose every word thrills us, who are incapable of dullness or the commoner kinds of stupidity, even though they may be guilty of greater crimes. All this, along with his wickedness, is part of the man we somehow value and feel for. "Most royal sir," says the First Murderer, "Fleance is scap'd"; and Macbeth answers,

Then comes my fit again.

No one will entertain for a moment the possibility that Macbeth might have said: "Then my fit comes again." Shakespeare wrote the perfect version: but, for us, Macbeth speaks it. It is the perfection that conceals art, if you like; but it is an inherent part, an essential part, of the character of Macbeth as we know it, of the imaginative conception we thrill to and are moved by, this perfection of poetic utterance. That such a man should sacrifice all the wealth of his human spirit—his kindness, his love, his very soul—to become a victim to continual fears, a tyrant ruthlessly murdering in the vain attempt to feel safe, finally to be killed like a foul beast of prey—this is terrible, and pitiful, too. Shakespeare has here achieved for us most poignantly the ambivalence of the tragic effect Aristotle described. We see the necessity of Macbeth's destruction; we acquiesce in his punishment unreservedly; and yet we would find whatever excuses for him we can, because we admire the Promethean quality of his courage, because we recognize his conscience as like our own, and because we share his guilt.

3. *Othello* and *Macbeth*

The foregoing analysis has attempted mainly to establish the Christian assumptions that control the thought and mood of *Othello*; no one denies their force in *Macbeth*.[22] In both plays we watch, with increasing dismay, the progress of the hero towards his destruction, in this world, and, as each of them thinks, in the next as well. Othello's story is more painful than Macbeth's, though both of them are grim enough; but the suffering of Othello and Desdemona seems the less supportable because they are chiefly the victims of evil, whereas Macbeth and Lady Macbeth choose their lot and invite the consequences they suffer; nor is there any vision of peace at the end of *Othello*, as Bradley has noted,[23] whereas in *Macbeth* the land is restored to health and "the time is free."

There is, indeed, more than one kind of parallelism observable among the four plays we have thus far considered. In *Romeo and Juliet* and *Othello*, the protagonists suffer unwittingly—Romeo and Juliet are sacrificed in their families' quarrel; Desdemona and Othello suffer largely through the malice of Iago—whereas in *Hamlet* and *Macbeth*, the land is restored from sickness to health through the purging of human wickedness, and a divine shaping of events is discernible in each play. Yet the more significant relation of mood and emphasis is between *Macbeth* and *Othello*. It is as if Shakespeare had sought, in each of these two plays, to deepen the sense of tragedy through emphasizing the role of deliberate malice in human events: the malice of Iago and of Othello (though blindly ignorant he is still guilty of malice), and the effect of that malice upon the innocent Desdemona, upon Cassio, upon the foolish Roderigo, most of all upon Othello himself; the calculating malice of Macbeth and Lady Macbeth, and its effect upon them and upon the whole state which they afflict. In *Romeo and Juliet,* no one fully intends, much less foresees, the tragic outcome, while in *Hamlet* the tragic responsibility is not concentrated simply in Claudius but is the common burden of the knowing and the unknowing, of the whole human society of the play. From this point of view, *Romeo and Juliet* and *Hamlet* might be called "public" tragedies, whereas *Othello* and *Macbeth* are "private" ones; that is, in the two former, the tragic guilt is distributed and shared by the whole of society (as represented in the plays), while in the two latter it is more personal, it is studied with closer reference to individuals. Yet the distinction is but provisionally useful, because in all four plays we recognize as the more important principle the universality of human guilt, in which we ourselves share; and this constitutes the essential matter of their poignancy and of our sorrow.

The context of Christian thought and feeling in all four plays implies a paradox which remains unresolved. The most uncompromising individual tragedy, the wilfulness and despair of Macbeth, shows us the vindication of divine justice and the benefit of the human society which Macbeth afflicts; but our sympathy for him runs counter to this good and robs the ending of any sense of exaltation, of humanity ennobled through some brave or generous act. The bravery is there, even the potentiality of noble conduct in the imaginative energy of the man; but his nature is infected, and we watch the tragic progress of his disease until it issues, inevitably, in his destruction. We are not greatly edified by the corresponding triumph of Malcolm or the freeing of Scotland from tyranny. These events are not central in our concern but seem like consequences implied in the moral design of Macbeth's sin and punishment. The effect is like an indictment of human nature; we share in Macbeth's guilt and we recognize his damnation as just, rather than triumphing in the reassertion of a moral order which is divinely imposed. The paradox is indeed inherent in the sinful nature of man, as Christianity views it: the wages of sin is death, and there is no evading that conclusion, no mitigation, no consolation, no hope whatever in this tragic catastrophe.

Yet tragedy, we may feel, in its highest reaches, nevertheless, can achieve an effect of triumphant affirmation. This is what we miss in *Othello* and *Macbeth*, otherwise among the very greatest of Shakespeare's tragedies, or of all tragedies, and certainly among the most powerful in their effect upon us. In both plays, we must recognize the full responsibility of the tragic protagonist for the catastrophe he suffers—and this means much more, in its Christian context, than Aristotle could possibly have comprehended in his notion of the tragic "flaw"; we must recognize the responsibility of Othello almost as fully as that of Macbeth, because human blindness is no excuse for the malice that moves Othello at the end, it is no excuse for the working of terrible evil. Yet, in spite of our understanding of all this, we are more pained by the evil that lays hold on Othello and Desdemona than by the deliberate self-involvement in evil of Macbeth and Lady Macbeth, because we hate most to see human goodness suffer. Yet human goodness *must* suffer, in the Christian conception of tragedy; no human being is good enough to escape its consequences, not even Shakespeare's innocents, Romeo and Juliet, Ophelia, Desdemona. All are touched with the original taint, all must bear the common burden of sin, if only by inheritance. The Christian view permits no reconcilement with the central fact of human guilt, and in tragedy that shows a Christian bias the positive values are seen to lie not in human wills or human efforts, which are blind or perverse, but in a divine ordering of events the ultimate resolution of which lies beyond the scope of tragedy and pertains to the affirmations of Christian faith:

> All is best, though oft we doubt
> What th' unsearchable dispose
> Of highest wisdom brings about. . . .

These are the ordinary limits of the tragic experience within a Christian context that confines itself to the moral world of man. And if Shakespeare was to enlarge that tragic experience, without undertaking to dramatize a specifically religious theme, it was necessary for him to contemplate another moral plane—natural morality but not overtly Christian morality—as he does in the group of tragedies we shall consider in the following chapters.

THE ORDER OF NATURE

THESIS: *JULIUS CAESAR* AND *CORIOLANUS*

1. *Julius Caesar*

IN *Julius Caesar*, Shakespeare makes a fresh start in the tragic form. The play differs radically from the tragedy that precedes it chronologically, *Romeo and Juliet*, in subject-matter, in the tragic conception, and, for the most part, in technical execution. *Romeo and Juliet* belongs to the matter of romance, matter that Shakespeare could freely alter to suit his conception, as he did by inventing characters and complications not found in his source, by directing the action in a schematic pattern that emphasizes the parts played by chance and a higher destiny and that shows a providential purpose controlling the whole action. *Hamlet* and *Othello* are likewise the matter of romance and here again Shakespeare shapes the matter to suit the design of his Christian conception, of providence and divine justice; *Macbeth* is so freely compounded of different materials found in Holinshed and elsewhere that we may consider it in the same way.[1]

Julius Caesar draws upon the historical authority of Plutarch, as do the later Roman tragedies, an authority which the Elizabethans held in great veneration. Shakespeare doubtless felt freer to alter the materials of Holinshed for his dramatic purposes;[2] at least, his Roman plays follow Plutarch for the most part with close fidelity.[3] Furthermore, the very name of tragedy, for Shakespeare's age, summoned up the authority both of ancient matter and of ancient dramatic form—the formal precedent, that is, of Seneca mainly, which makes itself felt throughout the tragedies of Shakespeare, as in those of Chapman and others of Shakespeare's contemporaries. The treating of familiar themes drawn from ancient history and "climbing to the height of Seneca his style" became almost as much an obligation for the popular dramatist of the end of Elizabeth's reign as it was within the coterie of the

Countess of Pembroke. It was to be expected that Shakespeare, as a practising dramatist, would turn his hand to something in the classical manner, or what would be accepted as the classical manner. Actually, the treatment of the theme would be in the tradition of the living theatre of Shakespeare's day, and just as truly aimed at popular appeal as was *Romeo and Juliet* or *Hamlet*: in the hands of Shakespeare the treatment would be incomparably more skilful than the academic exercises of the English Senecans; but it would also, and necessarily, bid for the attention of the learned—Ben Jonson's scornful comment about "Caesar did never wrong but with just cause" is well known—and Shakespeare doubtless felt some constraint in undertaking it. Certainly, it is one of his most careful pieces of workmanship, as we now have it.

The play centres upon what Shakespeare's age probably considered the most famous event of ancient history, as it was set forth in the pages of their favourite moralist among the ancient historians, whom Shakespeare read in Sir Thomas North's fine version. It was a theme full of political and moral import for Shakespeare's time, the story of the assassination of a dictator, the grandeur of whose personality has impressed succeeding ages like that of no other man. Caesar's murder changed the mightiest of states from a republic of free men who ruled the world to an empire which rapidly degenerated into tyranny. So Shakespeare endeavoured to comprehend it.

His task, in constructing a tragedy upon this theme, was one of historical interpretation. Undoubtedly Shakespeare made a careful effort of historical imagination for *Julius Caesar* and his other Roman plays, thinking himself back into the time of Cicero and Brutus, Cleopatra and Octavius Caesar, Aufidius and Coriolanus, trying to feel their motives and to think their thoughts, as he found them suggested in Plutarch. Shakespeare's Romans are by no means Elizabethans; they are *men*, of course, as Dr. Johnson remarked; for Shakespeare, human nature is universally the same; but Shakespeare's Romans do not have the outlook and attitudes of Christians, nor do they recognize the same political motives and values as Elizabethans, or share recognizably kindred tastes. Shakespeare, in fact, is very careful in *Julius Caesar* and the other

Roman plays to avoid anachronisms—witness the difference in such plays as *Troilus and Cressida* (where the atmosphere is mediaeval) or in *The Winter's Tale* (where anachronism seems to be a calculated part of the effect). He is not so learned as Ben Jonson; there is no special attempt to create historical atmosphere; but Shakespeare is clearly trying to interpret the actual motives and point of view of historical persons in *Julius Caesar, Antony and Cleopatra,* and *Coriolanus,* to make us understand, with his artist's imagination, how the events which Plutarch records, in his interesting but limited historian's way, really came about. He takes minor liberties with Plutarch's data—especially with the chronology, in the service of his dramatic narrative—as he did with the events of the English history plays; but he is remarkably faithful, on the whole, to the main lines of Plutarch's narrative, even to the extent of transferring whole passages of North's prose into verse, almost word for word, as has often been remarked.

To the writing of *Julius Caesar*, Shakespeare brought the rich experience of the English history plays he had already produced. *Julius Caesar* belongs to the period of the two parts of *Henry IV* and *Henry V* and contains minor reminiscences of *1 Henry IV.*[4] There is the same effort of historical imagination; but *Julius Caesar* lacks the immediacy and warmth of patriotic feeling that we sense throughout the plays dealing with English history. There is a cool detachment about *Julius Caesar,* a dispassionate study of incident and motive and character. Human nature is displayed with profound insight, as always with Shakespeare; but the actors move in a context of political concepts in some degree alien to Shakespeare the Elizabethan and patriot of the English histories; and there is a pervasive irony, characteristic of Shakespeare's dealings with antiquity generally, which controls the mood of the whole.

In this mood of ironic contemplation, of disinterested reflection upon the great persons and happenings of an age that had vanished, Shakespeare follows the pattern of events with a clear and untroubled gaze. It is a pattern of moral causes and their effects in this world. There are no theological, no metaphysical preconceptions. The world of *Julius Caesar*—as of *Antony and Cleopatra* and *Coriolanus*—is the natural order of man, which is a moral order, but the religious sanction of that order is not invoked. It is simply man's world as he knows it by the light of natural reason—as Plutarch knew it, and Julius Caesar, Brutus, Cassius, and the rest. In this world there are no significant chains of accident, as we have observed them in *Romeo and Juliet* and *Hamlet*. The moments of choice are clear and emphatic: Brutus's soliloquy (II, i), Caesar's disregard of Calphurnia's foreboding dream, Brutus's overbearing Cassius's judgment about Antony and about the battle of Philippi; even the lack of judgment in the Roman mob has its sequent penalty. The action does, of course, imply a superhuman order of justice and retribution; only we must not think of sin and punishment, if they carry any Christian implications for us, but rather of *ate* (the mad folly that comes upon proud men), *hybris* (arrogance), and *nemesis* (the inescapable consequences of *ate* and *hybris*). Shakespeare invokes no other explanation of events, and even these Greek conceptions we must invoke for ourselves; but they best fit the course of events in Shakespeare's Roman plays. What he shows us is a moral pattern of human history, a sequence of human causes and their effects. The supernatural portents in *Julius Caesar*, even the ghost of Caesar before Philippi, are not agents in the drama. They are present for atmospheric effect, and because they figure in Plutarch's account; we may take them as symbolic of the moral event, or not, as we please; but they do not determine anything. The moral outcome is clearly enough determined by the characters of the drama as they feel and think and act before our eyes.

The unifying principle of conception and execution in *Julius Caesar* has troubled a good many critics, the fate of Caesar and that of Brutus (or Brutus and Cassius) being thought to constitute two centres of interest not altogether reconciled; and Fleay's suggestion that we should regard the play as an amalgamation of two earlier ones—a "Death of Caesar" and a "Revenge of Caesar"—has been followed by even wilder hypotheses.[5] There are those who regard the play as essentially Brutus's tragedy,[6] and those for whom the theme is "Caesar and Caesarism."[7] Nor is Professor Kittredge's view that the supernaturalism of the play is the clue to its unity very satisfactory: "Caesar vanquishes Brutus and Cassius at Philippi as truly as he vanquishes Pompey at Pharsalus. Antony and Octavius are not Caesar's avengers; they are merely Caesar's agents; he avenges himself. . . . Caesar, alive or dead, pervades and operates the drama—and not less after his death than in his life."[8] This view exaggerates the importance of the theme of revenge, which is hardly more than incidental to the action; and whether we regard the act of revenge as Caesar's or his successors', such an interpretation differs but little from Fleay's suggestion. Dover Wilson seems much nearer the mark in stressing the political implications, for the play is in some sense Rome's tragedy, as much as Brutus's or Caesar's. But we must necessarily take account of Brutus's centrality in the action, for he is the most impressive figure in it, and the spotlight is on him at the end.

Actually, the play is more complex than any of these suggestions would indicate. We feel its unity readily enough as we read it or see it acted, but when we try to find a verbal approximation for this effect, we may easily overlook some of the significant interrelations of its parts. We may try to express the unity of its theme in a question: Was the murder of Caesar justified? The implied answer develops two levels of significance—like *The Faerie Queene*, except that *Julius Caesar* does not employ the method of allegory. The political issue provides the major and enveloping theme that comprehends all the actors in their relation to the state; among them Caesar is the dominant figure, for he is the occasion of the action, influences its course whether living or dead (as Professor Kittredge has said), and illustrates the tendency, in a republic, for the ablest man to seek absolute power, and the consequent struggle, the anarchy and reversion to a worse form of tyranny which may ensue upon his overthrow. The political tragedy of the Roman state and of Caesar are, for the purposes of the play, identical; the play is thus well named, because the fortunes of Rome reach their highest point, and their turning point, in the fall of Caesar. This political tragedy involves as a consequence the moral tragedy of Brutus; and Brutus's moral tragedy, in turn, is mirrored in Caesar's; for Brutus's act is no better justified in its outcome than Caesar's aims, perhaps less justified. Brutus's wrong choice arises from the "flaw" (in the sense of an ineluctable blindness) of his character. "The noblest Roman of them all," he is nevertheless blind to his own limitations and the guiding motives of other men; with steadfast confidence in his own ideals and his own rightness, he misses the mark completely and without realizing that he has done so. The overweening pride of Caesar during his last days shows us the ground of Brutus's fears for the future and influences his decision: had Caesar not been ambitious, Brutus had never fallen. The fault of one provokes the fault of the other. And yet, the political argument holds as a generalization, without depending upon the personal characters of the protagonists; for if Caesar had not aspired to absolute power, so the political argument would go, sooner or later some other would: he would have found his opposer, and in the resulting conflict Rome would still have fallen. The principals are exemplary of a profound comment upon states and upon individuals; and the two themes, the political and the moral, parallel and complement each other in an ironic yet deeply understanding study of the blindness and futility of men's strivings as they try to act according to their own righteousness and to impose their personal wills in a universe which sets little store by merely human pretensions.

Julius Caesar opens with the tribunes' foreboding of Caesar's mounting ambition and the contrasting irresponsibility of the plebeian crowd; it closes with the victory of the triumvirate over Brutus and Cassius. This is cause and effect, the epitome of the political scale of the action. In between these poles, we have the fall of Caesar and the moral tragedy of Brutus which it entails. The fall of Brutus parallels that of Caesar; Caesar falls through obstinate pride and Brutus through his own blindness—the Greek *hybris* comprehends both varieties of human culpability. But both of these men, in their falls, show us what is happening to the Roman state. Having made himself dictator, Caesar, "the greatest man in all this world," naturally aspires to the final step, the absolute and permanent power of a king; and ironically, it is just such a benevolent autocrat as he would make that the careless Roman populace need to rule them, and, in their fickleness, would readily welcome. Brutus, in attempting to uphold the traditional republican ideals of Rome by leading the conspiracy against Caesar, actually delivers Rome into the power of the opportunist Antony and the coldly astute Octavius, neither of whom has either the disinterested devotion to his country of Brutus or the magnanimity of Caesar. Such is the pattern of human history that *Julius Caesar* presents to us.

The portrait of Caesar in his last days which the play affords, of a man physically infirm—even Cassius's exaggeration of these infirmities (I, ii, 100 ff.), though we discern his envy of Caesar's greatness in the account, has its derogatory weight—easily swayed by Calphurnia's fears or Decius's flattery, and vain to the point of infatuation, has been variously accounted for. The traits of the braggart, for instance, have been traced to the Senecan *Julius Caesar* of Muretus and the tradition descending therefrom;[9] and, as Granville Barker has remarked, Caesar must be played down if he is to die in the third act, or the play would end in anticlimax.[10] Yet more significant is the fact that Shakespeare does choose to kill Caesar in the middle of the play rather than at the end. Evidently, Shakespeare does not take sides, nor is the play simply a study of characters in conflict. Caesar's character in the play is more than a device of dramatic balance or a heritage of Senecan bias; it is part of Shakespeare's reading of the tragic pattern of history, a pattern in which no man, however great, is entirely self-sufficient.

Something of Caesar's true stature emerges from the spell his spirit casts over the drama: he seems to us greater dead than living. With Caesar living, there is no particular subtlety. His is the fault of pride, of *hybris* in its familiar classical lineaments. "What, is the fellow mad?" asks Caesar, with blandly unconscious irony, as Artemidorus presses the paper upon him informing him of the conspiracy. And the extraordinary vaunt of

> But I am constant as the Northern Star,
> Of whose true-fix'd and resting quality
> There is no fellow in the firmament . . .

seems in itself enough to provoke the thrusts of the conspirators. This is all heightened for dramatic effect, no doubt, for it is hard to believe that the Caesar of the *Commentaries* ever talked in quite this vein; though in the calculated understatements of Caesar's surviving accounts of his conquests we may perhaps catch an echo of the Thrasonical *veni*, *vidi*, *vici*, which, together with his genius for politics, his intellect, and his magnanimity, we may consider, as Shakespeare apparently did, to constitute the complex nature of the man.

Caesar, Brutus, and Cassius are the greatest figures of the play; Octavius, and even Antony,[11] are minor by comparison. Caesar's arrogance and Caesar's fall are the occasion, or the provocation, for the fall of Cassius and Brutus. The dominant note of Cassius's character is plainly envy:

> Such men as he be never at heart's ease,
> Whiles they behold a greater than themselves.

He is the sort of man who takes everything personally, always prone to suppose that someone has slighted or injured him, even his best friends.

> I have not from your eyes that gentleness
> And show of love as I was wont to have,

are his opening words to Brutus (I, ii, 33–34); and he begins the quarrel scene,

> Most noble brother, you have done me wrong!

Especially revealing is his soliloquy after he has first broached the conspiracy to Brutus:

> If I were Brutus now and he were Cassius,
> He should not humour me. . . .

The personal favour of Caesar would, for him, have overborne his resentment of Caesar's tyrannous ways, or so he thinks, for the sake of asserting to himself his superior shrewdness. Yet his resentment of Caesar is something more than personal spite. Cassius, we eventually come to feel, is indeed, as Brutus calls him, "The last of all the Romans" (meaning the great ones), excepting Brutus himself. Cassius is able, far abler than Brutus as a tactician; he is brave; in his way, he is devoted to the ideal of Roman freedom;

he is warm-hearted, and knows something of his own faults; and most of us probably feel that, as a friend, we should much prefer the choleric and not altogether high-souled Cassius to the noble Brutus—at least, as Shakespeare imagines them. But Cassius's faults are enough, and more than enough, to bring about his downfall. We recognize the justice and inevitability of his end:

> Caesar, thou art reveng'd
> Even with the sword that kill'd thee;

and the irony of it, for he has despaired of the fluctuating battle too soon.

The justice and the irony of Brutus's end are very much subtler. His integrity is unimpeachable. In his personal character, he approaches Plato's ideal of the philosopher-statesman, disinterested and unsusceptible to passion, devoted to the welfare of his country, the *res publica* which his ancestors had founded and which he is ready to defend at whatever personal cost. No one can doubt that he joins the conspiracy through devotion to his republican principles which, he honestly thinks, are jeopardized by Caesar's continued existence, and despite his friendship and admiration for the man. What Brutus feels about Caesar as a man we may gather from his incidental tributes to him: "O that we then could come by Caesar's spirit, And not dismember Caesar" (II, i, 169–70); "I, that did love Caesar when I struck him" (III, i, 182); "The foremost man of all this world" (IV, iii, 22). Brutus's friendship for Cassius is of the same stuff. "You love me not!" cries Cassius, at the height of their quarrel, when he has been humiliated to the breaking point by Brutus's inflexible insistence upon Cassius's deviations from Brutus's strict code of honourable dealing; and Brutus's reply comes with chilling emphasis: "I do not like your faults." Brutus cares less for persons than for ideas; he has an unshakable conviction of his own virtue; and he demands that the same virtue should be in other men:

> There is no terror, Cassius, in your threats;
> For I am arm'd so strong in honesty
> That they pass by me as the idle wind
> Which I respect not.

His view of the conspiracy is of like simplicity:

> Did not great Julius bleed for justice sake?
> What villain touch'd his body that did stab
> And not for justice?

which we may place beside Antony's final verdict:

> All the conspirators save only he
> Did what they did in envy of great Caesar.

Brutus's motives are unselfish; his integrity is complete; and yet he is infatuated, with an infatuation like Caesar's in degree, if not in kind—indeed, more terrible, because Caesar's vanity (as Shakespeare imagines it) has something of a child's boastfulness,[12] while Brutus's opinion of his own honesty is well founded.[13] His fault lies in his superb confidence. The ancients taught that no mortal could afford such self-sufficiency: "Think as a mortal," the maxim has it;[14] and Brutus's pride is of the type that Montaigne so strongly censured in the peroration to the most famous of his essays.[15]

Brutus's pride betrays him. Once in the conspiracy, his reputation, and his sublime assurance of his own rightness (an assurance which Cassius, for all his passionate intensity, never dreamed of possessing, or of questioning in Brutus, either), impose him as the leader. With unerring insight, Shakespeare fixes upon this trait to explain Brutus's fatal mistake as he found it described in Plutarch:

> All the conspirators but Brutus, determining upon this matter, thought it good also to kill Antonius, because he was a wicked man, and that in nature favoured tyranny; besides also, for that he was in great estimation with soldiers, having been conversant of long time amongst them: and specially having a mind bent to great enterprises, he was also of great authority at that time, being Consul with Caesar. But Brutus would not agree to it. First, for that he said it was not honest: secondly, because he told them there was hope of change in him. For he did not mistrust, but that Antonius, being a noble-minded and courageous man (when he should know that Caesar was dead) would willingly help his country to recover her liberty, having them as an example unto him, to follow their courage and virtue. So Brutus by this means saved Antonius's life. . . .[16]

To this flagrant misjudgment of Plutarch's Brutus, Shakespeare adds the weight of Brutus's assurance as he overbears the shrewder judgment of Cassius not merely in the matter of sparing Antony

(II, i, 162 ff.) but in the plan of tactics for their last battle as well (IV, iii, 196 ff.).[17] And the crowning irony is Brutus's unawareness of his fault, or of the venality that vitiates his cause. This blindness is that "missing of the mark" (ἁμάρτημα) which is at least part of what Aristotle had in mind in that troublesome passage of the *Poetics* on dramatic character,[18] and which, in the severest tragic conception of the Greeks, above all of Sophocles, the gods punish as inevitably as the faults of passion. As Granville Barker excellently puts it, "it is not . . . passions that blind [Brutus], but principles";[19] and his fault is more awe-inspiring than the passion of Cassius because it is the excess of his virtue: in his serene sense of that virtue, he never knows that he does wrong.

In Brutus, we cannot trace a process of ennoblement through suffering, as we can in Hamlet, and perhaps even in Mark Antony of *Antony and Cleopatra*. The end of *Julius Caesar* shows, among other things, how unchanged Brutus is by all that has happened. We can hardly feel sorry for him. His motives, his principles, his acts are all of a piece throughout, and he dies in defence of the same principle of Roman liberty that had led him in the first place to join the conspirators. He commits suicide against his Stoic code (V, i, 100 ff.), but this is to avoid what for a Roman was unbearable disgrace, to be led as a victim in a Roman triumph. It is perhaps a final irony that the rational Brutus should be influenced by the ghost of Caesar to take his life at Philippi. But Brutus's suicide was also his last act in defence of liberty, and in this sense the final assertion of his principles.

Brutus's tragedy is personal in its cause, human blindness, but it is not deep personal tragedy, the tragedy of divided motives; the deeper tragedy lies in the public consequences of his acts. In a great crisis of the world's history, Brutus, despite his complete personal integrity, lacked the wisdom necessary to the high role he felt called upon to fill, adjudicator in the issue of what form of government made for justice. He committed murder, and without achieving the results he hoped for. The consequences, like nemesis, were civil war for Rome, death for Brutus and the other conspirators, and an eventual reign of tyranny compared with which the rule of Julius Caesar had been benevolent and wise.

In the political consequences of the play lies its ultimate significance. If Brutus had been at all venal—if, as the analogy of Cassius suggests to us, the personal favour he enjoyed from Caesar had weighed with him more than the cause of liberty—his personal tragedy might have been avoided. His plight is that he had the virtue of disinterestedness without the wisdom—that is, the understanding of himself and other men—necessary to give his disinterestedness political effectiveness. He is as noble, essentially, as a man can be; his tragedy is that he is, after all, human, and he aspired to play the role of a god.

Brutus commands our admiration rather than our full sympathy. At bottom, he was infatuated, no better than a fool—as Caesar was in a different way, and as many another great man has been, before and since; and when they die through their own folly, we cannot deplore their loss. What is most fully tragic about the play is the effect of Brutus's conduct, for it influenced the lives of all his fellow beings, the Roman commonweal. Ironically, his act of killing Caesar brought upon Rome the very tyranny he planned to do away with. Yet we cannot say that the tyranny which followed is wholly Brutus's fault, either. He became the guiding spirit of the conspiracy, and so we may speak as if it were his agency. But he was not its cause. If Brutus and Cassius had not murdered Caesar, others probably would have; for his arrogance (in a state accustomed to the maximum of liberty for the citizens) cried out for such a check.

This is the design, then, of political events and their outcome which Shakespeare presents to us in the play. The human ideal of liberty is incompatible with the limits of human wisdom, the human capacity of self-knowledge and self-rule. This fact is tragic for the noble-minded idealist like Brutus and for the great statesman like Caesar; and it is tragic for the state, for each member of it has his share of responsibility in the catastrophe, from Caesar and Brutus, Caesar's supporters and Brutus's supporters, on down to the humblest of the Roman mob, who make holiday when Caesar triumphs over the sons of Pompey and would indifferently accept Caesar or Brutus for their king.

This play contains perhaps the most philosophical of all Shakespeare's dramatic interpretations of human history. Plainly, it is the most detached; there was nothing to engage Shakespeare's partisanship, and he views both the imperial ambitions of Caesar and the republican ardour of Brutus with a gravely ironic impartiality. The irony is deeply understanding; he studies not only the vicissitudes of the Roman state in its moment of greatest crisis but also the personal tragedies of its citizens. Brutus and Caesar, Cassius and Antony, Titinius and Lucilius and even the slave Strato who holds the sword for Brutus are all vividly realized for us as human beings. The detachment, the serene and impartial understanding of the artist and the thinker—for this is more a play of thought than of passion—is the leading quality of this work; and, as we grow older, at least, it leaves us filled with admiration for the artist's genius but comparatively unmoved—unmoved, that is, compared with the effects we experience in the great tragedies that followed *Julius Caesar*. It is an excellent play for young students, because here they may discover the beautiful comprehensiveness of Shakespeare's mind and the constructive genius of his dramatic art displayed with relative simplicity, without the subtler ambiguities of motive he delighted to study in the psychologically more complex of his tragedies and without the headier intoxication of his most splendid poetry. There was nothing in the theme of *Julius Caesar* to arouse Shakespeare's highest poetic energies, most deeply stirred by romantic rather than historical themes. On the other hand, we find a simplicity of style admirably suited to the subject, a severe logic of construction,[20] and a pervasive irony in the development of the motives and the action not unworthy to rank with the work of the supreme master of dramatic irony, Sophocles. *Julius Caesar* is far from the greatest of Shakespeare's own tragedies; nor is it so learned an invocation of classical antiquity as Ben Jonson's *Sejanus*: yet it is a very much greater play. It is, among English plays, the one best informed with the qualities we call "classical"—a perfection of structure, a severe and restrained beauty of style, deeply contemplative insight. In this sense, it is the best classical tragedy in English.

2. *Coriolanus*

Certain affiliations of *Coriolanus* with *Julius Caesar* are easily apparent. The same mob of humble Roman folk—or tradesmen of Shakespeare's London, for that matter[21]—meet us in the opening of the play, merry and good-humoured, but also dangerous in their irresponsible and easily swayed simplicity; the same furtive and cunning pair of tribunes, jealous of their own prestige and that of their class; the same contrast of conservative dignity in the senatorial rank. The senators of *Julius Caesar* are members of a legislative body whose present function is simply to give effect to the will of a dictator, while in *Coriolanus,* though the senators actually exercise the legislative power, the tribunes, representing the mass of the plebeians, have the right of veto and important judicial powers. The earlier society of republican Rome is much more democratic than the later. In *Julius Caesar,* the struggle is between two parties of the senatorial class, Caesar's party and the conspirators; in *Coriolanus,* the political issue is between patricians and plebeians.

Both plays represent a political conflict; but in *Julius Caesar* the political tragedy comprehends and subsumes the tragedy of individuals, whereas the political struggle of *Coriolanus* is rather the background for the central tragedy of the hero. Coriolanus's tragedy issues from the political situation of the play, is conditioned by the struggle for power between plebeians and patricians; but his tragic career also runs counter to that struggle, and, in a sense, transcends it. His powerful figure aggravates the political conflict in Rome, but his death does not change the political situation: the city is saved, but the rivalry of patricians and plebeians continues, as far as we can judge. Rome is saved, at the cost of its hero's life; and the tragic concern of the play is with his loss.

It has, indeed, been argued that the dramatic interest of the play centres about Shakespeare's attitude to the common people of Rome—in effect, that Shakespeare is on the side of the common people against Coriolanus, or vice versa;[22] and it has been suggested, with a good deal less simplicity, that the play dramatizes a theory of the state which is common to all of Shakespeare's plays dealing with Greek and Roman themes.[23] Here, the view of Swinburne, and more particularly, of Bradley is preferred;[24] that Coriolanus's personal tragedy is central throughout, specifically for the following reasons.

From Coriolanus's point of view, the struggle in which he becomes involved is not a political issue but a personal one. He is not really the representative or spokesman of the patrician class. He himself belongs to what Shakespeare thinks of as the most exclusive group within that class, the "old nobility" (IV, vii, 29–30), and he has been brought up as a soldier rather than as a politician. He stands for the consulship because it is expected of a man of his rank and attainments, and especially to please his mother Volumnia; but, for his own part, he despises the false position in which the custom of the election puts him of seeming to flatter the common people and advertise his heroic deeds for their support. His proud spirit loathes this display:

> Better it is to die, better to starve,
> Than crave the hire which first we do deserve.
> Why in this wolvish toge should I stand here
> To beg of Hob and Dick that do appear
> Their needless vouches? Custom calls me to't.
> What custom wills, in all things should we do't,
> The dust on antique time would lie unswept,
> And mountainous error be too highly heapt
> For truth to o'erpeer. Rather than fool it so,
> Let the high office and the honour go
> To one that would do thus.

We understand the proud impatience of the man; we may even sympathize with it; but we must recognize the political irresponsibility of it, too.

Coriolanus, in the opening of the play, vehemently disapproves the free distribution of corn by which the senators have appeased the agitations of the plebeians (I, i, 171 ff), because they have not borne their share against Rome's enemies; in effect, he denies that they have any rights in the state except upon the ground of military service. If he has any policy, it is that of a military dictator. But he is not really systematic in his politics. He is for making his own rules rather than recognizing party lines or the authority of Roman custom as over-riding the will of the individual. He has no real comprehension of the need for mutual tolerance and co-operation in a state composed of two parties. His idea of "co-operation" is to force the plebeians to do as he desires. And he has no discretion. In his passion, he even goes so far as to attack the office of the tribunes and to urge the abolition of their place and authority as representatives of the common people—a position which the senators never dream of endorsing; which they must, in fact, repudiate.

Politically, Coriolanus is impossible, and, while he is in Rome, a grave embarrassment to the patricians. When the tribunes pronounce his sentence of banishment, he flashes back at them

> You common cry of curs, whose breath I hate
> As reek o' th' rotten fens, whose loves I prize
> As the dead carcasses of unburied men
> That do corrupt my air, I banish you!

In Antium, he speaks of his party as

> our dastard nobles, who
> Have all forsook me;

and he sets himself to destroy all Rome as his personal vengeance for the wrong he has suffered. There is no political issue here. Coriolanus has no politics, no programme save his own authority, his own vindication, his own revenge. He stands alone, against plebeians and patricians alike, against mother, wife, and child, against his country. This is his tragedy, and it is purely personal.

If this be so, then we can hardly speak as if the tragedy involved the city of Rome. Potentially, it does; but, as it turns out, not so. The whole point of the play is that catastrophe for Rome is averted through the sacrifice of Coriolanus, by the sacrifice of his pride and by the heroic self-denial of his own will, as he chooses to spare Rome in the clear understanding of what the consequence of his choice is likely to be. There is neither a sacrifice nor a triumph for plebeians or patricians; they are gravely threatened, but they suffer no real harm. The tragedy is not theirs; it is the tragedy of the man they have wronged—though it is hard to see how they could have helped wronging him.

Coriolanus, then, is central in the tragedy, and it is essential to see his character and motives clearly. They are displayed for us with care, and we may pursue the comparison with *Julius Caesar* by contrasting him with Brutus. The contrast is in many ways revealing.

The leading quality of both of them is a sterling honesty. Brutus, the thinker, is impersonally devoted to an ideal of justice; he wholeheartedly serves the Roman state; and he errs through insufficient knowledge of himself and others, through mistakes of tactics and practical judgment. Coriolanus, the blunt soldier and man of action, knows his own qualities and limitations very well; he stands for inequality, the traditional privileges of his aristocratic class and the supremacy of military virtue; his allegiance is not so much to a state (whether actual or ideal) as to his caste of the military nobility, to his family, and at last and above all—until he yields to the climactic appeal of his mother—to himself, to the idea of his own integrity. Politically, he is at least as unpractical as Brutus; indeed, more so, and in precisely the opposite way: Brutus has sublime faith in the people and their devotion to justice; Coriolanus, a blazing contempt for the people and all their ways—and whereas Brutus acts only upon careful reflection and with a studious dispassionateness, Coriolanus characteristically acts in passion, heedless and headlong in expressing the principles and biases of his upbringing. Yet one is as unswerving in his principles as the other, and both of them fail of a full grasp of the political situation that confronts them. In their falls, we observe the same grave irony and impartiality of the dramatist; the end of neither is very deeply moving, though full of the keenest interest. For most people, perhaps, Brutus seems the nobler figure in his tragic fall; his faults are less obvious to us and less irritating than the arrogance of Coriolanus. Yet Coriolanus had the harder choice, in renouncing his vengeance, without even the consolation of a dignified end, like Brutus's; and though he dies as the victim of Aufidius's base contriving, in a huddled brawl, his end was the more purely heroic, the more self-effacing.

Coriolanus is an even simpler play than *Julius Caesar* in its organization and design. The economy of the play's construction is masterly. The opening gives us the situation between the two political parties of Rome in the plebeians' demand for the free distribution of corn; and the good-humoured remonstrance of Menenius Agrippa with the agitators—his fable of the rebellion of the body's members against the belly—prepares us to observe by contrast the impatient arrogance of Caius Marcius, who intervenes with violent reproaches to confirm the impression of the poorer citizens and their tribunes that he is their enemy. But he is summoned to defend Rome against the Volsces, and we see the other side of him, his invincible valour, and learn of his standing rivalry with the Volscian hero Aufidius, which is further emphasized in the following scene of the Volscian preparations in Corioli. Scene iii gives us the remaining, and most vital, element in the exposition, the picture of the hero's relation to his mother Volumnia, that redoubtable Roman matron who has trained her son for the wars and sent him at a tender age "to let him seek danger where he was like to find fame," who exults in his battle scars, and sees him, even now,

> pluck Aufidius down by th' hair;
> As children from a bear, the Volsces shunning him.
> Methinks I see him stamp thus, and call thus:
> "Come on, you cowards! You were got in fear,
> Though you were born in Rome." His bloody brow
> With his mail'd hand then wiping, forth he goes,
> Like to a harvestman that's task'd to mow
> Or all or lose his hire.

The scene is wonderfully skilful, with its contrast between the proud and fierce old mother and the gentle and fearful wife Virgilia, while their gracious visitor, the lady Valeria, acts as a foil for each; and in its suggestion that the son is what his mother has made him. The following battle with the Volscians bears out the spirit of Volumnia's prophecy. Caius Marcius is the animating force on the Roman side. Almost single-handed he takes Corioli, rallies and leads the other part of the Roman forces to victory, and is acclaimed "Coriolanus" for his unexampled heroism as he returns from victory over Aufidius and the Volscians to Rome.

In this workmanlike exposition of the first act, all the elements of the approaching conflict are foreshadowed: the political division of Rome, with Coriolanus's pride and scorn of the plebeians as an aggravating cause of its continuance; the heroic services of Coriolanus to Rome as a ground of his contempt for the common people, too faint-hearted to defend the city that supports them—or so Coriolanus thinks; Coriolanus's own character as a bold and uncompromising soldier, reared by his mother in a severe and arrogant military discipline, scorning to hear himself praised or to flatter others, whose very pride and inability to compromise are but the excess of his unparalleled virtue of courage; there is even the foreshadowing of Aufidius's ultimate treachery to Coriolanus, in his bitter reflections upon his defeat and the vow:

> Where I find him, were it
> At home, upon my brother's guard, even there
> Against the hospitable canon, would I
> Wash my fierce hand in's heart.

These are the materials of tragedy in the state of Roman and Volscian affairs with which the play deals.

The action develops in three orderly stages, each stage contrived to exploit the fullest dramatic effect of suspense and reversal. The first stage centres about the battle of the first act, in which Coriolanus is shut within the gates of Corioli and apparently lost, only to emerge bloody but victorious and to continue to complete success. The two latter stages reverse the pattern of apparent defeat followed by success. In the second, Coriolanus offers himself for the consulship and is apparently to be approved, only to be ultimately rejected and banished, indeed all but condemned to be hurled from the Tarpeian Rock. The final stage of the action, Coriolanus's invasion of Rome and its consequences, has really two reversals, though the second is foreshadowed and diminished in a deliberate anticlimax. Coriolanus advances upon Rome, apparently invincible and impervious to every plea, only to yield to his mother's impassioned appeal; and, in the sequel, there is some prospect that he may satisfy the Volsces with the terms of the humiliating peace Rome has been obliged to accept, until the envy of Aufidius brings about his assassination. From beginning to end, the play is a sustained and vigorous action; yet the heart of the tragedy lies in the study of the hero's character and of the ineluctable causes of his fall.

The materials of this central concern are all in Plutarch's life of Coriolanus, with its emphasis upon the moral evaluation of Coriolanus's character and conduct. Shakespeare is very faithful to his source throughout; nevertheless, here and there, he alters the tone or the emphasis, he provides a deeper insight into situation or motive, with the result that he is able to show a tragic dignity in Coriolanus of which Plutarch, in his sober and severe summing up of that hero, hardly conceived.

Plutarch mentions, near the beginning of his life of Coriolanus, the detail that Shakespeare fixed upon as most significant in Coriolanus's background:

> Caius Martius, whose life we intend now to write, being left an orphan by his father, was brought up under his mother, a widow, who taught us by experience, that orphanage bringeth many discommodities to a child, but doth not hinder him to become an honest man, and to excel in virtue above the common sort. . . . But Martius thinking all due to his mother, that had been also due to his father if he had lived: did not only content himself to rejoice and honour her, but at her desire took a wife also, by whom he had two children, and yet never left his mother's house therefore. . . .[25]

From this text, Shakespeare reveals to us dramatically, and by degrees, how Coriolanus's beliefs and attitudes, his character and conduct, have been shaped by his mother's teaching, and how he remains her devoted son to the end. Volumnia made him the hero of Corioli; but she also made him the victim of the pride that cost him his life. She taught him to be inflexible in opposition to his enemies, and he brought the same attitude to his treatment of the tribunes, Brutus and Sicinius. There seems to have been a certain inconsistency, or at least a fatal source of conflict, all unforeseen, in Volumnia's doctrine. She taught her son that to be true to his aristocratic code and class was to be true to the state. But the state of Rome was a republic, very nearly a democracy, in which the plebeians, through their tribunes, had real power and interest; in such a state, the aristocratic code, the aristocratic interest and authority, were only partially valid. Hence Volumnia's son, if he were to be faithful to his mother's teaching, was bound, sooner or later, to come into conflict with the plebeian interest. With such a temperament as Shakespeare imagines him to have, that conflict was apt to be sudden and violent. Shakespeare delicately indicates this inconsistency in Volumnia's arbitrary appeals to her son that he humble himself to sue for the consulship: "Thy valiantness was mine," she taunts him, when he vows he will not humiliate himself before the common people, "but owe thy pride thyself" (III, ii, 129–30). The example Volumnia has hitherto given in this regard, however, we gather from Coriolanus's ingenuous wonder at his mother's disapproval of him, a little earlier (III, ii, 7–13):

> I muse my mother
> Does not approve me further, who was wont
> To call them woollen vassals, things created
> To buy and sell with groats, to show bare heads
> In congregations, to yawn, be still, and wonder
> When one but of my ordinance stood up
> To speak of peace or war.

Volumnia is one of those parents who take all the credit for their children's successes but will have nothing to do with their failures. She, indeed, is willing to stoop for victory:

> I would dissemble with my nature where
> My fortunes and my friends at stake requir'd
> I should do so in honour,

she urges, and goes on to coach Coriolanus in the policy he should use to win his end—or rather hers, for the consulship is her ambition, not her son's:

I prithee, now, my son,
Go to them, with thy bonnet in thy hand;
And thus far having stretch'd it (here be with them),
Thy knee bussing the stones (for in such business
Action is eloquence, and the eyes of th' ignorant
More learned than the ears), waving thy head,
Which often, thus, correcting thy stout heart,
Now humble as the ripest mulberry
That will not hold the handling—say to them
Thou art their soldier, and, being bred in broils,
Hast not the soft way which, thou dost confess,
Were fit for thee to use, as they to claim,
In asking their good loves; but thou wilt frame
Thyself (forsooth) hereafter theirs, so far
As thou hast power and person.

It is shrewd advice. Had Coriolanus been able to follow it, he might have recovered everything. Had Volumnia been in her son's place, there would have been no difficulties; she would have been more than equal to the occasion, more than a match for the wily tribunes, and yet have had her own way, too. Coriolanus does his best to obey his mother, not because he wants the consulship but because he has never failed in his filial duty. He even summons a rueful humour in giving way, and a prophetic irony:

Pray be content.
Mother, I am going to the market place.
Chide me no more. I'll mountebank their loves,
Cog their hearts from them, and come home belov'd
Of all the trades in Rome. Look, I am going.
Commend me to my wife. I'll return consul.
Or never trust to what my tongue can do
I' th' way of flattery further.

It is of no use. The tribunes are too much for Coriolanus. They know their man:

Put him to choler straight. He hath been us'd
Ever to conquer, and to have his worth
Of contradiction. Being once chaf'd, he cannot
Be rein'd again to temperance; then he speaks
What's in his heart, and that is there which looks
With us to break his neck.

The charge of "traitor" rouses him to fury, and his frantic defiance of the tribunes and people delivers him into their hands. Sicinius and Brutus could hound him to his death, out of hand. They are content, being better politicians than Coriolanus, to decree his banishment; and his defiant acceptance of it assures the end they had all along intended.

It is an irony that so ambitious a mother as Volumnia should have reared a son so incapable of policy or pretence as Coriolanus, who yet worships her with unquestioning devotion; that in urging her indomitable will upon her son Volumnia should fail fully to understand the nature of the man she has so largely shaped. The despised tribunes understand him better. That they should overreach Coriolanus is a foregone conclusion; but in so doing, they also overreach Volumnia, who has taught Coriolanus to despise them. The ultimate irony is that their successful efforts should make necessary the mother's sacrifice of the son she has reared to the glory of Rome as the price of that city's safety.

In the final crisis, when Coriolanus, at the head of the Volscians, approaches Rome sweeping all before him, Volumnia shows the same heroic fibre as her son. She has been, in large part, the architect of his present fortune; and in the approaching tragedy she shares. She loves her son; and, in her final appeal to him, she must choose between him and Rome. This last appeal is from the text of her earlier profession of faith (I, iii, 15 ff.):

> VOL. . . . To a cruel war I sent him, from whence he return'd, his brows bound with oak. I tell thee, daughter, I sprang not more in joy at first hearing he was a man-child than now in first seeing he had prov'd himself a man.
>
> VIR. But had he died in the business, madam, how then?
>
> VOL. Then his good report should have been my son; I therein would have found issue. Hear me profess sincerely, had I a dozen sons, each in my love alike, and none less dear than thine and my good Marcius, I had rather had eleven die nobly for their country than one voluptuously surfeit out of action.

With the same stern devotion of the Roman matron who sent her son to the wars to learn to die nobly, if need be, for Rome, she now instructs him in his last duty to her and to the state. Coriolanus has been hitherto invincible against Rome, impervious to every appeal; we get the measure of his rage from the account of his former general and comrade-in-arms, Cominius; of his determination, from the rebuff of kindly old Menenius Agrippa. Coriolanus is fully committed to the Volscians; in the appeal of his family lies the city's last faint hope. Volumnia does not underestimate the difficulty. She knows how to direct her eloquence with masterly strategy, with the same care for gesture as for word that she had urged upon her son in dealing with the plebeians, with the same tactics we have already seen her use to win him to forgo his pride in seeking the consulship.[26] She is as persuasive in her suppliant's gesture of kneeling as in what she says; and now her plea to her son is surer, as she makes it not on her own behalf but for their country, appealing to his integrity, to his willingness to set aside his revenge for the sake of his family, of his fame, of his duty to her in which he has never failed. It is an appeal backed by all the emotional force of which she is capable, by her orator's skill, and by her love—for her love of her son is, in the final test, heroically unselfish; it is united with her love for Rome, so that for her the honour of Rome and of Coriolanus are one and the same; so she endeavours to persuade him. She does not win easily. The dramatic art of this great climactic scene is implicit in the whole previous study of the relation between mother and son; and the principles for which Volumnia has stood are vindicated in the strength of her appeal and in the sacrifice her son accepts.

Volumnia pleads first through the ties of family affection, describing the plight of Coriolanus's family, who must bow in shame to see the father, husband, son led in chains through the streets of Rome, or die in the triumph of his conquest; and even the timid Virgilia seconds this plea. Still Coriolanus is firm: "I have sat too long," he says, attempting to make his escape. But Volumnia holds him. If you reconcile the Volscians and Romans, she urges, you will be blest by both sides; if you persist in your revenge, the success is uncertain, but the infamy that will follow your name through history is certain: you will be abhorred to all after times as the would-be destroyer of your country, even though your attempt should fail. Then she sounds again the personal note, deeper this time:

Daughter, speak you.
He cares not for your weeping. Speak thou, boy.
Perhaps thy childishness will move him more
Than can our reasons. There's no man in the world
More bound to's mother; yet here he lets me prate
Like one i' th' stocks. . . .
Say my request's unjust,
And spurn me back. But if it be not so,
Thou art not honest, and the gods will plague thee
That thou restrain'st from me the duty which
To a mother's part belongs. He turns away.
Down, ladies! Let us shame him with our knees. . . .

As Coriolanus still hesitates, in turning from her, she rises for the last bitter stroke:

This fellow had a Volscian for his mother;
His wife is in Corioles, and this child
Like him by chance. Yet give us our despatch.
I am hush'd until our city be afire.
And then I'll speak a little.

And Coriolanus abruptly yields, unconditionally, with the courage, the generosity, and the grace that are the foundations of his real character, for he knows well the price of his yielding:

O, mother, mother!
What have you done? Behold, the heavens do ope,
The gods look down, and this unnatural scene
They laugh at. O my mother, mother! O!
You have won a happy victory to Rome;
But for your son—believe it, O believe it!—
Most dangerously you have with him prevail'd,
If not most mortal to him. But let it come. . . .

It is a victory for everyone but Coriolanus; a moral victory for him, too, indeed the greatest of all; but at a tragic cost. Bradley has eloquently summed it up:

The whole interest towards the close has been concentrated on the question whether the hero will persist in his revengeful design of storming and burning his native city, or whether better feelings will at last overpower his resentment and pride. He stands on the edge of a crime beside which, at least in outward dreadfulness, the slaughter of an individual looks insignificant. And when, at the sound of his mother's voice and the sight of his wife and child, nature asserts itself and he gives way, although we know he will lose his life, we care little for that: he has saved his soul. Our relief, and our exultation in the power of goodness, are so great that the actual catastrophe which follows and mingles sadness with these feelings leaves them but little diminished, and as we close the book we feel, it seems to me, more as we do at the close of *Cymbeline* than as we do at the close of *Othello*. . . .[27]

The contrast with the effect of *Othello* is indeed valid. And yet we may be more aware of tragic irony in *Coriolanus* than of the mood of reconciliation which Bradley finds in the play. Coriolanus's decision is magnificent, and so is Volumnia's appeal. But we have seen how Volumnia has shaped her son's nature, how her ambition for the consulship has put it in the power of the tribunes to banish him; how she must, in the end, sacrifice her son to save Rome. The same qualities in Coriolanus that have made him terrible to Rome's enemies make him, in turn, terrible towards Rome; and his self-vindication he must forgo, to suffer an ignominious death in Corioli.

> The gods look down, and this unnatural scene
> They laugh at.

Rome is spared. It is right that Coriolanus should yield to Volumnia's plea. No man's pride is worth a city, least of all for the sake of gratifying so ignoble a passion as revenge. But we may find little to rejoice at when Rome escapes. Coriolanus is not reconciled to Rome; we are not reconciled to his end, or fully satisfied that any lasting good has come of his sacrifice. There has been good for Coriolanus, indeed; it is good that he should conquer his pride; it is good that after ages should have his example and that they should remember it; but it is all at the cost of his life, and he is greater than those whom he saves. We see nothing to make us hope for better things in either Rome or Corioli, as a result of his loss. They are much alike, and it seems probable that they will continue in their habitual courses of envy, political scheming, and strife; Coriolanus's murder in Corioli has much in common with the previous spectacle of his banishment from Rome. Both cities have used him for their own ends—the only truly heroic man among them—and then cast him aside. We cannot excuse Coriolanus completely, by any means. He himself has provoked his fate by his pride, his unmanageable impetuousness, his impractical folly. Here is the same irony that we find in *Julius Caesar*, the irony which consists in the perception, the pitiless perception, of how common humanity defeats its own loftiest aspirations, its own finest qualities—courage, generosity, the very capacity for self-sacrifice in the cause of the state—and not merely *common* humanity but likewise its heroes, a Julius Caesar, a Brutus, a Coriolanus; and all through the commonest of human failings, ignorance and pride.

This irony completely informs the dramatic action of *Coriolanus* from first to last, from the first act of arrogance that introduces us to the hero to the scene that marks his end; for the mocking irony of Aufidius's concluding speech must not escape us:

> My rage is gone,
> And I am struck with sorrow. Take him up.
> Help three o' th' chiefest soldiers. I'll be one.
> Beat thou the drum that it speak mournfully.
> Trail your steel pikes. Though in this city he
> Hath widowed and unchilded many a one
> Which to this hour bewail the injury,
> Yet he shall have a noble memory.
> Assist.

It sounds like a generous tribute. Yet, but a moment before, Aufidius has successfully completed an act of political treachery in bringing about the assassination of Coriolanus which plainly parallels the earlier machinations of the tribunes against Coriolanus in Rome. There is the same careful preparation (V, vi, 1 ff); the same provocation of the hero on his most vulnerable side, with the taunts of "Traitor!" and "Boy!" (V, vi, 85, 99); the same inciting of the hostile mob (V, vi, 116, ff). The hypocrisy of Aufidius is palpable in this last scene, he who does not dare to provoke Coriolanus man to man but must play the politician with his insinuations and distortions of the truth to win the support he needs to betray the man he envies and hates; and we recall his earlier vow:

> Where I find him, were it
> At home, upon my brother's guard, even there,
> Against the hospitable canon, would I
> Wash my fierce hand in's heart.

Aufidius's final tribute to Coriolanus is but the concluding stroke of his "policy." The more magnanimous of the Volscian lords have been shocked at the sudden and violent attack upon the man who has won for them their greatest victory:

> 1 LORD. O Tullus!
> 2 LORD. Thou hast done a deed whereat valour will weep.
> 3 LORD. Tread not upon him. Masters all, be quiet!
> Put up your swords.

Coriolanus's murder has been the unexpected coup of a political cabal, of Aufidius's military faction; and Aufidius, as their leader, capitalizes upon the consternation of the other lords by himself assuming the generosity of their feelings in his pretended remorse for his deed of malignant treachery. It is easy to be magnanimous after winning one's end. We may be reminded of the conclusion of many a political campaign. Once the electors have returned him, the successful candidate, who has consistently vilified his opponent in his campaign speeches with every accusation and insinuation his advantage or his malice can suggest to him, now pays a delayed tribute to his defeated rival; he remembers certain merits in the opponent who is no longer dangerous to his own ambitions; he extends to him, perhaps, his sympathy in defeat and a certain carefully qualified praise for the fight he has waged; thus the electors may observe the generosity in victory of their new representative and reflect with satisfaction that they have chosen the better man. Aufidius is doubtless as sincere in his tribute to Coriolanus as is the modern politician in the circumstances that have just been described.

An anticlimax, Granville Barker calls the ending of *Coriolanus*.[28]

Such an anticlimax is inherent in the whole story, in the first outburst of Caius Marcius against the tribunes, in Volumnia's pride in her son and her indomitable will that he shall be consul, in the very eloquence of her pleading that he shall forgo his victory over Rome, in the hero's final ignominious destruction. It is the sort of anticlimax inherent in the day-to-day activities of common humanity, if we can view them with any detachment; and, when our emotions are not deeply engaged, as they are not in this play, we might almost as well speak of the "human comedy" as of tragedy. This ambivalence of the human situation is the theme, *par excellence*, of satire; and *Coriolanus* comes as close to satire, almost, as to tragedy, though the satire is qualified for us by the impression of human nobility that emerges as we watch a great man destroy himself.

3. *Julius Caesar* and *Coriolanus*

In *Julius Caesar* and *Coriolanus* certain positive values are paramount, though the mood of both plays is also deeply ironic. The world of the two is a moral order in which the principle of justice is seen as operative with a serene and impartial certainty that disregards the wills and pretensions of great men and factions, of Caesar and Brutus and Cassius, of Coriolanus and the tribunes Sicinius and Brutus, of Volumnia (who would have liked to see her son a consul), of Menenius Agrippa (who thought his friendship and influence all-powerful with Coriolanus), of the Volsces who would have liked to burn and pillage Rome. The operation of moral law in these two plays may be likened to the second law of thermodynamics: if anything leads you to question it—taking Sir Arthur Eddington's word for it[29]—you must be wrong, you have missed the point. It is a grave and ironic thing to contemplate, this necessary and certain operation of moral law, as we see it in these plays; it is neither something to rejoice over, nor something to feel particularly sad about. The point is that this is the nature of things, that this principle of an inevitable justice really does operate in common human experience, as we find it recorded in the pages of history. Sooner or later, the too ambitious man meets a fall, like Julius Caesar; so does the impractical idealist, like Brutus, or the proud and violent man, like Coriolanus. Cities and states are not exempt from this inexorable operation of nemesis. All must suffer for human limitations, for human pride or folly.

But this is not the whole. There are no villains in these two plays, for even Aufidius, if unprincipled, is but a simple and primitive fighting man, after all. There are degrees of human imperfection and folly, but no one is very wicked. The responsibility for the tragic catastrophe in each play is generalized, shared by the common humanity involved in the total action of each. No one is blameless, and no one is principally at fault. All are human and fallible, mortal men and women. Yet it is a conspicuous quality of both plays, too, that the heroes are noble men. Julius Caesar, Brutus, Coriolanus—they are all great men, beyond question, and their greatness is especially marked in their falls, even in their very errors. They share in common the faults of pride and ignorance, and of the two it is the latter, perhaps, that is ultimately the more impressive. Julius Caesar has no fear of the consequences of his arrogance, does not realize, perhaps, that he is arrogant. Brutus walks in utter darkness, bemused by his vision of an unreal world. Coriolanus is swept along in a red rage of passion, in which he neither sees nor understands. And yet they are all men we are somehow proud of, men whose deeds and sufferings have conferred dignity upon humanity.

This, then, is a positive element in Shakespeare's tragic vision, though verging upon satire; the movement referred to in the introductory chapter, from thesis to antithesis, is especially apparent in the group of four plays—*Julius Caesar*, *Coriolanus*, *Troilus and Cressida*, *Timon of Athens*—with which we are concerned in this chapter and the next. *Julius Caesar*, and more particularly, *Coriolanus*, approach the line which separates tragedy from satire, and pause just short of it. This line is, of course, imaginary; but it is useful to refer to as a critical hypothesis, in the subsequent discussion of this group of plays. For *Troilus and Cressida* and *Timon*, it will be argued, are plays which do cross this line, which we may consider as "satiric tragedies," though coming within the category of "tragedy" properly enough, too.

ANTITHESIS: *TROILUS AND CRESSIDA* AND *TIMON OF ATHENS*

1. *Troilus and Cressida*

IF *Troilus and Cressida* is a tragedy,[1] it is a tragedy in no conventional mode. Writing in 1916, in the light of his own elaborate study of the background of the play, J. S. P. Tatlock called *Troilus and Cressida* "the chief problem in Shakespeare";[2] and a dozen years later, Peter Alexander introduced his acute examination of the bibliographical puzzles of the play by observing that "*Troilus and Cressida* presents a group of problems not the most difficult or important but perhaps the most varied that requires consideration from the student of Shakespeare's text."[3] Since then, bibliographers have made notable progress in solving the problems of the text, and while they cannot be said to have disposed of all the questions that may be asked concerning the printing of the quarto and folio texts, their findings provide an indispensable initial guide to the critical consideration of this difficult play. These findings, and the ground they furnish for regarding the play as intended for a tragedy, have been set forth with admirable clarity by Sir Walter Greg.[4] We may here take for granted his rather technical discussion—to which the reader is herewith referred—and, armed with his authority, make no further apology for considering the play as a tragedy.

The story with which the play deals was of long-standing popularity, and Shakespeare's version presents material thoroughly familiar to his audience.[5] The current versions of the story derived from several famous mediaeval sources. Most famous of all was Chaucer's great narrative poem, *Troilus and Criseyde*, with its sequel in Robert Henryson's *Testament of Cresseid*, where Cressida, abandoned by Diomede, is punished for her unfaithfulness by being stricken with leprosy and dies of a broken heart when Troilus, returning from battle, fails to recognize her as he throws her his purse while she is sitting among beggars at the gates of Troy. This poem was printed with Chaucer's in the sixteenth-century editions of Chaucer's works and commonly accepted as fulfilling the poetic justice which his story was thought to require.[6] Particularly for the story of the Trojan War, popular sixteenth-century versions of the tale likewise derived importantly from John Lydgate's *Troy Book* and from Caxton's *Recuyell of the Historyes of Troye*, both of which stemmed, in turn, from the romantic narrative of Troy first recounted by Benoît de Ste-Maure in the twelfth century. Tatlock and Rollins have shown that versions of the Troy story, including the Troilus and Cressida episode, provided the matter of many popular narratives and plays from the reign of Henry VIII onward,[7] and the story seems to have enjoyed a particular vogue upon the stage at the turn of the century. The general tendency of these versions was to tell the whole story of Troy in order—that is, according to the mediaeval precedents followed—and as it was not available in Homer, Virgil, or Ovid, who tell only parts of it. The influence of the Homeric epic scarcely figured in this mediaeval tradition, formed in a time largely without benefit of Greek learning or of adequate translations of the *Iliad* or *Odyssey*. The first instalment of George Chapman's translation of the *Iliad* did not appear until 1598, and the veneration for the heroic age of antiquity with which we are familiar belongs to a still later period. The mediaeval versions of this "matter of Troy," however, whether as drama or as narrative, were widely familiar and enjoyed great popularity at the time Shakespeare undertook his play. In *Troilus and Cressida*, he was dealing with one of the best known stories of his time.

We have a fine example of the kind of drama on the popular Trojan War theme that flourished during Shakespeare's dramatic career, and beyond it, in Thomas Heywood's play in two parts called *The Iron Age*, itself the culmination of a cycle of five plays bearing the titles of the Hesiodic "ages" and reviewing the whole compass of ancient myth down to the last of the "returns" of the Greek heroes who fought at Troy.[8] Heywood's plays of the Ages were published between 1611 and 1632, but there is evidence that parts of them, particularly a version of *1* and *2 Iron Age* probably corresponding to a play called *Troy* recorded in Henslowe's diary, may be dated as early as 1595–96.[9] Of the long-continued popularity of *1* and *2 Iron Age* (which may have been revised and augmented during their stage career), Heywood writes in the preface to the edition of 1632:

> Lastly I desire thee to take notice, that these were the Playes often (and not with the least applause) Publickely Acted by two Companies, vppon one Stage at once, and haue at sundry times thronged three seuerell Theaters, with numerous and mighty Auditories. . . .[10]

These two plays are constructed in the form of a running chronicle of episodes, from the opening council at Troy where it is decided that Paris shall sail to Sparta to carry off Menelaus's queen in retaliation for the earlier rape of Hesione,[11] through the invasion of Troy by the Greeks, Hector's challenge and combat with Ajax, Achilles' refraining from battle for love of Polyxena, the love of Troilus and Cressida and her falsing him for Diomede, the base slaying of Hector by Achilles and his Myrmidons, the slaying of Achilles by Paris, the rivalry of Ulysses and Ajax for Achilles' armour and the death of Ajax by his own hand, with which Part One concludes. Part Two contains the stratagem of the Wooden Horse, with Synon as the villain of the action and Pyrrhus as the ruthless champion of the Greeks. Thersites, who first appears as a dignified if bitter commentator on the Greek side in Part One, degenerates during the course of the plays into a mischievous railer, with all the indiscriminate malice, if less of the wit and foulness of Shakespeare's character. In Part Two he becomes the companion of Synon, and, while continuing his bitter commentary, gradually lapses into ineffectual clowning and perishes ignominiously. A brief passage shows us the rejection of the false Cressid by Diomede, and an incidental reference is later made to her leprosy. The climax of the first three acts is the sack of Troy under the leadership of Pyrrhus, the vigour of which recalls the declamation of the First Player in *Hamlet*, though Heywood gains his effect through spectacular action rather than through the descriptive rhetoric of Shakespeare's lines.[12] Acts IV and V of *2 Iron Age* are really a separate playlet, tracing the nemesis that follows the Grecian conquerors—the slaying of Agamemnon by Clytemnestra and Aegisthus, the vengeance of Orestes, with a rather huddled holocaust in Act V, where Helen makes a speech of self-accusation and strangles herself, and all the surviving heroes perish except Ulysses, who apologizes, in an epilogue, for the bloodiness of the catastrophe and the unusual length of the action:

> Much matter in few words, hee [the author] bad me say,
> Are hard to express, that lengthned out our Play.

Here was typically popular theatre fare in the era that saw the vogue of the chronicle histories upon the Elizabethan stage. The loosely flowing episodic structure was easy to follow. It provided a crowded and spectacular action with simple and energetic characterization of figures well known to the audience: the crafty Ulysses, the bully Achilles who takes so mean an advantage of the magnanimous Hector, Troilus second only to his brother Hector in heroic deeds and his equal in indomitable valour but shamefully betrayed in love, the mighty and dull-witted Ajax, Thersites the malcontent, ironist, and buffoon, were all abundantly familiar to Elizabethan audiences before Shakespeare undertook to present them in his own play.

The resemblances between Heywood's plays of the *Iron Age* and Shakespeare's *Troilus and Cressida* are indeed far too close and striking to be fortuitous. Almost every scene of the war story in Shakespeare's play finds a parallel in *1 Iron Age*; the only notable difference in subject-matter between the two plays is that Shakespeare has given the love story much greater prominence anp elaboration, and his account of the war ends with the event that opens Act IV, Part One, of Heywood's play, the death of Hector.[13] Moreover, as Tatlock points out, the *dramatis personae* of the two plays are nearly identical, the similar role and utterance of Thersites, Achilles, and Ajax being especially striking. Finally, amid many less notable verbal resemblances,[14] the following is unmistakable (in both cases Hector is the speaker):

> And Cuz, by Ioue thou hast a braue aspect,
> It cheeres my blood to looke on such a foe:

I would there ran none of our Troian blood
In all thy veines, or that it were diuided
From that which thou receiuest from *Telamon*:
Were I assured our blood possest one side,
And that the other; by Olimpicke *Ioue*,
I'd thrill my Iauelin at the *Grecian* moysture,
And spare the Troian blood; Aiax I loue it
Too deare to shed it . . .
Then here's thy cousins hand
By *Ioue* thou hast a lusty pondrous arme.
(*1 Iron Age*, end of act II)[15]

Thou art, great lord, my father's sister's son
A cousin german to great Priam's seed.
The obligation of our blood forbids
A gory emulation 'twixt us twain.
Were thy commixtion Greek and Troyan so
That thou couldst say "This hand is Grecian all,
And this is Troyan; the sinews of this leg
All Greek, and this all Troy; my mother's blood
Runs on the dexter cheek, and this sinister
Bounds in my father's;" by Jove multipotent,
Thou shouldst not bear from me a Greekish member
Wherein my sword had not impressure made
Of our rank feud; but the just gods gainsay
That any drop thou borrow'dst from thy mother,
My sacred aunt, should by my mortal sword
Be drained! Let me embrace thee, Ajax.
By him that thunders, thou hast lusty arms!
(*Troilus and Cressida*, IV, v, 120–36)

Concerning these resemblances, Tatlock concludes: "While most of the parallelism in larger contexts is due to the fact that both follow Caxton, as to the smaller points one thing seems certain; without insisting on any one, they cannot all be due to coincidence, or to any known source, or to any sort of common fund of material generally traditional in Trojan plays. The remaining possibilities are that one borrowed from the other directly, or through an intermediary play, or that both made use of a third play."

It is hardly conceivable that so simple a chronicle as *1 Iron Age* could have borrowed from Shakespeare's play without taking account of its two most distinctive features—the structural parallel and balancing of the war story with the love story of Troilus and Cressida, and the way in which Hector's challenge is linked with Ulysses' scheme to rouse Achilles by putting forward Ajax as his rival. Tatlock finds it hard to believe that Shakespeare drew upon Heywood's version because he cannot conceive how Shakespeare, in or about 1601 when he was presumably working on *Troilus and Cressida*, might have known Heywood's play or studied its manuscript, since presumably it belonged to Henslowe's company. If Heywood's play was being popularly performed at least five years earlier than Shakespeare's by the chief rivals of Shakespeare's company, the Admiral's Men, however, and if it had been a considerable success, Shakespeare would certainly hear of it; and what was to prevent his going to see it performed—we can hardly suppose that he never went outside his own theatre, or that he failed to take a lively interest in the productions of his competitors. Again, some of the performances "by two Companies vppon one Stage at once," to which Heywood refers in the preface to the published edition of *The Iron Age*, may even have drawn upon the resources of Shakespeare's company before Shakespeare decided to prepare his own version of the Troy story. On the whole, it seems more than likely that Heywood's *Iron Age*, at least in an early version, was among the sources upon which Shakespeare levied for *Troilus and Cressida*. Tatlock prefers to suppose that both authors drew upon a common source which has not survived. Such an hypothesis is cautious, but it seems in this case cumbersome and unnecessarily speculative.

In the two plays, thus closely linked, we appear to have, then, the interesting and by no means uncommon situation of a highly popular play by a respectable but very run-of-the-mill dramatist providing a working model for the supreme dramatist of his time, who produces, in his turn, a play which must have been "caviare to the general." If we keep in mind the analogy of Heywood's play as we study Shakespeare's, we shall have not merely a valuable clue to the common tradition of the mediaevalized Trojan War story which both plays reflect but also a measure of the individuality of form and purpose distinguishing *Troilus and Cressida* from what we may regard as a normal specimen of Elizabethan tragedy in the popular chronicle form.

The two parts of *The Iron Age* conform to the conception of tragedy explained in *The Monk's Tale* and still widely current in Elizabethan drama:

> Tragedie is to seyn a certayn storie,
> As olde bookes maken us memorie,
> Of hym that stood in greet prosperitee,
> And is yfallen out of heigh degree
> Into myserie, and endeth wrecchedly.

Part One contains the deaths of Hector, Troilus, Achilles, and Ajax; Part Two ends with the deaths of all the heroes except Ulysses; and in the preface to the second part, Heywood distinguishes his serious treatment of the heroic matter of his plays of the Ages from the "Satirica Dictaeria, and Comica Scommata [which] are now in request: For mine owne part, I neuer affected either. . . ."[16] It might, of course, be argued that Heywood is here thinking of the contrast offered by Shakespeare's play in particular—of the same elements praised in the preface to the 1609 quarto of *Troilus and Cressida*. But it seems more likely that in 1632 Heywood might have in mind the mock-heroics of Beaumont and Fletcher and kindred theatrical fare then so much in fashion, rather than the unmistakably serious, and probably unfashionable, *Troilus and Cressida* of Shakespeare. At all events, it seems clear that Shakespeare's play follows the traditional conception of genre as represented in Heywood's plays of the Ages while extending the limits of that genre to include an irony subtler than anything Heywood could have conceived, or, indeed, than can be found in other preceding exemplars of that tradition.

In Heywood's version of the story and other versions of Heywood's predecessors, then, Shakespeare found a material precedent for the treatment of his theme. The lumbering arrogance of Ajax and Achilles, the base slaughter of Hector by Achilles' Myrmidons, the railing of Thersites,[17] all belong in the high and heroic matter of tragedy, according to the mediaeval tradition. This matter represents a semi-fabulous and heroic age in which various famous but faulty heroes flourish for a time, and, with the turn of Fortune's wheel, regulated in accord with a rough poetic justice, at length meet unhappy ends.[18]

But if Shakespeare's play belongs in this popular tradition by reason of its subject-matter, we shall not find Shakespeare's unifying tragic conception in any such scheme as contented Heywood and the simpler folk of the Elizabethan audience for whom he mainly wrote. Shakespeare's tragic design in *Troilus and Cressida* is much more complex, and much less orthodox by popular Elizabethan standards. Hector, to be sure, dies in the last act; but Troilus is left alive, bitter and defiant. And what of the nemesis that poetic justice required to fall upon Cressida and Achilles, to say nothing of lesser figures—the nemesis that the tradition itself supplied and that the popular audience had every ground to expect? Clearly, this is no conventional tragedy, even by the comparatively sophisticated standards of the Elizabethans, nor is it a play aimed primarily at pleasing a popular audience. There is no design of poetic justice here (unless by way of an implicit and highly refined irony), no conventional catastrophe. If the matter of *Troilus and Cressida* is traditional, Shakespeare shaped the play according to his own rather unconventional notions. It is surely a mistake to think of him as constantly aiming at popularity; almost as great a mistake as is the baseless idea, now fortunately passing out of fashion but once taken for granted, that Shakespeare was primarily an "improver" of other men's plays, a dramatist who followed the changing theatrical vogue but never led it.[19] If, then, we wish to understand Shakespeare's *Troilus and Cressida*, we must take account of the tradition from which his material derives, for this establishes the material limits of his conception, but we must guard against the easy mistake of assuming that because the material is derivative the form is necessarily derivative too; in other words, we must look for Shakespeare's formal design not in some precedent supplied by Heywood or Chapman or Ben Jonson, by Chaucer or Lydgate or Caxton or any other part of the stock from which Shakespeare drew his material, but in the unique construction of his own imagination.

When we look at Shakespeare's play as a whole in comparison with Heywood's, it is clear that the essential respect in which it differs structurally from *1 Iron Age*—as from any of the other versions which may have figured among Shakespeare's sources—is the way in which the two main elements of the plot, the war story and the love story, are balanced and interrelated. Instead of providing us with a chronicle, Shakespeare frames the story of the lovers within the story of the war so that the one mirrors the other—a technique that may remind us in one way of *Julius Caesar* and in another of *King Lear*, though neither parallel could be pressed too far; no two of the tragedies are structurally very much alike.

In *Troilus and Cressida*, the tragic effect does not concern the fortunes of any one central figure, his rise and fall; rather, it relates to the plight of mankind as represented in the play, of the human society which it pictures. This effect is achieved through the study of two common human situations: a man in love with a woman, two peoples at war. These situations are interrelated as microcosm and macrocosm; the causes and effects of the one are seen to be reflected and magnified in the other—the ethical situation of individuals in the social context of war—so that we receive the impression of a common and all-pervading pattern in human affairs. It is a pattern of betrayal and counter-betrayal. Helen betrays Menelaus; Cressida betrays Troilus. The Trojans wrong the Greeks by keeping Helen, prompted by a false sense of honour; the Greeks retaliate, through Achilles, with the dishonourable slaying of Hector. Similarly with the aims of the heroes. Troilus burns to enjoy the love of Cressida and is frustrated through her wantonness; Ajax would fain outshine Achilles, and is frustrated by his own stupidity and by Hector's extravagant generosity; in turn, the generosity of Hector towards Achilles in battle merely reserves Hector as the prey of Achilles' Myrmidons; finally, the master stratagem, Ulysses' plan to arouse the indifferent Achilles, is rendered nugatory by the unforeseen death of Patroclus. All is lust and vanity and frustration; and throughout, like a low comedy chorus, runs the foul and gloating commentary of Thersites: "All the argument is a cuckold and a whore!" "Nothing but lechery! All incontinent varlets!" "Lechery, lechery; still wars and lechery; nothing else holds fashion. A burning devil take them!"

Yet this is only one aspect of the whole. Thersites sees the situations of the lovers and the heroes in all their triviality—the pride, the lust, the vanity of their various aims; he strips them of every dignity, of every heroic pretension. But he interprets everything maliciously, vindictively, with an extravagant vehemence that renders *him* an object of our mirth in the furious career of his invective. As he tends more and more to the obscene, he provides the safety-valve for our disgust; he is the clown whose very excesses warn us against laughing merely derisively, or in the wrong place.

For the action is not simply travesty, nor are the heroes merely ridiculous. The Trojans fare better than the Greeks; like his mediaeval predecessors, Shakespeare remembers his Trojan ancestry. But even the Trojans are tragically mistaken in their aims, the victims of their own false ideals.

It is instructive concerning Shakespeare's purpose to compare his version of the Troilus and Cressida story with Chaucer's. The tale had undergone great transformation between Chaucer's day and Shakespeare's, especially in the degeneration of Cressida as represented in Henryson's *Testament of Cresseid*; but Shakespeare, in telling the story at much greater length than it appears in Heywood's *Iron Age* or in most of the other contemporary versions, drew directly upon Chaucer's poem, and, had he seen fit, could have told the story of the lovers much more sympathetically than he chose to. That his version is not circumscribed within the limits indicated by his own play is clear from the reference of Ancient Pistol to the "lazar-kite of Cressid's kind" (*Henry V,* II, i, 80) which shows his familiarity with Henryson's sequel to Chaucer's story.

How different Shakespeare's reading of the story is from Chaucer's —or from Henryson's, either—may surprise anyone who turns directly from a reading of the poems to the play. In Chaucer, the love of Troilus for Cressida is a beautiful thing, an ennobling discipline. In his zeal to merit the lady's approval, Troilus becomes the pattern of valour and knightly courtesy:

> But Troilus lay tho no lenger down,
> But up anon upon his stede bay,
> And in the feld he pleyde the leoun;
> Wo was that Grek that with hym mette a-day!
> And in the town his manere tho forth ay
> Soo goodly was, and gat hym so in grace,
> That ecch hym loved that loked on his face.
>
> For he bicom the friendlieste wighte,
> The gentilest, and ek the mooste fre,
> The thriftiest and oon the beste knyght,
> That in his tyme was or myghte be.
> Dede were his japes and his cruelte,
> His heighe port and his manere estraunge,
> And ecch of tho gan for a vertu chaunge.

Chaucer requires two whole books to tell of the young lover's trials and sufferings in the effort to prove his worthiness, and another to represent the difficulty of winning his lady. His theme is the serious and exacting course of a true love, demanding, as it does, the utmost devotion and unselfishness and courage of both lovers, and the tragedy that results when one of them proves unequal to its severest demands. Criseyde's falseness is not so much a betrayal as a failure, failure in the resourcefulness and strength of character necessary to manage her return to Troilus which she had so easily promised. It is a fault of her yieldingness—otherwise so appealing—rather than of her intention. Once she has returned to her father, her escape is too difficult for her to manage; she had not foreseen the difficulties, she had over-estimated her own powers, she had persuaded herself and Troilus that what they both wished would easily come to pass; in the event, she yields to the force of circumstance; hardly realizing how she does so, she follows the easier way. Chaucer is unwilling to blame her harshly for it. Nor is Troilus easy to sympathize with in grief; he embraces it so freely, we half suspect him of enjoying it. The sadness of the story, and its irony, lies in the inadequacy of human love, of human lovers:

> O yonge, fresshe folkes, he or she,
> In which that love up groweth with youre age,
> Repeyreth hom fro worldly vanyte,
> And of youre herte up casteth the visage
> To thilke God that after his ymage
> Yow made, and thinketh al nys but a faire
> This world, that passeth soone as floures faire . . .

But there is no bitterness in the tale.

Shakespeare gives us his view of the story in the first two scenes of the play. He passes over Troilus's trial of devotion, which figures so prominently in Chaucer. The issue is no longer Troilus's worthiness but Cressida's unworthiness; and we first see the youthful Troilus, "mad in Cressid's love," burning with an ungratified passion for a wanton who, in his innocence, he supposes to be hard to win. His illusions are carefully cherished by Cressida's uncle, Pandarus, whose name, in Shakespeare, is eloquent of his nature. Cressida's real motives, amply suggested in her flippant parrying of her uncle Pandar's solicitations on Troilus's behalf, are explicitly stated for us in her soliloquy after Pandarus leaves her:

> Words, vows, gifts, tears, and love's full sacrifice
> He offers in another's enterprise.
> But more in Troilus thousandfold I see
> Than in the glass of Pandar's praise may be.
> Yet hold I off. Women are angels, wooing:
> Things won are done; joy's soul lies in the doing.
> That she belov'd knows naught that knows not this:
> Men prize the thing ungain'd more than it is.
> That she was never yet that ever knew
> Love got so sweet as when desire did sue.
> Therefore this maxim out of love I teach:
> Achievement is command; ungain'd, beseech.
> Then, though my heart's content firm love doth bear,
> Nothing of that shall from mine eyes appear.

Her yielding to Troilus is a foregone conclusion, a matter of tactics, not at all of worthiness, or of scruples to be overcome.

After this brief but sufficient exposition of the lovers' relationship, we turn to the war story, which is elaborated at much greater length, involving as it does the status of the war in the Greek camp and in Troy. When the love story resumes (III, i), the assignation of the lovers has been arranged by the eager Pandar, who comes with ridiculous affectation of archness to request Paris and Helen to make Troilus's excuses at supper to King Priam. Pandar's leers and winks need no stage direction, as the scene subtly suggests the parallel, in the approaching meeting of Troilus and Cressida, with the falseness of Helen and the infatuated sensuality of Paris. Troilus comes to his love with sense-intoxicated naïveté:

> I am as true as truth's simplicity,
> And simpler than the infancy of truth.

Cressida invokes a catalogue of comparisons to witness the impossibility of her playing false, and Pandarus joins their hands with an emblem-like prophecy:

> If ever you play false to one another, since I have taken such pains to bring you together, let all pitiful goers-between be call'd to the world's end after my name; call them all Pandars. Let all constant men be Troiluses, and all false women Cressids, and all brokers-between Pandars! Say "Amen."

The scene is a masterpiece of iterative irony.

The turn of the lovers' fortunes immediately follows, with the request of Calchas for his daughter and the despatch of Diomede to bring Cressida to the Greek camp. At her parting with Troilus the irony of her coming betrayal of him is deepened in the eloquence of her protestations:

> I have forgot my father;
> I know no touch of consanguinity,
> No kin, no love, no blood, no soul so near me
> As the sweet Troilus. O you gods divine,
> Make Cressid's name the very crown of falsehood
> If ever she leave Troilus! Time, force, and death,
> Do to this body what extremes you can,
> But the strong base and building of my love
> Is as the very centre of the earth,
> Drawing all things to it. I'll go in and weep—

But in the actual leave-taking, she is calmly self-possessed, a little impatient of Troilus's anxious need for further assurances from her—"O heavens! 'be true' again!"; once more the coquette—"O heavens! you love me not!"; and pleased to be so much the centre of masculine attention: all of which prepares us for Ulysses' summary comment:

> Fie, fie upon her!
> There's language in her eye, her cheek, her lip;
> Nay, her foot speaks. Her wanton spirits look out
> At every joint and motive of her body.
> O, these encounterers so glib of tongue,
> That give accosting welcome ere it comes
> And wide unclasp the tables of their thoughts
> To every ticklish reader—set them down
> For sluttish spoils of opportunity
> And daughters of the game!

Over her betrayal of Troilus, Ulysses presides. His praise of Troilus affords us the measure by which we are to judge Troilus's role in the double catastrophe that he suffers, the loss of his love and the loss of Hector:

> The youngest son of Priam, a true knight;
> Not yet mature, yet matchless; firm of word;
> Speaking in deeds and deedless in his tongue;
> Not soon provok'd, nor being provok'd soon calm'd;
> His heart and hand both open and both free.
> For what he has he gives, what thinks he shows,
> Yet gives he not till judgment guide his bounty,
> Nor dignifies an impair thought with breath;
> Manly as Hector, but more dangerous;
> For Hector in his blaze of wrath subscribes
> To tender objects, but he in heat of action
> Is more vindicative than jealous love.
> They call him Troilus, and on him erect
> A second hope as fairly built as Hector.

It is fitting that Ulysses, the advocate of order, the symbol of reason, and the man who has read Cressida at a glance, should act as mentor to Troilus's disillusionment. The scene is a variation upon the play-within-a-play convention, with Cressida and Diomede at a distance acting out the spectacle, and Ulysses, Troilus, and Thersites giving us the commentary in the foreground; and, to the scene of Troilus's union with Cressida, it is a parallel and contrasting symbolic tableau, with Ulysses parting the union that Pandar had made, and with the addition of Thersites as ribald chorus. As Cressida dallies with Diomede—a gallant who knows well how to counter her coquetry with the firmness of his threatened indifference, and who thus draws her into giving him Troilus's love-pledge of the sleeve—we witness Troilus's struggle to deny the evidence of his senses, a struggle at once absurd and pathetic:

> This she? no, this is Diomed's Cressida.
> If beauty have a soul, this is not she.
> If souls guide vows, if vows have sanctimony,
> If sanctimony be the gods' delight,
> If there be rule in unity itself—
> This is not she.

The quiet irony of Ulysses' firm rationality: "I cannot conjure, Troyan . . . Cressid was here but now," gives us one measure of the import of the scene, and Thersites' "Will he swagger himself out on's own eyes!" another. But after Troilus's hopeless attempt to deny the situation itself, after his recriminations, his bitterness issues in a resolve:

> Farewell, revolted fair! and, Diomed,
> Stand fast, and wear a castle on thy head.

Here is one strand of the rejection theme. Troilus has mistaken a sensual infatuation for an ideal relationship of devotion and trust. When Cressida plays him false, he has nothing but the will to resist, to strike back against the personal agents of his betrayal. He is powerless against the cause of it, human weakness and perfidy. Ulysses, Troilus, Thersites: in each of them we may see reflected an aspect of the situation symbolized by Cressida's betrayal—Ulysses, who understands and reveals, but cannot help; Troilus, who acts, but without fully comprehending, simply with the will to reject, to oppose; and Thersites, who accepts it all as meat for his own foul appetite for human degradation. These three suggest the degrees of reason, will, and debased appetite in man; and the only value that emerges is the motive of repudiation, Troilus's will to resist the fact of human baseness.

In the story of the siege of Troy, the theme is enlarged to comprehend the whole world of the play. In the scene of the Greek council, first, we learn the cause that impedes the Greek prosecution of the war, in Ulysses' speech on degree: Achilles, in his tent, "grows dainty of his worth," and with his minion Patroclus mocks Agamemnon, Nestor, and the other leaders, while Ajax (we see him in the next scene, like a dazed bull parrying Thersites' jibes) and many another, infected by Achilles' example, grow equally self-willed and overweening. In the long truce between the two sides, all order and discipline in the Greek camp have been overthrown. The challenge to a trial of arms arrives from Hector—for we are in the world of mediaeval chivalry, of Lydgate and Caxton rather than of Homer—and provides the occasion for Ulysses' clever plan to arouse Achilles' envy by the choice of Ajax as the Greek champion.

In Troy, the parallel council scene shows an even deeper-lying disorder. The issue is the return of Helen to the Greeks. The Greek leaders are willing to make peace if she is given back, and without further reparations, a generous offer. Fairly and reasonably, Hector gives the grounds for accepting: keeping Helen means the continuation of the war, with all its hazards, and already she has cost the life of many a brave man: "She is not worth what she doth cost the holding."[21] He is seconded by his brother, the priest Helenus. The opposition is hotly taken up by Troilus. First he belittles reason as a guide:

> Nay, if we talk of reason,
> Let's shut our gates and sleep. Manhood and honour
> Should have hare hearts, would they but fat their thoughts
> With this cramm'd reason. Reason and respect
> Make livers pale and lustihood deject.

The value of Helen, he urges, lies in the valuer; and we catch the echo of Marlowe's Faustus in his tribute to Helen,

> Why, she is a pearl,
> Whose price hath launch'd above a thousand ships,
> And turn'd crown'd kings to merchants—

with an ironic substitution for the suppressed "And burnt the topless towers of Ilion"—an implication made explicit in the following prophecy of Cassandra. Troilus's main argument is a double sophistry: the Greeks, he says, committed the first wrong in carrying off Hesione, and thus justified the rape of Helen; once having supported this act, the Trojans are bound in honour to maintain it, cowards if they do not.

Hereupon Cassandra enters, bitterly declaiming her prophecy of the disaster to fall upon Troy:

> Our firebrand brother, Paris, burns us all.
> Cry, Trojans, cry! A Helen and a woe!
> Cry, cry! Troy burns, or else let Helen go.

The irony here, or rather the double irony—for Cassandra, we remember, is the prophetess inspired by Apollo and doomed to be disbelieved—is that her appeal really turns the scale. Troilus scornfully rejects her mad ravings; Paris takes heart to speak in his own defence and in support of Troilus, since Cassandra has attacked him; and Hector makes the fateful decision, while judging the issue clearly:

> If Helen then be wife to Sparta's king,
> As it is known she is, these moral laws
> Of nature and of nations speak aloud
> To have her back return'd. Thus to persist
> In doing wrong extenuates not wrong,
> But makes it much more heavy. Yet ne'ertheless,
> My spritely brethren, I propend to you
> In resolution to keep Helen still;
> For 'tis a cause that hath no mean dependence
> Upon our joint and several dignities.

Indeed, he has already prejudged the outcome, for he has sent a "roisting challenge" among the Greeks, as he now boasts, the challenge which issues in the fiasco of the later encounter with Ajax:

> Hector, in view of Troyans and of Greeks,
> Shall make it good, or do his best to do it,
> He hath a lady, wiser, fairer, truer,
> Than ever Greek did compass in his arms,

And will tomorrow with his trumpet call
Midway between your tents and walls of Troy,
To rouse a Grecian that is true in love.
If any come, Hector shall honour him;
If none, he'll say in Troy when he retires,
The Grecian dames are sunburnt and not worth
The splinter of a lance.

The whole scene emphasizes the wilful disregard of reason, the reversal of the due order of the human faculties: the will defying reason, and prompted by the passions—by the lust of Paris and Troilus, by the rash pride (however spirited or magnanimous) of Troilus and Hector. Certainly, Shakespeare here is not thinking of Homer and the heroic age of Greece—though we need not assume that he was ignorant of them, either. He is thinking rather of the mediaeval world of chivalry and its values; of the romantic past as pictured by Lydgate and Caxton, and by the simpler tales of Amadis and Palmerin and the Knight of the Sun that still delighted and edified the Citizen and his wife in *The Knight of the Burning Pestle*; of the heroics of a Hotspur, which he had viewed with half-affectionate irony in the first part of *Henry IV*; perhaps even of such a contemporary figure as the Earl of Essex, with his romantic gestures, his generosity and heroism, and his fatal lack of judgment and self-command. Shakespeare weighs this world of rash and chivalrous "honour" and rejects it, though not altogether without sympathy, in his picture of the Trojan cause and the Trojan motives, just as he exposes and rejects, with less sympathy, what he represents as the false values of *amour courtois* in the story of Troilus and Cressida.

If Shakespeare's ironic portrait of the Trojan chivalry is sympathetic, he is all but pitiless towards the Greeks. Ulysses gives us the measure of the disorder in the Greek camp, and we see for ourselves the disparities of ceremonious and ineffectual dignity in the grave Agamemnon and the garrulous Nestor; ludicrous stupidity in Ajax; wanton rudeness, pride, and despicable treachery in Achilles, as he lolls mockingly in his tent with his darling, his "masculine whore" Patroclus, insults Hector, the guest of the Greeks, with his vaunts, or finally surrounds him with his Myrmidons, slaughters him, and drags his body over the field tied to his horse's tail.

The action that concerns the war develops an ironic pattern involving both sides. Ulysses proposes to use the challenge of Hector to rouse Achilles from his mocking indolence through an appeal to his pride. Ajax is preferred as champion of the Greeks against Hector; and Ulysses devotes the full powers of his diplomatic eloquence to the attempt to stir Achilles' envy:

> Time hath, my lord, a wallet at his back,
> Wherein he puts alms for oblivion,
> A great siz'd monster of ingratitude. . . .

Even Patroclus is stirred by Ulysses' appeal and begs Achilles to vindicate both their honours. But Ulysses misjudges his man. Achilles is scarcely aware of Ulysses' too subtle innuendoes. It has never occurred to him that anyone could think ill of him:

> I see my reputation is at stake,
> My fame is shrewdly gor'd;

and with bland condescension he resolves to invite Hector to visit him peacefully at his tent after the combat with Ajax! We notice the studied contrast to Hector: Hector with his too great regard for honour; Achilles with his brutal insensibility to honour, as to courtesy, or any other knightly virtue. Ulysses' beautiful plan comes to nothing; or rather, it has consequences that he could neither intend nor foresee. The combat between Hector and Ajax resolves itself into an occasion for the display of Hector's characteristic generosity—which is to be ultimately his undoing—as he clasps his kinsman Ajax in his arms instead of fighting with him. The peaceful visit of the Trojans follows, when Hector is insulted by Achilles and Troilus sees Cressida betray him.

And thus we come to the final stage of the action, which begins in Act V, Scene iii. It used to be a common opinion that the last scenes of the play, or most of them, crowded as they are with successive situations, with fragments of a confusing struggle (as it was thought), and undistinguished by any remarkable verse, were unworthy of Shakespeare. This was the huddled close which Dr. Johnson had so emphatically censured;[22] or, worse still, perhaps, here were the hasty additions of an inept reviser of the play.[23] But the whole preceding action of the Trojan War theme has led up to and prepared for this anticlimax. The contrast between Hector and Achilles, Greeks and Trojans, now finds its fitting culmination. The play would indeed be fragmentary and enigmatic without these scenes. They are essential in completing the ironic design of the whole. And if these scenes are crowded with action—a sustained and unbroken action, of course, upon the Elizabethan stage—this is a fitting contrast for the final effect of a play that has been throughout most of its extent unusually thoughtful and discursive, a prolonged analytic argument, almost, containing some of the most impressive of Shakespeare's poetic meditations. The bearing of these final scenes upon the whole design and purport of the play deserves careful attention.

The opening of Act V is merely a transition from the peaceful issue of the trial of arms between Hector and Ajax. Achilles, having greeted Hector with boasts of his own superiority and the promise to meet him in battle on the morrow, here lightly abandons his challenge upon receiving a secret letter from Hecuba, charging him in the name of his love Polyxena to refrain from fighting. Hector's entertainment by the Greeks is abridged by the representation of his departure from the Greek camp; and this leads us to the climax of the love story—Ulysses' exposure of Cressida's treachery to Troilus, in Scene ii.

The culminating episode begins with the arming of Hector before the next day's battle. Lest we should have missed the point of Hector's vulnerability hitherto, and to heighten the contrast of his approaching fall, every effort is made to keep him from fighting that day. Andromache and Hecuba have dreamed prophetic dreams; Cassandra raises again the strain of her fruitless forebodings; even Priam lends his authority to their urgings; to all of which, Hector steadfastly opposes his "honour": "Mine honour keeps the weather of my fate . . . I am i' th' vein of chivalry today . . . I must not break my faith." With ironic foreshadowing, he urges Troilus (who is to survive him) to remain at home; and Troilus, impetuously seconding Hector's resolve to fight, unwittingly foretells the very ground of Hector's destruction in expostulating with him for his "vice of mercy," which is to lead him to decline his first encounter with Achilles.

The ensuing scenes offer a kaleidoscopic review of all the themes of the action: Thersites railing; Troilus seeking vengeance on Diomede and losing his horse to him instead; Agamemnon and Nestor trying vainly to rally and direct the Greek forces; Ulysses bringing word that the death of Patroclus has at last roused Achilles to fury and he is coming to fight—the incidental irony here is that Ulysses' earlier attempt to rouse Achilles has brought Patroclus to join the battle, lose his life at Hector's hands, and thus bring Achilles against Hector, after all. Hector carries all before him, chivalrously sparing Achilles on their first encounter (he has likewise spared Thersites, earlier!), because that hero, as Hector thinks, is at a disadvantage through his lack of recent warlike exercise; at length he is himself beguiled by the rich armour of his latest victim to expose himself unarmed to the treachery of Achilles and his Myrmidons. Hector's motives have been exactly reversed by his conqueror. The generosity and heedless courage of the Trojan hero have been checkmated by the cowardly and circumspect advantage taken of him by the Greek, who with final indignity ties his victim's lifeless body to his horse's tail.

This is all at the opposite pole from the heroic anger, and the magnanimity, of the hero of the *Iliad*; and Shakespeare must have been aware of the contrast his story offered with the Homeric account. The first version of George Chapman's translation of the *Iliad*, when it appeared in 1598, constituted a major literary event; it may even have provided a stimulus for the production of Shakespeare's play; but it could hardly have figured as an influential source for Shakespeare's conception, unless by way of contrast.[24] The mood of *Troilus and Cressida* is consistently ironic, so much so that the last speech of Troilus,

> You vile abominable tents,
> Thus proudly pight upon our Phrygian plains,
> Let Titan rise as early as he dare,
> I'll through and through you! And, thou great-siz'd coward,
> No space of earth shall sunder our two hates;

> I'll haunt thee like a wicked conscience still,
> That mouldeth goblins swift as frenzy's thoughts.
> Strike a free march to Troy! With comfort go.
> Hope of revenge shall hide our inward woe . . .,

which sounds like the note the tragedy was originally designed to end with, was apparently supplemented, on at least one occasion, by Pandarus's mocking epilogue on the pox. In the Folio text, the dismissal of Pandarus,

> Hence brother lackey! Ignomy and shame
> Pursue thy life, and live aye with thy name,

occurs at the end of V, iii. These lines, improved to read, "Hence, broker! lackey! . . ." and with the further ribald injunctions of Pandarus to the audience, occur as an epilogue following Troilus's last speech in the Quarto, and so in modern editions of the play. But the final speech of Troilus is the fitting end of the tragedy; he is, too, the character of highest rank in this final scene. If Shakespeare did write Pandarus's epilogue, as seems likely, it sounds as if it were intended for a special occasion. It is easily detachable, and a producer of the play may well question its appropriateness in a modern production. At least, it is an irrelevance in the tragic design, though characteristic enough of the prevailing mood of bitter disillusionment which is felt throughout the play.

The reversal of human values has been complete. The Trojan War which might have ended with the restoration of Helen, goes on. Paris keeps Menelaus's queen, and the wrong is perpetuated. The faith of Troilus lies bleeding, betrayed by the wantonness of Cressida; she is won and held by a man of her own kind, and Troilus is not even able to avenge himself upon Diomede. The honour of Hector succumbs to the brutal treachery of Achilles, and the doom of Troy is clearly foreshadowed. Brutality, treachery, lust are everywhere in the ascendant; the forces of disorder and dishonour have triumphed. We have seen the amiable weaknesses through which the Trojans succumb—Hector's imprudent sense of honour, the rash inexperience of Troilus in both love and war; but the successful forces are wholly odious—the shrewd licentiousness of Diomede, the heartlessness of Cressida, the impudent and brutal pride of Achilles. These are all simply human motives. There is nowhere any implication of a power that transcends the human measure. This is the world of men, and it is a disordered world, as Ulysses' thematic speech pictures it:

> Take but degree away, untune that string,
> And hark what discord follows! Each thing meets
> In mere oppugnancy. The bounded waters
> Should lift their bosoms higher than the shores
> And make a sop of all this solid globe;
> Strength should be lord of imbecility,
> And the rude son should strike his father dead;
> Force should be right; or rather, right and wrong
> (Between whose endless jar justice resides)
> Should lose their names, and so should justice too.
> Then everything includes itself in power,
> Power into will, will into appetite;
> And appetite, an universal wolf,
> So doubly seconded with will and power,
> Must make perforce an universal prey,
> And last eat up himself.

In the mood of this play we are aware of certain potentialities of goodness and nobility in man but likewise recognize with merciless vividness that they may be of no avail against disordered physical force, wayward lust, and calculating treachery. This is a satiric mood, of the grimmest sort; for good-humoured satire implies a measure of possible human reformation and exposes human follies to laughter. But this play is concerned with more than follies. We might try to imagine the degree of reformation possible in Paris and Helen, Diomede and Cressida, Ajax and Thersites and Achilles, as they are here represented; as well imagine the reformation of Swift's Yahoos. And there is nothing very amusing about Achilles' vanity; he is simply brutish: and his success is complete. This is not comedy, unless in the sense that the fourth book of *Gulliver's Travels* is also comedy; and the Elizabethans did not ordinarily conceive of the comic genre in this way, least of all Shakespeare himself. The only value that survives in the play lies in the final defiance of Troilus, the impulse to reject, to say that these things shall not be. This is not the comic mood; there is too much bitterness, and such laughter as there is—the giggles and sidelong leers of Pandarus in the epilogue, and the guffaws of the gallants to whom his antics are directed—is not silvery. It is a sorry spectacle. We are not deeply touched; nothing is here for pity or for tears. The story is not fully tragic, but its blend of satire—of savage, bitter laughter and disgust—with the mood of disillusionment and sadness approximates the effect of tragedy in its gloomiest mood.

2. *Timon of Athens*

One of the most stimulating discussions of *Timon of Athens* in recent times is that of Wilson Knight.[25] He has interpreted the play as a vital and intensely imaginative experience, and, though we may not be able to follow him all the way in his admiration for it,[26] we may yet find the main lines of his interpretation of great help. In no other play of Shakespeare, perhaps, is the "spatial" effect, as Mr. Knight has happily termed it, more marked; like a painting or tapestry that unfolds in a succession of tableaux, with Timon's mighty invective rolling and echoing, a mounting and menacing thunder through its desolate landscape, yet with the symbolic promise of purification, as the barren prospect of man's greed and ugliness is blotted out in the healing waters of oblivion:

> Timon hath made his everlasting mansion
> Upon the beached verge of the salt flood,
> Who once a day with his embossed froth
> The turbulent surge shall cover. Thither come,
> And let my gravestone be your oracle.
> Lips, let sour words go by and language end.
> What is amiss, plague and infection mend!
> Graves only be men's works, and death their gain.
> Sun, hide thy beams! Timon hath done his reign.

The textual faultiness of *Timon* is apparent. In the First Folio text there are mislineations, irregularly divided lines, prose speeches printed as verse and verse rendered as prose; and the poetic quality of the play is uneven, though a great deal of it, and above all the speeches of Timon himself, reflect Shakespeare's fullest poetic power. The play was given to the printer of the First Folio to fill up the place left among the tragedies when the printing of *Troilus and Cressida* was held up.[27] This *Timon of Athens* does not completely do; and the state of the text, as E. K. Chambers notices, suggests that the printer's copy was a rough one, with marginal insertions, perhaps a draft recovered from Shakespeare's posthumous papers, though there are some careful stage directions framed with a view to production. Attempts to consider the play as a work of collaboration or an incomplete draft finished for the stage by a reviser are conflicting and unsatisfactory. It seems clear that Shakespeare is responsible for the design of the whole; and we may wish to follow Chambers in regarding the play as unfinished work of Shakespeare's, possibly a first draft in which he concentrated upon the main lines of his poetic conception and left details of stagecraft for subsequent attention which he was ultimately unable to give.[28] These observations, at any rate, are significant chiefly with reference to the play as designed for the stage: as an imaginative conception, as a symbolic poem, *Timon* is splendidly complete in its effect. We may begin by considering it as an action to be presented upon the stage. Faulty and strange though it may be in this respect, it is full of dramatic interest.

The play opens with a projection of the design of the action. Amid a group of Timon's suitors waiting to take advantage of his well-known generosity, a poet describes to a painter the poem he is about to present to Timon. In it he has represented Fortune throned upon a hill up which struggle a throng of all conditions of men, among whom she beckons Timon to her; when, with sudden change of mood, she spurns him from her,

> all his dependents,
> Which labour'd after him to the mountain's top
> Even on their knees and hands, let him slip down,
> Not one accompanying his declining foot.

It is perhaps a sign of incompleteness in this opening tableau that there is no overt suggestion of the sycophantic nature of the poet, though this is later made clear in V, i. Here he figures simply as an informal prologue to the ensuing action. Timon, when he enters, magnificently,[29] accepts the poem with a casual indication that he will reward it but takes no further notice of its contents.

With Timon's entrance, we see at once his extravagant generosity in his payment of a debt of five talents to release his friend Ventidius from prison, and of a substantial sum to enable his servant Lucilius to marry. The motive of this generosity is emphasized in the next scene. When Ventidius, having come into a fortune, tries to repay, Timon answers,

> You mistake my love.
> I gave it freely ever; and there's none
> Can truly say he gives, if he receives;

and to the other friends clustered about him,

> More welcome are ye to my fortunes
> Than my fortunes to me.

Timon is a lover of his fellow man. He gives of his love and his wealth without thought of return, keeps a table for all Athens, and overwhelms alike with gifts the calculating Lucullus who sends him presents to elicit richer in return and the soldier Alcibiades whose only fortune is his martial prowess; he even bears good-humouredly with the taunts of the surly Apemantus because he is an Athenian.

As a counter-movement in the exposition runs the foreshadowing of Timon's approaching fall: in the anticipation of the poet's prologue, in the misgiving expressed by Timon's steward Flavius, above all in the gibes of Apemantus: "O you gods, what a number of men eats Timon, and he sees 'em not!" "Thou giv'st so long, Timon, I fear me thou wilt give away thyself in paper shortly. . . ."

> Thou wilt not hear me now; thou shalt not then.
> I'll lock thy heaven from thee.
> O that men's ears should be
> To counsel deaf but not to flattery!

Act II shows bankruptcy closing in on Timon. The usurers send to dun him, and Timon's faithful steward enters "with many bills in his hand":

No care, no stop! So senseless of expense
That he will neither know how to maintain it
Nor cease his flow of riot. . . .

When Flavius reproaches his master, Timon is obliged at last to recognize his pressing need, but he still feels secure in his motives,

No villainous bounty yet hath pass'd my heart;
Unwisely, not ignobly, have I given.

He has done such service to Athens that the Senate, he thinks, will send him a thousand talents. Flavius tells him that they have already rejected his petition for even a part of that sum.[30] Still confident, Timon sends to his rich friends, especially Ventidius. One by one, they evade Timon's request. Lucullus tries to bribe Timon's man to say that he has not seen him; Lucius sends word he has no ready money; Sempronius pretends to take offence that he was not asked first; and even Ventidius refuses the appeal. The baseness of each rejection is underlined by the scorn of Timon's servants and by the comment of "Three Strangers" upon Lucius's ingratitude. In this contrast, we see that Timon's reckless generosity has made him the victim of the worst kind of men, just as Hector's generosity in *Troilus and Cressida* makes him the victim of the worst kind of treachery.

The critical turn comes midway in Act III. Denied by all, and as the usuerers' men press their claims upon him, Timon gives a foretaste of his rage and disgust: "Tell out my blood!" "Tear me, take me, and the gods fall upon you!" "They have e'en put my breath from me, the slaves! Creditors? Devils!" And he invites all his false friends to his last banquet (III, iv).

At this point, Shakespeare takes up the parallel of Alcibiades (III, v). Hitherto, he has been introduced simply as one of Timon's friends, a captain who would rather dine upon his enemies in the field than at Timon's own table. Now Alcibiades appeals to the same senators who have repulsed Timon for the life of one of his men who has killed a fellow Athenian in hot blood. Alcibiades urges the man's act in self-defence, his valiant services to Athens, Alcibiades' own interest with the state in the victories he has secured. The senators remain inflexible for the letter of the law; and when

Alcibiades will not desist from urging, they banish him forever. As a self-contained action, the scene is well dramatized: Alcibiades begins his plea confidently, is moved to eloquence by his first rebuff, is unable to believe in the refusal or accept it, is finally enraged by the sentence of banishment, and returns to calm cheerfulness in his resolve:

> I have kept back their foes,
> While they have told their money and let out
> Their coin upon large interest. All those for this?
> Is this the balsam that the usuring senate
> Pours into captains' wounds? Banishment!
> It comes not ill. I hate not to be banish'd.
> It is a cause worthy my spleen and fury,
> That I may strike at Athens. I'll cheer up
> My discontented troops and lay for hearts.
> 'Tis honour with most lands to be at odds.
> Soldiers should brook as little wrongs as gods.

The parallel and contrast with Timon's situation are obvious, but they do not help us to interpret the role of Alcibiades himself in this scene. How are we to take his resolve? We may be reminded of the somewhat comparable situation of Coriolanus, but whether this parallel is significant or not the role of Alcibiades in the play is too slight and imperfect to show clearly.

Timon's mood and his resolve are shown in the following episode of the mock banquet. He overwhelms his guests with the beginnings of his invective:

> Most smiling, smooth, detested parasites,
> Courteous destroyers, affable wolves, meek bears,
> You fools of fortune, trencher friends, time's flies,
> Cap-and-knee slaves, vapours, and minute-jacks!

and he concludes,

> Burn house! Sink Athens! Henceforth hated be
> Of Timon man and all humanity.

If the preceding scene of Alcibiades is in itself obscure, it is eloquent in the parallel and contrast it affords for Timon. Both Alcibiades and Timon suffer ingratitude from Athens. Alcibiades has been banished, and Timon banishes himself. The contrast lies in their different responses. Alcibiades is moved to oppose, to fight the ingratitude of Athens, but with no more than passing bitterness and indignation. Timon is moved to reject not merely Athens but all mankind. As he has been wholehearted in his philanthropy, so now his misanthropy is equally unqualified; and he has no resort but to withdraw from human society and curse it.

Acts IV and V are largely a lyrical rhapsody upon this latter theme, the climax towards which the action has been building all along, a torrent of dithyrambic hate and loathing of mankind. It is crossed by the contrasting movement of Alcibiades' humbling of Athens, but the two themes are by no means equal and the contrast is but fitfully sustained. The prevailing movement develops as a series of interviews with Timon in the woods outside Athens, where, as he bitterly digs for roots, he finds gold. First comes Alcibiades, marching gaily against Athens with his army and his whores, Timandra and Phrynia; Timon gives them curses, and gold to visit men with wars and diseases. Then there is the long exchange of abuse between Timon and Apemantus; the appeal of the faithful Flavius still to serve Timon, the reward of his fidelity with gold, and his rejection by his master; the bestowal of gold upon the banditti to further their "mystery"; the stoning away of the fawning poet and painter; and finally the repulse of the humbled senators who come to beg Timon to protect Athens against Alcibiades. Through it all runs the impassioned strain of Timon's maledictions, in which the dominant images are of man's degradation to beastliness. The theme is not so much the disgustingness of beasts in themselves—though Shakespeare's images of the dog, invoked here and elsewhere, and especially in application to Apemantus, are of the fawning, snarling, or revolting[31] —as the worse disgustingness of men degraded to beasts. Timon finds

> Th' unkindest beast more kinder than mankind;

and pictures men more savage than beasts of prey, devouring their own kind. He himself goes to the forest to embrace beastliness; and he answers Alcibiades' startled inquiry at the sight of his transformation:

ALCIB. What art thou there? Speak.
TIMON. A beast, as thou art.

Timon's fury subsides, after his final outburst against the senators, with the forecast of his death (V, i, 218 ff.). The denouement is perfunctory. Alcibiades receives the submission of Athens, on condition that those who have wronged him and Timon shall be punished. Timon's death is reported (with two versions of his epitaph),[32] and Alcibiades gives the closing comment:

> Though thou abhorr'dst in us our human griefs,
> Scorn'dst our brine's flow and those our droplets which
> From niggard nature fall, yet rich conceit
> Taught thee to make vast Neptune weep for aye
> On thy low grave, on faults forgiven. Dead
> Is noble Timon, of whose memory
> Hereafter more.

In this structure, Timon is central throughout. Alcibiades and his story do not really counterbalance Timon's. Alcibiades does not become active in the plot until the crisis is reached, when his rejection by the Athenian senators sets in stronger relief the particular quality of Timon's response to the same ingratitude. Alcibiades moves to retaliate; Timon withdraws. Again, Timon's encounter with Alcibiades in Act IV is one of a series testing Timon's misanthropy from different points of view; and Alcibiades serves to vindicate Timon against Athens in the end. But there is no attempt to pursue a systematic parallel or contrast in their careers or their attitudes. The character of Alcibiades undergoes no change throughout the play. He remains the soldier and man of action who resents a wrong and promptly takes measures to correct it. Like Apemantus, like Flavius and the other servants, like the friends and usurious creditors of Timon, he is a foil or mirror to set Timon in stronger dramatic relief, as he is studied from different angles, in his motives and his change from philanthropy to misanthropy.

The peculiarity of this method is that it provides hardly any scope for dramatic conflict in the ordinary sense; that is, of protagonist and antagonist. The distinction is a fine one, but it seems worth making. We may say that Timon acts against the forces of moral ugliness in man, that his struggle against human greed and hypocrisy *is* the central dramatic conflict of the play. If it is, then this conflict is not resolved, unless in the rather special sense that it kills Timon. But this way of looking at the play tends to stultify Timon as a moral agent. In fact, he takes his own life, or so we assume. It is as if Timon were to say: "I am sick to death of this false world, and just to show that I mean what I say, I'll die."

Perhaps this is why some people regard the play as a satire upon Timon—a view which surely places a banal construction upon it. There is indeed a temptation to hold Timon himself chiefly to blame: he is heedless and prodigal, and he gets the treatment his folly merits. But we must consider the effect that such a construction attributes to the play as a whole. Is the play meant to be simply a dramatic exemplum against prodigality? Then Timon's diatribes, which constitute the lyrical climax towards which the drama builds, the texture and substance of the play as a sustained poem, these rhapsodies of invective are surely excessive and poetically otiose, if their only point is to underline Timon's bathos. We may consider the play ill-made; but we cannot dismiss it, if we have any taste or perception, as merely silly. It contains some of Shakespeare's most concentrated poetic utterance; its poetic seriousness is unmistakable; and Timon, as a symbol of human love confronted with human baseness and turning, as a result, to hate, is not meant to be ridiculous.

We cannot, then, consider that Timon himself is the object of the play's satire, for this would be to reduce the play to mock heroics. Clearly, however, Timon is the protagonist, the centre of our interest from beginning to end. Wherein, then, does the conflict of the protagonist lie? If we agree that Timon is central and Alcibiades but a foil for him, we may test the issue by asking what Timon, as protagonist, *does* in the play. We see examples of his extravagant generosity, and his bankruptcy is foreshadowed from the beginning. The reversal that comes is in his attitude: he turns from loving men to hating them. The only action he takes is to withdraw from men; and he keeps on passionately asserting his will to withdraw, his desire simply to be left alone, to be allowed to repudiate humanity and all human associations, despite every inducement to the contrary—the finding of new wealth; the offered comradeship and support of the martial Alcibiades; the taunts of Apemantus; the humble appeal of Flavius; the grovelling petition of Athens itself through the very body of senators who have hitherto scorned and abused him; until at last he finds release in death.

Among all Shakespeare's plays, *Timon of Athens* may most aptly be called the dramatization of a state of mind, or rather, of the change from one state of mind to another, with its logical outcome in death. At the outset, Timon is a lover of his kind, a lofty if impractical idealist who believes that the practice of virtue lies in giving, and who is innocent enough to suppose that other men share his feelings and his aims, who is blind to human self-interest because he has little or none of it himself. When he discovers the baseness of normal human motives, he cannot compromise, and he swings from extreme philanthropy to extreme misanthropy. The other characters provide no model of an acceptable compromise, not even the devoted Flavius, who is all for living discreetly, putting up with men's faults, and carefully husbanding one's wealth. According to Timon's standards, all the other characters are venal, even Flavius in accepting Timon's gold. Timon alone is faithful to the principle of unselfishness—quite as much in his retirement from men as in his life among them. But the rest of mankind will not leave him alone, even in his wish to withdraw—it is a motif that Aldous Huxley has exploited with another kind of savagery in *Brave New World*. Timon's only release lies in death. In this conception, the tragic effect resides: we are shown what it would be like for a man to take a stand of uncompromising idealism and stick to it, in a society chiefly made up of hypocrites, usurers, and whores. It would be different if he were supported by some religious hope, some precedent for suffering the evil that men do meekly, some religious sanction for humility and love. But Timon has no such hope, no such precedent, no religious sanction whatever. He has only mankind as he finds it in Athens—which is the world of Shakespeare's London, too, or any modern city. Without a religious support, Timon has no other recourse but death, no other escape. His story may remind us of the text: "Blessed are ye, when men shall revile you and persecute you . . ."; but the story is utterly detached from such a Christian context.

The prevailing effect is thus the development of Timon's mood of disgust in his rejection of man. There is no attempt to interest us through an exciting or hazardous conflict. The appeal of the play is almost wholly thoughtful, almost wholly poetic, the action but a pretext for elaborating the mood that the poetry induces, in Shakespeare's inexhaustible resources of lyrical invective. The play takes us as far as the drama can in the mood of rejection, of negation—far beyond *Troilus and Cressida*, where there is still the will to oppose the evil in man. In *Timon*, the evil that men do is not accepted, but neither is it opposed; there is simply a withdrawal from it, as from a bad dream that issues in oblivion.

Timon, then, is a great poem rather than a great play; for once in a way, Charles Lamb's paradox may stand: *Timon* is a greater imaginative experience when it is read than when it is acted. The play was performed at the Old Vic in the summer of 1952. It was directed by Tyrone Guthrie, in keeping with the distinguished tradition of the Old Vic, with André Morell in the title role. The director and his cast did as much for *Timon of Athens*, probably, as can be done; but they could not transcend the dramatic limitations of the text itself, as the performance witnessed by this writer amply demonstrated.

The director intended that the play should be regarded as a satire, upon Timon as well as upon the Athens that rejected him. "Timon is not a hero in whose sufferings we are supposed to share with pity and with terror," the programme notes stated.

He is the spoiled darling of Fortune, whom Fortune suddenly spurns—the allegory of the Poet in the first scene of the play is intended as an extremely literal clue to the course of the story. In misfortune Timon shows unmistakably that he is not of heroic stature. He is peevish, hysterical; he adopts the cynicism of Apemantus not from intellectual or moral conviction but as a kind of compensatory gesture against society; it is, to quote Apemantus, "a poor unmanly melancholy sprung from change of fortune." His death is a symbolical gesture of purification. . . .

In the performance, however, the impression created was very nearly the opposite. As played by Mr. Morell, Timon seemed neither ridiculous nor contemptible; his generosity, if prodigal, was frank and magnanimous; he dominated every scene, spoke the most impressive lines, seemed evidently to be the only character in the play whose motives were thoroughly disinterested; one was necessarily drawn to him from the beginning, in contrast with the various kinds of self-interest and hypocrisy with which he was surrounded; and the action of the latter part of the play, representing Timon's revulsion from this society, did not offer any ground for a change of sympathy. His estimate of Athens seemed thoroughly justified, and consequently his revulsion from mankind as represented in the play; the vigour of his diatribes was satisfying.

The manifest embarrassment of the production, however, was that the story afforded little in the way of dramatic movement, and the cast were put to it to supply this element adventitiously. There was an engaging attempt, in the beginning, to differentiate the crowd of Timon's flatterers. Lucullus was Mr. Chadband in a toga; Lucius skipped and fluttered about the stage like a character strayed out of *The Mikado*; and Ventidius was the ubiquitous "yes-man" to be found in every generation. This was the more acceptable because, while Timon was always the centre of the spectacle, he had little to do in the earlier scenes but move about the stage making large gestures, and the flatterers really kept the play going. But the effect was a little incongruous, like a three-ring circus with the clowns threatening to eclipse the main business in the centre.

The mood underwent a decided change in the latter half of the play. As he recoiled from his hypocritical friends, Timon became more interesting. Bitter and misanthropic, he assumed full command of the dramatic situation; but far from seeming "peevish and hysterical," he grew in dignity and impressiveness as he waxed more bitter, in his retirement from Athens. Mr. Morell made eloquent the sense of Timon's utter disgust with man, that he was "sick of this false world," filled with loathing, though still spirited enough to find a sharp relish in the irony of his rejection of the procession of visitors to his cave—it was somewhat like the procession of visitors to Cloudcuckooland in the *Birds* of Aristophanes. Timon's impassioned lines, beautifully spoken, rendered him wholly sympathetic, though without arousing distress about his plight. He seemed to be fully master of the successive situations. His visitors were all very interesting, and there was still some danger that the play would be amusing in the wrong place.

Compared with Timon, Apemantus resembled nothing so much as a grizzled rat—it is surprising that Timon does not think of awarding him this epithet, among the other animal imagery with which he invests him—envious, poisonous, his teeth showing, taking his brute satisfaction in hurting wherever he dared. He is, of course, the type of the cynic, which meant, for Shakespeare, quite literally "the dog." Obviously, he came to the woods to torment Timon, to gloat over his fallen state, and to assure himself that he was Timon's moral superior; and his taunts were unapt, compound of pure malice: "Thou'dst courtier be again," he growled, "wert thou not beggar"—and there before us (though hidden from Apemantus's sight) was Timon's new found gold. And Timon demolished him with a single question:

What hast thou given?

This was all serious, and finely acted. Timon at length dismissed Apemantus with a crowning comment—"Away, thou issue of a mangy dog!"—and pelted him with stones. He was quite right. Apemantus seemed, as Shakespeare surely meant him to seem, the most loathsome of all the foul company.

To the woods also came the faithful steward Flavius, to offer Timon what money he had, and to serve him, if Timon would let him. Timon was moved:

> Forgive my general and exceptless rashness,
> You perpetual-sober gods. I do proclaim
> One honest man. Mistake me not—but one!

He pressed upon Flavius the rest of his gold. And here the Old Vic production introduced a surely gratuitous piece of business—there is no warrant for it in the directions of the Folio text. Flavius stepped over to the wing, heaved the chest from him with a crash, and returned to beseech Timon,

> O let me stay
> And comfort you, my master.

Timon rejected him, though with less loathing than the others:

> If thou hat'st
> Curses, stay not. Fly whilst thou art blest and free.
> Ne'er see thou man, and let me ne'er see thee.

And Flavius turned sadly away, without the chest. It would surely have been more appropriate if Flavius had left sadly, but carrying the chest under his arm. He returned later, shepherding in the repentant senators who came to solicit Timon to help them against Alcibiades, quite the man of substance, and quite as much interested in the senators' appeal to Timon as the senators themselves.

Of Alcibiades, Dr. Guthrie wrote,

> The same idea of purification is, I think, exemplified in the character of Alcibiades. It is a rather sketchy portrait, but obviously intended to be one of the principal figures in the play's design. One thing that emerges unmistakably—he is meant to represent the Soldier, the Man of Action. My belief is that, at the end of the play, it is Shakespeare's intention to suggest that a corrupt materialism, symbolized by the Government of the Senators, can only be purged by violent action; its guilt can only be washed away in blood. Bloodletting is avoided only by the total surrender of the Senators to the Man of Action. Perhaps it is an implicit part of the satire, that Alcibiades is not represented as having any constructive or imaginative ideas. There is no evidence whatever that Athens, under his military protectorship, will be a better place to live in than before.

In the production, Alcibiades was the most theatrical member of the cast, with his shining breastplate and helmet, yet the least satisfactory—though this was hardly the actor's fault. Nor was it the director's, whose remarks about Alcibiades constitute a heroic attempt to make something coherent of his role. But Alcibiades' role is not by any means on the same plane with Timon's. He appears in the first scene as an almost unobtrusive addition to the company of Timon's flatterers; and if Alcibiades does not flatter Timon, he nevertheless seems to enjoy being entertained by him quite as much as the flatterers do. In the performance one could hardly distinguish him from the flatterers, at first, except that he was less amusing. In the scene which Alcibiades had to himself, with the senators, he had his only chance to do an effective piece of acting, and here he was adequate. Elsewhere he was not.

When Alcibiades, accompanied by his soldiers and his whores, met Timon at his cave, he was no match for the misanthrope; indeed, he seemed almost comically at a loss throughout the whole encounter. The whores served with equal woodenness the symbolic purposes of the scene; and while this was in keeping with the prevailing mood and technique, one could not help regretting the absence of such vitality and interest as Doll Tearsheet might have lent to the occasion. Timon enjoined Alcibiades and his companions to afflict mankind with wars and diseases, loaded them with gold and curses, and they went out solemnly beating their drums and waving their banners amid a profound sense of anticlimax.

Finally, Alcibiades' conquest of Athens was necessarily perfunctory. Alcibiades seemed very much the stage soldier as he summoned the trembling senators to capitulate—about as impressive, from a military point of view, as the Queen of Hearts in *Alice*. And as for "purification" in Alcibiades' role, Dr. Guthrie seems to answer himself: "There is no evidence whatever that Athens, under [Alcibiades'] military protectorship, will be a better place to live in than before." His enemies, and Timon's, were to be punished; and who cared? All that mattered, at the end, was the report of Timon's death, which the Old Vic production tactfully curtailed to one epitaph:

> Here lie I, Timon, who alive all living men did hate,
> Pass by, and curse thy fill; but pass, and stay not here thy gait.

This brief review is not intended to belittle the highly intelligent production of *Timon* at the Old Vic; indeed, in view of the difficulties inherent in the undertaking and the limited basis of the play's appeal, the production was exceptionally commendable, something to feel thankful for. It is always a privilege to see the less familiar plays of Shakespeare intelligently performed; and there is always the possibility that a competent production will show unrealized dramatic possibilities in seemingly unpromising material. But here the production was competent, and the dramatist, in his dramatic function, at least, for once was not. Throughout the play, Shakespeare is intent upon a poetic, and above all a symbolic effect. There was a curious masque-like quality about many of the scenes, especially in the latter part; and yet the production as a whole was not keyed to a mood of deliberate unreality. It was as if the dramatist had neglected the dramatic demands of his theme in the attempt to achieve a symbolic effect, rather than making the dramatic medium serve his symbolic purposes, as he was to do so much more effectively in his final plays. As a stage play, *Timon* is a very odd and interesting failure; but it is definitely a failure.

Yet whatever its inadequacies on the stage, *Timon of Athens* is a most impressive poem. In reading, we are not troubled by the incongruities or the woodenness of the spectacle, and we are borne along by the poetry of Timon's mounting denunciation, with its rich symbolic suggestiveness. Wilson Knight's account of this can hardly be bettered here, and to that account the reader who is not already familiar with it should turn. What now follows is by way of a footnote to what Mr. Knight has written.

Timon, in his quest for oblivion, as Mr. Knight argues, is a symbol of man's striving to be free of the limitations and vileness of the flesh, to become one with the purely spiritual, the universal reality. This aspiration is no part of the "argument" of the play as we have it, or of its dramatic action; here is nothing but the repudiation of humanity, as we commonly find it in this world, with its greed for material possessions, its trickery and hypocrisy by which men grow rich, its lust that afflicts it with diseases, its wars and conquests that destroy it, its very pride in laughing at its own cupidity and lust and treachery, epitomized in the obscene figure of Apemantus. But in the building of the poetic mood of the play, with all its relentless emphasis upon human degradation, there is a context. It is the context of the Christian tradition, *de contemptu mundi*, which was still a vital tradition in Shakespeare's day and which finds impressive utterance in the disguised Duke's homily to Claudio in *Measure for Measure* (III, i, 6 ff.). *Timon of Athens*, it has already been suggested, recalls the text: "Blessed are ye, when men shall revile you, and persecute you. . . ." It recalls, even more emphatically: "Lay not up for yourselves treasures upon earth, where moth and rust doth corrupt, and where thieves break through and steal: But lay up for yourselves treasures in heaven, where neither moth nor rust doth corrupt, and where thieves do not break through nor steal: For where your treasure is, there will your heart be also."

But that context, which would soften the indictment of *Timon of Athens* or qualify it, we are left free to neglect. Shakespeare has chosen to write his *De Contemptu Mundi* without affording any ground of reconciliation or compromise in the explicit content of the play itself—from what motive or out of what mood of personal bitterness it is now idle to speculate. The mood is easily recognizable in any age, whether we look to the ancients, or to Shakespeare's time, or to our own; anyone who does not admit its power has not lived very fully, or very long. It is a part of the tragic experience, this repudiation of human value, and without it, Shakespeare's tragic interpretation of human life would be incomplete. *Timon of Athens* marks a limit beyond which tragic denial cannot go, and with reference to which we may trace Shakespeare's recovery of a balance in tragedy, the transcending of the denial, the reconciling of it. *King Lear*, which traverses the ground of *Timon of Athens* in the eloquence of Lear's wanderings in the storm, also shows us Lear passing out of that storm and transcending it. Timon exists at the storm's centre: he does not emerge from it. But Shakespeare's tragic genius weathered that storm, and out of the same elements of tragic agony projected in *Timon of Athens* he created the tragic grandeur of *King Lear*. Whether *Timon* preceded *King Lear* in order of composition or followed it is of no moment in this consideration;[33] the important point is that *Timon of Athens*, for all its faultiness, its bitterness, its denial of the value of human life, has an organic and indispensable function in the fulfilment of Shakespeare's tragic vision.

3. *Troilus and Cressida* and *Timon of Athens*

Troilus and Cressida and *Timon of Athens* are the bitterest of Shakespeare's plays. It seems unlikely that either was calculated to have any wide popular appeal.[34] Each play, by reason of its unconventionality, its deliberate flouting of human complacency and self-esteem, must have been a work to which Shakespeare attached a special importance; else why should he have bothered to write them? It is not generally profitable to make people as uncomfortable as these plays seem designed to do. Shakespeare must have written *Timon of Athens*, at least, mostly to satisfy himself—if there was any satisfaction in the writing of it.

Both plays, too, contain a peculiarly personal indictment of human baseness, of man's moral nature isolated in all its unloveliness and increasingly separated from complicating political implications. The indictment, to be sure, is not simply of individuals but of human society as made up of base or misguided individuals, of the *mores* of society exhibited in the contexts of lust and of war in *Troilus and Cressida*, of hypocrisy and greed in *Timon*.

In *Troilus and Cressida*, the groups of individuals represent the conflict of different social codes: the mistaken idealism of the Trojans against the brutish treachery of the Greeks; and Ulysses gives us a measure of "order" to set against the illusory "honour" of the chivalric tradition as represented by the foolhardy generosity of Hector and the cheapened love of Troilus and Cressida. But the disorder reflected in the motives and actions of Greeks and Trojans against the background of Ulysses' standard is a flouting of reason, of the moral order in the nature of man, rather than a political disorder which projects and subsumes the moral tragedies of individuals, as in *Julius Caesar*, or provides the occasion of the moral tragedy, as in *Coriolanus*. In *Troilus and Cressida*, the satiric objects are the follies and vices of man's nature which undermine social order rather than the political consequences of man's disordered nature.

In *Timon of Athens*, the political aspects of the action are quite disregarded. Again, the indictment is of human society, which is exhibited, in Timon's rejection of it, as wholly corrupt.

Apemantus, who gives us one measure of its corruption, and Alcibiades, who supplies another, really set in stronger relief the ground of Timon's loathing of mankind; Apemantus shows what it would be like if Timon had made a cynic's adjustment to human society; and Alcibiades, what might come of opposing it. The ironic contrast is apparent. But in using Alcibiades as a foil for Timon, Shakespeare has allowed his normal vision of an ordered society to lapse. Alcibiades' appeal for the life of his condemned officer, in III, v, is well argued: he states persuasively the case against the civilian who sits comfortably at home increasing his income while the soldier risks his life to preserve the business man's profits; and the senators to whom he appeals are also among Timon's usurous creditors, and wholly despicable. But the senators do represent the government and the law of Athens. In seeking to revenge himself upon them, Alcibiades practises treason against the city state where he was born and bred—and is wholly successful. If we turn from reading *Coriolanus* to this, it must surely impress us as very strange. The historical Alcibiades did indeed behave in something like this fashion towards Athens, though under stronger provocation than Shakespeare here adduces; and Alcibiades in the play is represented as trying to redress the ingratitude of the city's corrupt leaders towards Timon as well as towards himself. But elsewhere in Shakespeare the situation of an individual putting himself above the law and leading a rebellion against the state is regarded with abhorrence; and here, we can only suppose, it is not because Shakespeare wishes to condone Alcibiades' political conduct that he represents him as triumphing in the end, but for the sake of the ironic contrast his triumph affords with Timon's withdrawal—Alcibiades, the man of violence, triumphs by means of war and for simply selfish ends, while Timon, the idealist, in repudiating the selfish ways of man, can find peace only in death—and for the sake of emphasizing further the greed and meanness of the Athenians whom Alcibiades humbles. In its political aspect, however, if we attend to it, the solution remains a desperate expedient for Shakespeare.

As we turn from *Troilus and Cressida* to *Timon of Athens*, the mood alters from the restrained protest of irony and implied satire to that of unrestrained mockery in the savage outpouring of Timon's loathing for mankind. But in neither play is there anything much like the effects of pity and fear ascribed to tragedy in Aristotle's famous definition. There is little or nothing to appeal to our deeper sympathies—not Hector's too easy-going magnanimity, nor Troilus's rash impatience and naïveté, nor Timon's experience of man's ingratitude which he did all he could to bring on himself. There is nothing very pitiful in all this, nor much to inspire terror in the outcome. The prevailing moods are rather ironic amusement, anger, or disgust; and it may be objected that these are not the moods proper to tragedy in any strict sense. But the tragic genre comprises many other moods equally incompatible with Aristotle's definition. Who would ascribe pity and terror to many of the extant tragedies of Euripides—to the *Alcestis* or *Ion*, to *Helen* or even *Medea* with its strange translation of the heroine in her dragon-borne chariot at the end? The effects of Euripidean irony seem much closer to the mood of *Troilus and Cressida* and even, at times, to *Timon of Athens*—in the *Bacchae*, for instance—than the authentically Aristotelian effects of *Oedipus Tyrannus* or Shakespeare's own *Othello* and *Macbeth*. Shakespeare nowhere gives evidence of being unduly impressed by Aristotle's authority, and we must allow him to deviate from it for his own purposes without disqualifying as "tragedy" what he himself and his contemporaries apparently so regarded, if we may trust the classifications of the First Folio. We might, indeed, call *Troilus and Cressida* and *Timon of Athens* "melodrama": the term has been deemed more appropriate to designate the genre (or sub-genre) of some of the plays of Euripides in which the effect of irony is perhaps uppermost; but the term has a pejorative vagueness and seems inappropriate to describe the seriousness of the Shakespearian plays, if not those of Euripides as well. In the present study, the decisive consideration for calling *Troilus and Cressida* and *Timon of Athens* "tragedies" is that both of them belong as organic and essential parts in an emerging pattern of Shakespearian tragedy which is only complete with *Antony and Cleopatra* and *King Lear*. Here the effects of irony and bitterness are finally reconciled in a larger, more comprehensive tragic design.

SYNTHESIS

SYNTHESIS: *ANTONY AND CLEOPATRA* AND *KING LEAR*

1. *Antony and Cleopatra*

Antony and Cleopatra is the story of empire crossed with the story of love; and the empire of the love of Antony and Cleopatra, as Wilson Knight has emphasized,[1] extends beyond the reaches of this world; it expands to fill the universe itself, transcends the limitations of the flesh to inhabit the universe of the spirit. This is the prevailing symbolic effect of the play. It is a vision of love which glorifies man and woman, so that with all their faults of ambition and deceit, sensuality and careless pride, they yet rise to a tragic dignity, a tragic reconciliation and serenity, compared with which the dreams of earthly empire shrink almost into insignificance; ultimately, their love is everything, or all that matters, to them and to us.

But the world is ever present, too, throughout the play, its background and its splendid texture. The gorgeous opulence of the East is here, its sensuous mystery, its music of enchantment, in the pomp of glittering image and exotic name. Syria, Cyprus, Lydia; Media, Parthia, Armenia; Cilicia, Phoenicia, and Egypt of the Nile;

> Bocchus, the King of Libya; Archelaus,
> Of Cappadocia; Philadelphos, King
> Of Paphlagonia; the Thracian king, Adallus;
> King Malchus of Arabia; King of Pont;
> Herod of Jewry; Mithridates, king
> Of Comagene; Polemon and Amyntas,
> The kings of Mede and Lycaonia, with a
> More larger list of sceptres—

all these are tributaries of Antony and Cleopatra, or in their gift. They sit upon chairs of gold in the marketplace, distributing kingdoms; they give feasts that last the night through, and eight wild boars are roasted whole for their breakfast; Cleopatra drinks Antony to his bed, or rouses him to go rollicking through the city streets in disguise; she taunts him, plagues him with practical jokes, she is inexhaustible in her changes of mood, her anger, her laughter, her passion; and yet Antony remains an emperor over kings, the greatest soldier in the world, and wholly, devotedly Cleopatra's; she beckons, and he comes.

Against all this is arrayed the power of the West, the greatness of Rome as represented in the heir of Julius Caesar, calm, cold, judicious, ruthlessly efficient, far too astute to be beguiled either through his own vices or through trusting other men, a Caesar greater than Julius Caesar if success is the measure of greatness—as many think; a man who is lucky because he never forgets himself, never makes a mistake, never shows weakness, never yields an inch; a man who loves his sister Octavia because she is part of his own grandeur, because, even though she becomes the wife of Antony and loves him, she remains Caesar's sister, and everything that is Caesar's must be inviolate, sacred, the gaze and wonder of the world; a man who is terrible because he seems invincible, to himself as to us. He is apparently without scruple—he would delude Cleopatra with his seeming magnanimity and consideration for her dignity, to exhibit her in triumph on his return to Rome, if he could; little concerned with "honour," which Antony holds so high, he never considers Antony's challenge seriously, never thinks of an obligation of generosity to his foes—like Achilles in *Troilus and Cressida*, except that Achilles is a savage while Octavius is highly civilized, dignified, kingly, not without understanding of the greatness of Antony and of what his love for Cleopatra means, but utterly without love himself, unless for himself. Yet even self-love hardly seems a clue to Octavius, for self-love should signify vanity and he appears to have none. Rather, he has a god-like impersonality, an unassailable sense of righteousness in his dealings with Antony, a god-like singleness of purpose. There is no apparent irony in the portrait of Octavius; and we see that he *can* make his power prevail, that he *is* invincible. We know that the historical Octavius was not so great a man as Julius Caesar, and Shakespeare surely knew this, too; but it did not suit his dramatic purpose in this play to make Octavius fully understandable, with human weaknesses as well as formidable strength. He remains an enigmatic figure, implacable, menacing, cold, as the historical Octavius doubtless was; but a power rather than a person, a function of the developing action, the nemesis of Antony and Cleopatra, the tragic measure of their human limitation.

Antony and Cleopatra, who are fully realized for us dramatically, seem exceedingly human—though the exordium of the present chapter, lightly brushed by Wilson Knight's soaring wing, has spoken in somewhat exalted vein of the symbolic significance of their love—but they have no chance against the power of Octavius. They are like Othello and Desdemona against Iago, in a way—though in other ways the comparison is of course inappropriate. And symbolically, it is the ageless contrast and conflict of East and West; the East, with its mystery, its sensuous delights and rapturous abandonments, against the matter-of-fact, efficient, materially powerful West. Antony tries to mediate between the two. He fails. But he gains his love. And that is what finally counts in the play.

Antony and Cleopatra is sometimes spoken of as a sequel to *Julius Caesar*; in a limited sense, this is true. The main outline of a sequence of historical events is followed from one play to the other, and the portraiture of Antony in both plays shows certain traits in common: his resourcefulness, his skill and daring in diplomacy as revealed in his dealings with the conspirators in *Julius Caesar*, his handling of the delicate negotiations with Octavius and Pompey in the later play. But Shakespeare did not start with a conception of character and build his play to suit this conception in either *Julius Caesar* or *Antony and Cleopatra*: neither is his dramatic projection of character governed simply by his reading of Plutarch; rather he uses the materials of Plutarch in shaping his tragic conception, in each play. We may see this particularly well illustrated in the two treatments of Antony, if we compare them with Plutarch's narrative.

Plutarch tells us that Antony was wild and dissipated in his youth but that he became proficient as an orator in the florid

Asiatic manner and early distinguished himself for his military exploits and his capacity to endure cheerfully the hardships of a campaign; that "he was a plain man without subtlety . . . he had a noble mind, as well to punish offenders as to reward well-doers; and yet he did exceed more in giving, than in punishing."[2] By his marriage to the strong-minded Fulvia, Antony's wild courses were regulated, for Fulvia was "a woman not so basely minded to spend her time in spinning and housewifery, and was not contented to master her husband at home, but would also rule him in his office abroad, and command him, that commanded legions and great armies; so that Cleopatra was to give Fulvia thanks for that she had taught Antonius this obedience to women, that learned so well to be at their commandment."[3]

Of these traits, all of central importance in Plutarch's narrative, Shakespeare in *Julius Caesar* finds no use whatever for those which concern Antony's relations with women. We hear of him first as the careless and pleasure-loving friend of Caesar, "given to sports, to wildness, and much company";[4] then as the skilful opportunist who, though genuinely grieved by Caesar's death, capitalizes upon the chance provided by his funeral oration for Caesar to turn the citizens against the conspirators, and who, with Octavius and Lepidus, coldly marks the names of the proscribed, including that of his sister's son and this at the request of Lepidus whom he despises (IV, i). Finally, after he and Octavius have prevailed over Cassius and Brutus, Antony pronounces the eulogy of Brutus: "This was the noblest Roman of them all. . . ." It is a finely ironic touch, and anticipatory of the situation in *Antony and Cleopatra*, that though Antony pronounces Brutus's epitaph, a perfect one, Octavius has the last word in *Julius Caesar*.

All of the details about Antony in *Julius Caesar* are to be found in Plutarch, but they are selected from their context simply with an eye to the creation of a tragic effect in which Antony, save in the great scene of his oration, plays but a secondary and supporting part. The Antony of *Julius Caesar* is but partially drawn, like the figure of Octavius in *Antony and Cleopatra*. *Julius Caesar*, in its largest aspect, is the political tragedy of Rome that involves the personal tragedies of Caesar and Brutus; and there Antony, as a subsidiary figure, appears only in the political role he played. Nothing in the role is inconsistent with Plutarch's picture of the man, but the Plutarchan narrative concerning Antony is not fully utilized until we come to *Antony and Cleopatra*. Here, the theme is the conflict of world empire and human love, and Antony and Cleopatra together symbolize that conflict, and its issue. The portrayal of Antony is correspondingly enlarged to include all sides of the man presented in Plutarch's narrative—the politician, the soldier, the world commander, the lover; and yet Plutarch's narrative is but the material. Shakespeare gives the form, by the most skilful selection, abridgement, apportioning of emphasis, until a pattern of action emerges that is wholly Shakespeare's, wherein we see causes and consequences of which Plutarch never dreamed and experience the pathos of the conflict, and the tragic purification of that pathos, under the spell of some of Shakespeare's greatest poetry.

Antony's infatuation for Cleopatra receives strong emphasis in the opening of the play:

> Nay, but this dotage of our general's
> O'erflows the measure . . .;

and, as the supporting action to this prelude, Antony enters in the toils of Cleopatra. A remarkable aspect of Shakespeare's art is the way he can distinguish the effect of one character upon another. Prince Hal of the *Henry IV* plays is touched to finer issues of wit by Falstaff than in himself he seems capable of. One of the subtlest distinctions of these plays lies in the strained, "clever" wit of Hal beside the naturally overflowing wit of Falstaff, not simply witty in himself but the cause that wit is in other men; and appropriately, Henry V, without Falstaff, is not witty at all but an altogether serious young man, even in his wooing of Catherine, where the situation is funny rather than the wooer. So with the effect of Cleopatra upon Antony: we see the evidence of her enchantments displayed before our eyes, as she enters with Antony; but Antony out of the presence of Cleopatra is much more master of himself, firm, decisive, and commanding. When at length he breaks his strong Egyptian fetters and returns to his duties in Italy, his manly apologies, his urbanity and easy self-command in the deliberations of the triumvirate with Pompey show us that he is still the best man of them all; we feel this though Antony is obliged to make politic overtures to the heir of Caesar, and to recognize that in their relationship the luck is all with the younger man:

> The very dice obey him,
> And in our sports my better cunning faints
> Under his chance. If we draw lots, he speeds;
> His cocks do win the battle still of mine
> When it is all to naught, and his quails ever
> Beat mine, inhoop'd, at odds. I will to Egypt;
> And though I make this marriage for my peace,
> I' th' East my pleasure lies.

The delicate irony of the reconciliation of the triumvirs with Pompey (II, vii) shows us Pompey, flattered by the sense of his own importance, the geniality of the occasion as Antony makes sport of Lepidus, and a scruple of "honour," waving aside Menas' offer to make him "lord of the whole world," while Octavius uneasily countenances the "Egyptian Bacchanals" of Antony and Enobarbus until he can escape from this dangerous and unseemly revel, and Lepidus, "the third part of the world," is carried drunk to bed. Antony is lord of this occasion, and, though unwittingly, prepares the way for Octavius's subsequent disposal of both Pompey and Lepidus, which we learn of in III, v. But the whole scene parallels and foreshadows Antony's own fall. Pompey is a comically diminished Antony. As Pompey missed his great chance by not cutting the cable of his ship while the triumvirs were in his power, so Antony misses his advantage, later on, in a land battle with Octavius, and from the same motive of "honour" (III, vii, 28 ff.); and as Menas abandoned the failing fortunes of Pompey, so Enobarbus abandons the failing Antony. The parallel likewise enhances Antony's tragic stature: for Pompey's "honour," as we readily perceive, is but the excuse of his lack of imagination and force, while Antony's sense of honour, though impractical, springs from his strength and his generosity; and Pompey, in eclipse, is a negligible counter in the game of politics, while Antony in defeat is heroic. The scene heightens our sense of Octavius's formidable and unscrupulous power, and of the inevitability of Antony's fall.

It is not simply in the interest of dramatic condensation that Shakespeare passes briefly over Plutarch's account of Antony's stay in Rome and Athens after he married Octavia, of how she bore him three children and, during this time, reconciled a difference between Antony and Octavius which had nothing to do with Cleopatra.[5] In fact, Antony's second (and fatal) infatuation for Cleopatra occurred after an interval of some years, during which time, as far as we may judge from Plutarch's story, Antony had given up all serious thought of returning to her.[6] In the historical account, only when his affairs necessitated his going into Asia and thus leaving Octavia, did the impulse strike him to send for Cleopatra to join him in Syria. Shakespeare suggests that the spell Cleopatra cast upon Antony was never broken and thus avoids raising questions about his activities and motives that Plutarch never answers. For Shakespeare, Antony is even simpler than Plutarch represents him. From the beginning, Cleopatra has laid enchantment on him, and we see him rouse for a moment to shore the ruins of his empire against the ominously encroaching Octavius, only to revert to his "Egyptian dish" when all is quiet. The politic Antony who conciliates Octavius by marrying his sister is of a piece with the Antony who beguiles the conspirators in *Julius Caesar*; and yet we feel that, despite his greater prestige and experience, Antony has met more than his match in Octavius, that everything he does plays into Octavius's hands, arming that inflexible and far-sighted man with an impregnable pretext for repudiating Antony because he has deserted both his wife and his empire. Octavia tries, quite fruitlessly, to reconcile her brother to Antony (in the play) as Antony sets out to join Cleopatra (III, iv-vi). In Plutarch, Antony summons Cleopatra to Syria and there confers honours on her; in Shakespeare's emendation,

> Cleopatra
> Hath nodded him to her;

and, passing over Plutarch's account of Antony's heroic campaign against the Parthians, Shakespeare represents the *débâcle* of Actium as following close upon his final capitulation to Cleopatra's charms.

About Antony's decision to fight a sea battle, Plutarch says:

> Now Antony was made so subject to a woman's will, that though he was a great deal the stronger by land, yet for Cleopatra's sake he would needs have this battle tried by sea. . . . Cleopatra forced him to put all to the hazard of battle by sea; considering with herself how she might fly and provide for her safety, not to help him to win the victory, but to fly more easily after the battle lost.[7]

It is of no use quarrelling with Plutarch at this date; but it is a little hard to see how Cleopatra's motive could have been as simple as this last; she had no recourse, presumably, but to flee to her Egyptian stronghold, if Antony lost; and, if she wished to be thus safe, it would have been easier to stay away from the battle altogether. At all events, Shakespeare alters the emphasis of Plutarch's account. His Cleopatra, indeed, favours a sea battle and insists upon being present at it, but the decision to fight by sea is represented as Antony's alone:

> ANT. Canidius, we
> Will fight with him by sea.
> CLEO. By sea, what else?
> CAN. Why will my lord do so?
> ANT. For that he dares us to't.

And against Enobarbus's urging, and later that of one of his own soldiers, Antony insists upon it as a point of honour: "I'll fight at sea." Still later, lest there be any doubt about it, Enobarbus emphasizes Antony's full responsibility for the disaster of Actium:

> CLEO. What shall we do, Enobarbus?
> ENO. Think, and die.
> CLEO. Is Antony or we in fault for this?
> ENO. Antony only, that would make his will
> Lord of his reason.

In the battle itself, the infatuated Antony pursues the fleeing sails of Cleopatra; and there is a slightly false note in his lamentation over the loss of honour after the defeat, a failure to face his responsibility fairly in his reproach of the Queen:

ANT. I have offended reputation—
A most unnoble swerving.
EROS Sir, the Queen.
ANT. O, whither hast thou led me, Egypt. See
How I convey my shame out of thine eyes
By looking back what I have left behind
Stroy'd in dishonour.

Yet this is all part of his impetuousness and his simplicity, of a piece with his challenge of Octavius. Knowing Octavius as he does and after the loss of Actium, Antony nevertheless supposes he can find a response in him to his own sense of honour:

Tell him he wears the rose
Of youth upon him; from which the world should note
Something particular. His coin, ships, legions
May be a coward's, whose ministers would prevail
Under the service of a child as soon
As i' th' command of Caesar. I dare him therefore
To lay his gay comparisons apart
And answer me declin'd, sword against sword,
Ourselves alone. I'll write it. Follow me.

As Antony leaves, Enobarbus bitterly comments,

Yes, like enough high-battled Caesar will
Unstate his happiness and be stag'd to th' show
Against a sworder! I see men's judgments are
A parcel of their fortunes, and things outward
Do draw the inward quality after them
To suffer all alike. That he should dream,
Knowing all measures, the full Caesar will
Answer his emptiness! Caesar, thou hast subdu'd
His judgment too.

Octavius scornfully bears this out:

Let the old ruffian know
I have many other ways to die, meantime
Laugh at his challenge.[8]

In Plutarch's account, there is no implied irony in Antony's challenges; they are represented simply as part of Antony's heroic character.[9] Plutarch saw clearly enough Antony's infatuation for Cleopatra. He hardly suspected—what Shakespeare was so clearly to show us in his tragic hero—that the simplicity and impetuosity of Antony's love for Cleopatra went together with a rash and impetuous sense of honour that impaired his tactical judgment when he had need of his greatest skill.

Antony's love and his "honour"[10]—the one is a measure of the other. There is generosity in Antony's sense of honour, an unthinking generosity that speaks from the heart rather than the head; and so it is with his love. His bitter humiliation after Actium, and his reproaches of Cleopatra, dissolve at the sight of her tears:

> Fall not a tear, I say. One of them rates
> All that is won and lost. Give me a kiss.
> Even this repays me. . . .

If this is folly, it is on a magnificent scale. When Antony comes upon Octavius's messenger Thyreus kissing Cleopatra's hand, his physical violence spends itself upon the luckless messenger, but his denunciation of Cleopatra is equally savage. "You were half blasted ere I knew you. . . . You have been a boggler ever. . . .

> I found you as a morsel cold upon
> Dead Caesar's trencher. Nay, you were a fragment
> Of Gneius Pompey's, besides what hotter hours,
> Unregist'red in vulgar fame, you have
> Luxuriously pick'd out: for I am sure,
> Though you can guess what temperance should be,
> You know not what it is.

Cleopatra's harshest critic could not speak more plainly; her failings are no secret from Antony. Yet he is more enraged by the indignity of her giving her hand to be kissed than by the thought of her falseness. After his outburst, he is easily propitiated by Cleopatra's protestations; the violence of his passion has freed his spirit. He forgets his suspicions, challenges his coming fortune gaily:

> I will be treble-sinew'd, hearted, breath'd,
> And fight maliciously. For when mine hours
> Were nice and lucky, men did ransom lives

> Of me for jests; but now I'll set my teeth
> And send to darkness all that stop me. Come,
> Let's have one other gaudy night. Call to me
> All my sad captains; fill our bowls once more.
> Let's mock the midnight bell!

And Cleopatra discovers that it is her birthday!

It is folly, as Enobarbus sees. Still, it is easy to understand why men follow this general with blind devotion, why Enobarbus, deserting him, is stricken with such self-loathing that he takes his life.

In his last battle, as Cleopatra's ships desert to Octavius and with them all that remain of Antony's forces, Antony renews his bitterness: "This foul Egyptian hath betray'd me. . . . O this false soul of Egypt! this grave charm." When Cleopatra herself appears, he passionately denounces her:

> Vanish, or I shall give thee thy deserving
> And blemish Caesar's triumph!

Yet Antony's love is eloquent, even as he dwells upon his wrongs:

> I made these wars for Egypt; and the Queen—
> Whose heart I thought I had, for she had mine,
> Which, whilst it was mine, had annex'd unto't
> A million moe, now lost—she, Eros, has
> Pack'd cards with Caesar and false-play'd my glory
> Unto an enemy's triumph. . . .

And when Cleopatra, fled to her monument, sends the false report of her death, Antony's mood is transformed in the beautiful elegiac lines that begin,

> Unarm, Eros. The long day's task is done,
> And we must sleep. . . .

His feeling is touched with a grave unconscious irony, at which we can hardly smile:

> I will o'ertake thee, Cleopatra, and
> Weep for my pardon. So it must be, for now
> All length is torture. Since the torch is out,

Lie down, and stray no farther. Now all labour
Mars what it does; yea, very force entangles
Itself with strength. Seal then, and all is done.
Eros!—I come, my queen.—Eros!—Stay for me.
Where souls do couch on flowers, we'll hand in hand
And with our sprightly port make the ghosts gaze.
Dido and her Aeneas shall want troops,
And all the haunt be ours.

We remember that it is Aeneas who betrays Dido, in Virgil, though in the fulfilment of a higher duty; and we know that Cleopatra is safe in her monument as Antony speaks. Yet we are swept along by the lyrical beauty of Antony's mood, and exalted by it.

As Antony fumbles the act of killing himself, with characteristic impatience, and is borne wounded to the Queen, no thought of her duplicity any longer troubles him. Cleopatra pledges him with a more eloquent feeling than she has yet shown:

If knife, drugs, serpents have
Edge, sting, or operation, I am safe.

Antony's last thoughts are for Cleopatra—"Of Caesar seek your honour, with your safety. . . . None about Caesar trust but Proculeius"—and his last words are of unsurpassed dignity:

The miserable change now at my end
Lament nor sorrow at; but please your thoughts
In feeding them with those my former fortunes,
Wherein I liv'd the greatest prince o' th' world,
The noblest; and do now not basely die,
Not cowardly put off my helmet to
My countryman—a Roman by a Roman
Valiantly vanquish'd. Now my spirit is going.
I can no more.

We need not raise the question whether Cleopatra has indeed betrayed Antony to Octavius. We assume from what follows that she had not; but we can understand Antony's suspicions: constancy is not her strong point. Shakespeare, with fine artistry, ignores the issue. It does not matter, since in the outcome Cleopatra is magnificently true to Antony, equal to the love she has inspired in him. What we do see in Antony's last moments is that he triumphs over his suspicions through his love, rises superior to Octavius and to the world that he has lost, in his death. His love has ultimately the generosity of self-forgetfulness, and in his end we are aware only of his courage, his magnanimity, and his devotion.

Samuel Daniel's *Cleopatra*, in its opening speech, reads like a commentary upon the Cleopatra of Shakespeare's play. Daniel's tragedy, first published in 1594, was subsequently more than once revised;[11] but the affiliations of Shakespeare's play are more obviously with the text of the first edition, and we may confine our attention to that.

The opening speech of Daniel's heroine pictures her after Antony's death, as she resolves to take her life rather than be led in Caesar's triumph. She reviews her life with Antony and reveals that she has never loved him truly until now:

> I then thought all men must loue me of dutie,
> And I loue none. . . .

In their fortunate days, Antony's love for her was an enchantment she cast upon him, hers for him a part of her vanity; and her ambition brought ruin upon them both:

> the world doth know,
> That my mis-fortune hath procured thine,
> And my improuidence brought thee so low,
> To lose thy glory, and to ruine mine. . . .

Now, with remorse, she realizes her loss:

> Our like distress I feele doth sympathize,
> And euen affliction makes me truly loue thee . . .;

yet, in taking her life, she seeks also to be free, to remain a great queen: "Ile be my selfe," she concludes.[12]

It is scarcely likely that the sententious Cleopatra of Daniel's heavy-footed verse influenced Shakespeare very much; but Daniel's overt judgment of what her love for Antony amounted to provides a leading clue to Shakespeare's subtler conception. There is a principle of development, and of refinement, in the love of Shakespeare's heroine and in her tragic end, as there is in Antony's, though the one is not to be measured precisely by the other.

The vitality of Cleopatra is so great—like that of Hamlet and Falstaff, as Bradley finely remarks in his essay on *Antony and Cleopatra*[13]—that we may be in some danger, with Antony, of simply submitting to her spell; which might conceivably be the greater part of critical wisdom. But if we wish to be clear about our admiration for her, we must come to terms with the moral issue of her character and conduct as they are represented in the play, heavy-handed though this may seem; if we wish to claim for *Antony and Cleopatra* the high seriousness of great tragedy, we cannot avoid the issue: the role of Cleopatra involves not simply an aesthetic consideration of dramatic and poetic form but also a consideration of her place in the moral order which the play projects.

That stern moralist, George Bernard Shaw, upon whom the mantle of Dr. Johnson sometimes sat a little rakishly and awry, has memorably pronounced upon this matter:

> Shakspear's Antony and Cleopatra must needs be as intolerable to the true Puritan as it is vaguely distressing to the ordinary healthy citizen, because, after giving a faithful picture of the soldier broken down by debauchery, and the typical wanton in whose arms such men perish, Shakspear finally strains all his huge command of rhetoric and stage pathos to give theatrical sublimity to the wretched end of the business, and to persuade foolish spectators that the world was well lost by the twain.[14]

If we do not happen to be very puritanically inclined, or among the more robust members of society either, we may nevertheless feel that Shaw has admirably indicated for us the grounds on which we should wish to commend the play. Shakespeare *does* give sublimity to the end of *Antony and Cleopatra* and does indeed persuade us that the world was well lost by the twain.

We may begin with that essential quality of Cleopatra already mentioned, her vitality; and here the analogy of Falstaff is helpful. We are not shocked that Falstaff should be dishonest, solicitous of his own ease and well-being, an oppressor of poor Mistress

Quickly, a coward, a liar, a vagabond, and a thief; for the man is the embodiment of laughter and conviviality and his scandalous ways are a necessary part of the nature we rejoice in. It is a happiness to be in his company, and his lightest word, even if he be but talking to himself, is something for the generations to recall lovingly and to chuckle over. Prince Hal owes everything that endears him to us to the moments he spends with Falstaff; the abject Bardolph is glorified as Falstaff's servant; and Mistress Quickly would sell everything she has for an encouraging word from the knight. Like all great men, Sir John is over-weening; and inevitably, this over-weeningness brings his fall. But we need not grieve too deeply at this; for when he turns to Justice Shallow: "Master Shallow, I owe you a thousand pound," we know that there will still be means to support his excesses and that there will be laughter and rejoicing, though, for a time, in a muted key, wherever he goes.

So it is with Cleopatra, in a very different context. Her genius is to make men love her, and if they make fools of themselves on that account, it is not her fault. She was but fulfilling her destiny when Cneius Pompey loved her, and Julius Caesar, and Mark Antony. She is a woman worthy to be loved only by the greatest man in the world. She did not ruin Pompey or Caesar, and she did not ruin Antony; he ruined himself for her love—if we must look at the matter in this way. Antony lost the world, and the loss was his responsibility; but the gain was his glory.

Cleopatra lives for love, and she recognizes no other end. To rule Antony with her love is solely her aim from beginning to end. She never pleads, never admits a weakness. When Antony decides to return to Rome, she taunts him and dismisses him with icy dignity:

> Your honour calls you hence;
> Therefore be deaf to my unpitied folly,
> And all the gods go with you! Upon your sword
> Sit laurel victory, and smooth success
> Be strew'd before your feet!—

though she is afire to lure him back to her. His return is so much a foregone conclusion that Shakespeare can leave it to be reported.

In the war that follows, Cleopatra knows nothing of generalship or strategy—why should she? It is a woman's triumph for her to influence Antony to fight by sea and a tribute to her greatness as a queen (she never loses the sense of her dignity) that her Egyptian fleet should take the post of honour in the battle and herself in the midst! Here was Antony's cue to over-rule her ignorance; but it was *his* honour, as Shakespeare represents it, that really turned the balance. His following in the wake of the Queen's fleeing sails was a crowning infatuation; but again the blame was Antony's. He was the commander, not Cleopatra.

> I little thought
> You would have followed,

Cleopatra tells him when they meet after the battle; and Antony reproaches her:

> Egypt, thou knew'st too well
> My heart was to thy rudder tied by th' strings,
> And thou shouldst tow me after. O'er my spirit
> Thy full supremacy thou knew'st, and that
> Thy beck might from the bidding of the gods
> Command me.

This is the weakest strain in Antony, this disposition to find a scapegoat, to blame Cleopatra for his own folly; and it is at the root of his later distrust of her. But he surmounts it, too, with the magnificence of his

> Fall not a tear, I say. One of them rates
> All that is won and lost . . .

and in their final reconciliation.

Cleopatra shares Antony's downfall, suffers his reproaches and his suspicions; yet she never reproaches Antony for their ruin. Though she is full of wiles and evasions, she is stronger even than Antony; she heartens and inspires him against the most formidable odds. When all is finally lost, she protects herself against Antony's violence by deceit—it is part of her charm, in happier times, and now her only weapon; and even thus she helps Antony to achieve his final grandeur.

We must not be carried too far in admiration. There can be very little doubt that Cleopatra, as Shakespeare sees her, was capable of betraying Antony's memory almost to the end. Selfless devotion is not hers; she is the quintessence of feminine elusiveness, always to be won, never—or scarcely ever—to be held; and, if held, then not for long. We must not qualify her for sainthood, not even in the calendar of Cupid. But she is a magnificent woman. And the depth of feeling with which she finally speaks, when she has resolved to die, signifies a real change of heart:

> No more but e'en a woman, and commanded
> By such poor passion as the maid that milks
> And does the meanest chares. It were for me
> To throw my sceptre at the injurious gods,
> To tell them that this world did equal theirs
> Till they had stol'n our jewel. All's but naught.
> Patience is sottish, and impatience does
> Become a dog that's mad. Then is it sin
> To rush into the secret house of death
> Ere death dare come to us? How do you, women?
> What, what! good cheer! Why, how now, Charmian?
> My noble girls! Ah, women, women, look!
> Our lamp is spent, it's out! Good sirs, take heart.
> We'll bury him; and then, what's brave, what's noble,
> Let's do it after the high Roman fashion
> And make death proud to take us.

This is the final pledge of her love for Antony; Antony's example has moved in her a heroic firmness that equals his, or surpasses it.

Yet when she is trapped by Caesar's soldiers, she is her old self, keeping back some lady trifles and immoment toys from the account of her wealth, divining at once the cold calculation beneath Caesar's urbane courtesy:

> He words me, girls, he words me, that I should not
> Be noble to myself!

She casts her spell sufficiently upon Dolabella to make sure that Caesar means to lead her in triumph. But before this, she has made provision for her freedom, and the excellent countryman who wishes Cleopatra and her women "all joy of the worm" offers the fitting prelude to the dignity and beauty of Cleopatra's latest moments. Her last thought of Antony answers Antony's thought of her and redeems its irony:

> Give me my robe, put on my crown. I have
> Immortal longings in me. Now no more
> The juice of Egypt's grape shall moist this lip.
> Yare, yare, good Iras; quick. Methinks I hear
> Antony call. I see him rouse himself
> To praise my noble act. I hear him mock
> The luck of Caesar, which the gods give men
> To excuse their after wrath. Husband, I come!
> Now to that name my courage prove my title!
> I am fire and air; my other elements
> I give to baser life.

And Charmian, as she pays the final tribute to the Queen's dignity in straightening her crown, speaks with her dying breath the perfect epitaph upon this "lass unparallel'd":

> GUARD What work is here! Charmian, is this well done?
> CHAR. It is well done, and fitting for a princess
> Descended of so many royal kings.
> Ah, soldier!

Cleopatra remains true to herself. She is the living, and dying, embodiment of earthly love, with all its energy of variety and enchantment; she is its fulfilment. This love, like other human things, sooner or later reaches its limit. It overwhelms Antony, and eclipses Cleopatra herself. But it reaches its highest point, the fulfilment of all the noblest powers of human love, in its eclipse. The theme is fully tragic. Its scale is human: for the dream of the lovers of meeting in Elysium is the symbol of the lasting human memory of their final reconciliation and their faith. That reconciliation and that faith embody for us the most enduring value of human life. It is a shared fulfilment. We see how the love of Antony for Cleopatra is freed of suspicion and pride and becomes purely devoted and heroic, how it ennobles him; and how the example of Antony moves Cleopatra to become "marble-constant" —she who had ever been so devious and varying—to "mock the luck of Caesar" as she joins Antony in the dignity of death and their symbolic union.

So it is that the final mood of *Antony and Cleopatra* is triumphant. The play ends in serenity, not with pain but with grandeur. Here is the end towards which the greatest tragedy moves. Its materials are the passions, the imperfections, the griefs and sufferings of humanity; but these limitations are countered by some heroic action or example that reconciles us to the spectacle of human frailty. There is an ennoblement and a purification through suffering: an ennoblement for the tragic protagonists; a purification for us the spectators who share in their suffering vicariously and in their triumphant reconciliation. Both Antony and Cleopatra are mortal and fallible, exceedingly liable to acts of passion, of human folly, and to the sufferings which they entail. They are also great human beings, true to the grandeur of their aims. These aims surpass the human measure and the protagonists suffer tragic eclipse; but they have lived greatly; they are not pitiable in defeat; rather, they achieve the utmost human grandeur in their tragic eclipse and in their deaths affirm for us the supreme value—in this world—of human love. Though they show us the tragic frailty of mankind, even at its worthiest, yet this spectacle is inspiring, uplifting, an affirmation, at the same time, of human dignity, of the dignity of the love of man and woman. It is not too much, perhaps, to say that the play contains the greatest affirmation of this value in the world's literature.

The structure of *Antony and Cleopatra* has sometimes been considered loose and faulty. "The play was evidently hastily written," a distinguished Shakespearian scholar has said; "it is not worked down to the fine point of connection that marks *Macbeth* and *Coriolanus*. It lacks general plan. After the middle of the play, Shakespeare more or less puts Plutarch on the stage. There is a multitude of short scenes which reproduce the source almost literally, so that the play is comparatively confused in its dramaturgy."[15] Such a judgment, which goes back to Dr. Johnson,[16] is surely wide of the mark. Shakespeare "puts Plutarch upon the stage" throughout the play, but with constant modifications to suit his tragic conception, as has here been shown; and the "multitude of short scenes"—which are not "scenes" in our modern sense but rather signify the rapidly changing exits and entrances of different groups in agitated parts of the fluid action—are carefully designed to create an atmosphere of bustling action and excitement, especially, and appropriately, in the representation of battles.

The construction, though expansive and comprehensive—in keeping with the theme—rather than economically concentrated, causes the action to oscillate purposely between the two poles of Egypt and Rome, two ways of life in conflict; this is the inclusive setting of the whole: the civilized world, the world of the Mediterranean. The single setting is thought of, according to the convention of Shakespeare's unlocalized stage, as "the place of the action"; and the different parts of that action are to be located in it imaginatively by the audience according to the hints of the dialogue but without literal-minded precision. The action is fluid and poetic and dramatic, rather than pictorial and static. Octavius Caesar, when he comes against Antony, carries the world of Rome and its values with him, he himself embodies it; Cleopatra's world is the East; Antony tries to mediate between the two. This is the framework in which the story of the conflict between world empire and a great love is played out. Each step in the developing action follows logically. Antony first parts from Cleopatra and the East to defend his claims of empire successfully in the West. But the spell of Cleopatra is not really broken. He precipitates the tragic crisis by returning to his love, when all is quiet; whereupon Octavius marches against him for the final conflict of Actium and its aftermath, in which Antony loses the world but triumphs, with Cleopatra, in their love. The design has a firmness and clarity which persuades us of its inevitability. This is not merely history; it is the necessary pattern of human tragedy.

Not only is the construction masterly in its dynamic development of the main proportions; as Granville Barker has shown,[17] it is most carefully articulated. But the point may bear a little more insistence. When Antony leaves Egypt for Rome, he bears the image of Cleopatra with him, he feels the drawing power of her charm—and we are constantly reminded of it. Cleopatra sends "twenty several messengers" after him; Enobarbus describes her first appearance to Antony upon the Nile, in surpassing poetry (though the elements of it are all in North's Plutarch); Antony himself longs to return:

> I will to Egypt;
> And though I make this marriage for my peace
> I' th' East my pleasure lies.

In Egypt again, Antony feels the constantly encroaching menace of Octavius Caesar and of the Rome that he has so recklessly repudiated. No sooner do we see him back in Egypt than we hear of the approach of Octavius. He has taken Toryne. We immediately enter the stages of preparation for the decisive battle of Actium. The whole movement is swift and balanced and excellently clear. The crisis of Actium leads us immediately to the catastrophe of Antony in Act IV, upon which the catastrophe of Cleopatra logically follows in Act V. There is nothing loose or "confused" in this construction. The impression of a lack of order and cohesion arises mainly from the exigencies of presenting battle scenes upon the Elizabethan stage, where no representation of massed forces in conflict is feasible, and, for the reader, from the conventional (and irrelevant) divisions of our reading texts into "scenes"; but in an intelligent production, neither the limitations of Shakespeare's stage nor the conservatism of editors in retaining the traditional scene divisions need trouble us. A director with a talent for handling group movements can make the battles of *Antony and Cleopatra* impressive, clear, and fluid; and, through it all, Antony provides the unifying clue. We watch the decline of his fortunes through the effect of the battles upon him; and we are never left in doubt about how the conflict goes against him, or why.

The effect of the two climaxes of Acts IV and V is really continuous; for the reconciliation of Antony and Cleopatra, the highest point of their love, begins at the end of Act IV with the death of Antony and reaches its fulfilment with the death of

Cleopatra at the end of Act V. With splendid craftsmanship, Shakespeare apportions the deaths of Antony and Cleopatra to separate acts, so that the one becomes preparatory for the other and the transition from one to the other cumulative, a unified movement in which the devotion, the courage, and dignity of both the lovers is interacting and mutually ennobling; the death of Cleopatra gives final unity to the whole movement figuring as a reunion with Antony, the crowning symbol of their love triumphant. All this is a far cry from the divided effect of such early work as *Romeo and Juliet.* The construction of *Antony and Cleopatra* represents the consummate technical achievement of Shakespeare's artistic maturity.

"The greatness of Antony and Cleopatra in their fall," says Bradley, "is . . . heightened by contrast with the world they lose and the conqueror who wins it."[18] The world that Antony loses is not the world of the English history plays where an ideal of national unity is related to a traditional concept of political order and social hierarchy which is thought of as divinely sanctioned, established and maintained by a succession of English monarchs, their ministers, and their patriotic subjects, for the good of the commonweal and to the glory of God. In this order, the duty of the individual to the state, of the king himself to the order which he heads under God, is perfectly clear-cut. His political obligation takes precedence of every merely personal or private motive, or should do so. This normative value is an ordering principle throughout the sequence of the English history plays, as Dr. Tillyard has shown.[19]

The political world of *Antony and Cleopatra* is simply the scene of the struggle for power between the two antagonists, Antony and Octavius Caesar, with Lepidus as an ineffectual buffer between them—

> They are his shards, and he their beetle—

whom Octavius unscrupulously removes when it suits his purpose. The struggle between them is to the death, with the world as the spoil of victory for Octavius, the world and his love for Antony. They live in a time of political upheaval following upon the demise of the last vestiges of the Roman republican tradition with the deaths of the conspirators against Julius Caesar and the assassination of the only man who could then be deemed capable of unifying the world conquests of the Roman people in a stable and authoritative political order. That Octavius Caesar was later to head such an order, to found the destinies of the mighty Roman Empire which Virgil was to celebrate in the *Aeneid* and Horace in his great odes, has no relevance for Shakespeare's play. The political background of *Antony and Cleopatra* is a world uneasily divided among an unstable triumvirate; and the unresolved conflict between the real antagonists, Antony and Caesar, must be decided before there can be a stable and recognizable political order to which either of them can owe allegiance.

In the play, accordingly, the "imperial theme" is but the background against which the personal conflict of Antony and Octavius is worked out. The magnitude of the stake for which they struggle gives grandeur and dignity to their conflict, but the stage-play offers no basis for distinguishing the relative merits of their cause on political grounds. The values of the political situation are left undefined. What remains is the moral issue between the antagonists, the personal aims and values of Antony and Cleopatra against those of Octavius Caesar, the love of Antony and Cleopatra against the ambition of Caesar, with the world as the prize of the side that prevails.

That the love of Antony and Cleopatra cannot prevail against the ambition of Caesar is the tragic theme of the play But the greatness of their love shines forth the more clearly because the antagonist who defeats them, though shrewd, ruthless, lucky, and exceedingly formidable, is so obviously without a shred of the generosity, the heroic humanity, the careless grandeur of the lovers. Foolish mortals they are, and the gods punish them for their folly; but theirs is the kind of human dignity that the gods respect. The qualities of Octavius, we may recognize with chagrin, are the virtues that make for success in this world; but there need be no bitterness in the recognition, for we see likewise how paltry is the world of Octavius, as paltry as the man who wins it, whose unheroic measure is sufficiently indicated by the attempt to imagine him succeeding Antony as the lover of Cleopatra.

The love of Antony and Cleopatra is heroic. This is the essential difference between the story of their love, and that of Romeo and Juliet on the one hand, or of Troilus and Cressida on the other. The love of Romeo and Juliet is young and innocent, beautiful and touching; but it is immature. The love of Troilus and Cressida is a tale of youthful naïveté betrayed by wantonness. To one who did not find the story of Antony and Cleopatra sympathetic, it would be easy to discern a certain parallelism between it and the story of Troilus and Cressida: Antony is betrayed by the very faults of Troilus, a vain pride in his "honour" and an infatuation for a false woman, a "daughter of the game." The parallel would surely be misleading: it would overlook the greatness of Antony—Troilus is a petulant boy beside him; and to compare Cleopatra with Cressida would be so pointless that we need not dwell upon the superficiality of so doing.

And yet the comparison is instructive, for the sake of contrast. It suggests clearly the grandeur of scale in the love of Antony and Cleopatra, which includes, as it were, all the motives of Shakespeare's two other stories of tragic love[20]—the devotion of Romeo and Juliet, the rash impetuosity of Troilus, and what potentially, in a cheap and shallow woman, might become the wantonness of Cressida—and yet transmutes them into the heroic in an action that takes the whole world for its stage, to show how human love may make even the world that the lovers lose seem trifling in comparison with what they gain. This is the "tragic synthesis" that *Antony and Cleopatra* achieves.

2. *King Lear*

As Shakespeare tells it, the story of King Lear is a folktale, not simply in the opening scene, but throughout; and the dramatist has not wished to alter the folktale arbitrariness and simplicity of its archetypal form.[21] The naïveté of Lear's test of his daughters' love is not more unaccountable than the grounds of Gloucester's suspicions against Edgar, the needless preservation of Kent's incognito until the last scene of the play, Edmund's delay in sending to reprieve Lear and Cordelia, Albany's ingenuous explanation of his own and the others' unconcern about their fate: "Great things of us forgot!"—or any of a dozen other improbabilities and loose ends. Let us not be misled into supposing that these are merely signs of carelessness or an imperfect command of stagecraft in what is a great drama, now generally recognized as the highest reach of Shakespeare's dramatic achievement, the masterpiece which must take pride of place among all the other plays, whether we read it or see it acted—adequately acted, that is—upon the stage. The famous paradox of Charles Lamb—that the tragic effects of Shakespeare, and most notably in *King Lear*, are more securely attained through reading than through attending a theatrical performance—has been adequately answered by Granville Barker and by numerous recent and impressive productions of the play.

Plainly, however, the appeal of the play cannot be in the naturalistic virtues of its plot, which is, on the face of it, improbable, sometimes unclear in minor details, and arbitrary to the last degree. No more does it consist in the psychological subtlety of its characterization. There is virtually no attempt to study or account for the motivation of anyone but Lear, and, to a lesser extent, Gloucester as Lear's shadow; and little for either of them. Goneril and Regan are terrible figures of evil. Who can discover the cause in nature that makes these hard hearts? They are not accounted for; they are imposed upon us as symbols, the more monstrous for being inexplicable, to show us how sharper than a serpent's tooth it is to have a thankless child. As with Iago, the evil they represent is greater than they are. We forget them as people, while we contemplate the power of evil which they embody, while we feel the horror of it.

Cordelia may seem little more real to us than Spenser's Una. Except for the strange stubbornness of her opening defiance of her father, she is the symbolic figure of filial love, known to us as a woman by a single trait, which we are not likely to remark since we are not told of it until after her death, unless the actress, by an extraordinary feat, succeeds in impressing it upon us while still making herself heard:

Her voice was ever soft,
Gentle, and low—an excellent thing in woman.

But this exquisite touch is part of Lear's pathetic attempt to believe that she still lives—he would hear her answer, did she not speak so low—rather than a specific instruction to the actress. With this judgment of Cordelia some will doubtless disagree. To nineteenth-century critics, especially, Cordelia was often the favourite among Shakespeare's heroines; and in fact her role, in the latter part of the play, can be made very appealing by a talented actress. But it is as an ideal of feminine tenderness and filial devotion, and as the innocent victim of misfortune, that she moves us, rather than as an imperfect but lovely woman—like Desdemona, with her enchanting mixture of frankness and indirection; or like Cleopatra, with her inexhaustible variety. And Cordelia's very ideality is startlingly at odds with her inflexible pride in the opening of the play, a trait (so to regard it) which is utterly absent from her later behaviour. No doubt Cordelia's behaviour in this scene can be reconciled with her later character, after a fashion: by considering her replies to Lear's unreasonable demands ironical, let us say; but it is surely simpler, and more in keeping with the prevailing tenor of both action and characterization throughout the play, to regard Cordelia's role as fulfilling mainly a symbolic rather than a psychological function.

Kent is likewise a symbol, Lear's *fidus Achates*, the very embodiment of fidelity, though he has fire enough, and eloquence, in opposition. We cannot say we know the man, however, as we know Enobarbus or even Horatio, as individuals apart from Antony and Hamlet.[22] Rather, Kent is like Antigonus in *The Winter's Tale*, individualized and understandable up to a point, but, when he has served his purpose, fading unobtrusively from view—it is not quite unobtrusively in the case of Antigonus, who, as the tame bear chases him across the stage and out of our ken, leaves, like the Cheshire Cat, only a smile to remember him by. In *Lear*, of course, Shakespeare takes no such jocose liberty with his characters. When Kent announces his approaching death at the end of the play, we do not wonder at it or seek to understand it. We simply accept it, as we have his fidelity. That is all there is of the man. When the object of Fidelity ceases to exist (that is, Lear), it is fitting that Fidelity itself should cease to exist.

Edgar is bewildering in his changes. We scarcely know where to have him, as he shifts from the guileless victim of Edmund's betrayal, to Poor Tom, to the well-spoken countryman who lapses unaccountably into dialect, to the knight in shining armour. His is a fine role for an actor of versatile talent, but it hardly produces a unified impression of character. Edmund is more consistent. Considered apart from the real conflict projected through the symbolic design of the action and the poetry and subsuming this and other contributory themes, he and Edgar are the ostensible antagonists of the play; and, until his fall, Edmund pursues a consistent policy of villainy. But, faced with the need of his relenting, Shakespeare loses all interest in Edmund's "philosophy" or even in the consistency of his psychology, and uses him simply to forward the action at the appropriate point. His repentance is no more plausible than Iachimo's in *Cymbeline* (we may recall, by contrast, the terrible consistency of Iago), and we had better not ask why, if Edmund really is penitent, he does not sooner intervene to save Lear and Cordelia. His behaviour serves the complicated requirements of the catastrophe and is in keeping with the general air of strange and arbitrary happenings that pervades the whole play.

The catastrophe itself (V, iii) may remind us of *Cymbeline*, the technique of which is indeed more than once reminiscent of *King Lear*. At least sixteen different dramatic situations follow each other in rapid succession in the final scene of *Lear*, as compared with *Cymbeline*'s twenty-four. Reversals, recognitions, challenges, confessions, accidental judgments, casual slaughters—they are all here; from the improbability of Edmund's repentance and the still more unlikely dying confession of Goneril (with which we may compare the confession of the wicked Queen in *Cymbeline*) to the shock of Lear's entrance with Cordelia in his arms, we run the gamut of dramatic effects; and the last effect is so wonderful that we tend to forget the strange prolixity of happenings that has led up to it. This effect is profoundly true and right, and yet not logical or inevitable at all. It is the most purely tragic of Shakespeare's catastrophes, and one of the most artificially contrived.

In this play, it is the surpassing poetic utterance that, above all, transports us, and, rendered by a great actor in the role of Lear and an adequate supporting cast, the play cannot fail. The very violence and variety of the action—at the opposite pole from *Timon of Athens*, in this respect, though the resemblances, noted by Bradley,[23] are also striking—carry the mighty poetry and are needed to carry it; and every "inconsistency" that we notice in attentive reading, every implausibility, every convention of the symbolic portrayal of human experience, has its essential part in supporting the frame of the whole and creating its total effect. The imagined elemental grandeur of the outdoor setting of the greatest scenes, implying a calculated contrast between court and country, "art" and "nature," is the background. As in *Antony and Cleopatra*, we find two worlds, with the action oscillating between the two; but in *Lear*, these two worlds are on an even larger scale, symbolically, than in *Antony and Cleopatra*; there it is East and West; in *Lear*, man's little world of courts and intrigue and hypocritical pretence is contrasted with the elemental universe in which man is stripped of every artificiality. And, giving life and intensity to the whole, there echoes the passion that surges in Lear's mighty voice:

> Blow, winds, and crack your cheeks! rage! blow!
> You cataracts and hurricanoes spout
> Till you have drench'd our steeples, drown'd the cocks!
> You sulph'rous and thought-executing fires,
> Vaunt-couriers to oak-cleaving thunderbolts,
> Singe my white head! And thou, all-shaking thunder,
> Strike flat the thick rotundity o' th' world
> Crack Nature's moulds, all germains spill at once,
> That make ingrateful man!

Or the different passion of prose:

> Why, thou wert better in thy grave than to answer with thy uncover'd body this extremity of the skies. Is man no more than this? Consider him well. Thou

ow'st the worm no silk, the beast no hide, the sheep no wool, the cat no perfume. Ha! Here's three on's are sophisticated! Thou art the thing itself; unaccommodated man is no more but such a poor, bare, forked animal as thou art. Off, off, you lendings! Come, unbutton here.

Or the ineffable pathos of

> And my poor fool is hang'd! No, no, no life!
> Why should a dog, a horse, a rat, have life,
> And thou no breath at all? Thou'lt come no more,
> Never, never, never, never, never!
> Pray you undo this button. Thank you, sir.
> Do you see this? Look on her! look! her lips!
> Look there, look there!

To recall such passages, to hear them with the ear of imagination, is to answer the question of the play's unfailing power. This is Shakespeare's supreme mode of dramatic creation and expression, a mode which suits the action to the word, the setting and situation to the poetic mood, and constantly oversteps the bounds of nature to contrive a spell more potent than any impression of mere naturalism. By enlarging nature in a few swift strokes, it overwhelms us with the feeling of mysterious power, of profound truth, of truth embodied in sweeping grandeur and simplicity. The drama is not of the same kind that we get in *Hamlet* or *Othello* or *Antony and Cleopatra*; there is not the same sense of real life, of real people undergoing experiences we ourselves conceivably might have had. The method of *King Lear* eschews psychological realism, the nice analysis of motive, or any standard of historicity; it seems to cultivate deliberately a certain arbitrariness and illogicality in the contriving of the plot, the behaviour and interrelations of the characters; it invokes the simplicity of the folktale and draws constantly upon its resources—and it does all this to provide the proper vehicle for a *poetic* drama in which the impression of large, sometimes vague, but always imposing symbols and values symbolically projected, emerging from and dominating a radiant poetic vision, is the ultimate effect. Yet the play is intensely dramatic, as great poetry like that of the *Divine Comedy* or *Paradise Lost* is not. We do not feel that someone is telling us a story, whether the impersonal bard of the *Iliad*, the melancholy thinker of the *Aeneid*, the fiery prophet of the *Inferno*, or the inspired schoolmaster of *Paradise Lost*. We are not listening or being instructed; we are feeling and suffering with Lear, cursing Oswald with Kent, laughing with the Fool, building mad fancies with Poor Tom; yet not so much as people and individuals but as symbolic projections of our own deepest feelings, human passions, and ideals.

When we examine the play critically, we become aware of the art with which it is all done. How magnificently the opening scene builds its effect, with Goneril and Regan answering patly to their father's demand, and Cordelia standing ready, close-lipped and inflexible, with her

> Nothing, my lord.

Then Lear's anger slowly mounts, till it flames forth with the great outburst of his rejection of Cordelia:

> Let it be so! thy truth then be thy dower!
> For, by the sacred radiance of the sun,
> The mysteries of Hecate and the night;
> By all the operations of the orbs
> From whom we do exist and cease to be;
> Here I disclaim all my paternal care,
> Propinquity and property of blood,
> And as a stranger to my heart and me
> Hold thee from this forever. The barbarous Scythian,
> Or he that makes his generation messes
> To gorge his appetite, shall to my bosom
> Be as well neighbor'd, pitied, and reliev'd,
> As thou my sometime daughter.

From this point we are so carried along by the passionate eloquence of the language that we forget to observe the artifice with which the action itself is contrived.

Or take the prolonged crisis of the storm, a sustained pouring forth of impassioned poetry. It is a succession of arias for Lear on the themes of filial ingratitude, man's inhumanity to man, the pride of great ones, and the nothingness of man himself—the passionate counterpart of Hamlet's meditative musings—skilfully interspersed with the recitative of the Fool and Poor Tom, and the counterpoint of Gloucester's parallel story. It is schematic to the last degree, and yet intensely moving.

All this is but to say that *King Lear* creates its own mode, not to be measured by the customary criteria of tragedy or of Shakespeare's previous works in this kind. It is the perfect wedding of drama and poetry, in which poetry, the elder art, takes pride of place, yet not to the prejudice of the dramatic effect either—the mode of the dramatic poem, to which all his later plays in greater or less degree belong.

Lear is constructed, then, as a succession of tragic effects, carefully designed to build a mighty emotional pattern, an imaginative, poetic pattern, rather than as a piece of "realism," a situation taken from ordinary life in which the psychological implications of the action are studied with close attention to logical sequence and interconnection. It is of little avail to try to reduce the events of *King Lear* to a strict logical coherence, or to construct the motivation of Cordelia and Edgar and the rest from an imaginary account of their previous lives. Shakespeare himself offers us not the faintest suggestion as an encouragement for doing this. We do not know what kind of life Lear and his three daughters led together before the play opens, why Cordelia was his favourite (was it because she was most like her father or most different?), or how Lear could have been deceived for so many years by the hypocrisy of Goneril and Regan, while Cordelia was not. Gloucester is just as naïve regarding Edgar. We are given a situation which contains the passionate conflict of the forces of good and evil; we see these forces play themselves out to a tragic conclusion; and the emotional pattern this sequence of events creates for us issues in a mood of sublimity. Here is the "grandeur of conception" of which Longinus wrote; and the effect of awe is so securely achieved that the finer articulations of the parts do not concern us.

Since the tragic potentiality of *King Lear* lies in the antagonistic forces of good and evil represented in the families of Lear and Gloucester, any casual circumstance might serve to set these forces in conflict. The immediate cause does not matter very much; and so the folktale of the old king and his three daughters, with its parallel from the *Arcadia* of the episode of the King of Paphlagonia, will serve as well as any—better, perhaps, because of their simplicity—to set these forces working against each other. But the forces themselves must be great forces, if their conflict is to yield great tragedy. The wickedness of Goneril and Regan, Edmund and Cornwall, becomes a monstrous and inhuman wickedness which human nature itself repudiates, which invokes every comparison of the unnatural—of mankind turned beast or fiend or monster—and this the imagery of the play echoes and re-echoes, imposes and superimposes. With the "good" characters the method is somewhat different. We can hardly speak of "flaws" in Kent or Edgar or Cordelia; but they do make mistakes—Cordelia in her proud integrity in the beginning, Kent in his utter lack of tact or forbearance, Edgar in his unsuspecting simplicity—and these traits of their behaviour can be reconciled, after a fashion, with a prevailing conception of their "characters." But their mistakes are slips, innocent errors, or the excess of their virtues, and detract not a whit from their nobility; it would be perverse to regard their misfortunes as the punishment or even the necessary consequence of their shortcomings. There is no attempt to suggest a pattern of poetic justice in their sufferings. Clearly, they are intended to be wholly sympathetic and admirable, symbols of the human goodness that suffers in the conflict with dreadful forces of evil.

The essential conflict of the forces of good and evil finds its focus and centre in Lear, and his shadow Gloucester—for the method of the play, as everyone observes, is to tell the story on two planes of intensity and significance, so that what happens to Lear is reflected in what happens to Gloucester, yet with subtly varying contrast that greatly enlarges the significance of the story and gives it universality. This matter will be considered at greater length below; for the moment, we are concerned with the impression Lear makes upon us—not so much in his psychology, with which Shakespeare is but little concerned, as in what he stands for, the symbolic significance of his actions. In the opening situation of the play, it is made as emphatic as possible that Lear is committing an act of rash and headlong, even childish, folly. Kent's protests suggest that this angry tyrant is not altogether the normal Lear, that he is not characteristically so blind, so swept away by passion; yet Goneril's "the best and soundest of his time hath been but rash"; and Regan's " 'tis the infirmity of his age. . . . He hath ever but slenderly known himself," while testifying to their cold-heartedness, suggest that the rage which we have just witnessed and the fatally precipitate decision against Cordelia taken on the instant are acts by no means unparalleled in Lear's past career. He is presented to us as the type of folly in a monarch, lightly thinking to set aside his kingship and to divide his kingdom among his children—a dereliction of duty in a king still able to rule, according to Elizabethan views, and a grave departure from political wisdom, as testimony from Sackville and Norton's *Gorboduc* onward abundantly witnesses. To crown his act of political unwisdom in dividing his kingdom, Lear has chosen to dramatize it with the spectacle of his daughters' protestation of their love, an occasion calculated to provoke embarrassment or hypocrisy in them and chiefly to minister to the father's vanity. This king must be far gone in senility, we might think, were it not for the fiery and imaginative energy of Lear's denunciation of Cordelia. But Lear is a commanding figure, an imposing presence in his folly, and we cannot but recognize his greatness, even in an act that verges upon madness. We are horrified by his rashness, but our horror is mingled not with pity but with awe.

When we next see Lear (I, iv), he is still the impetuous and lordly monarch, energetically enjoying his relaxation from the cares of his kingdom, just returned from hunting, demanding his dinner and calling for his fool to divert him while it is making ready. He genially receives the disguised Kent into his service, and we have the first ominous note in the incident of Oswald's intended rudeness to Lear and Kent's summary tripping up of the steward's heels. Then the Fool enters. Swiftly, from this moment, begins the humiliation of Lear. The recurring and persistent note of the Fool's jibes is Lear's irretrievable folly. The Fool can stand for the accusing figure of Cordelia because he has loved her, and because, as a fool, he speaks without malice and without constraint. He is the voice of Lear's own conscience, reproaching him: "Can you make no use of nothing, nuncle?" Lear's reply,

> Why, no, boy. Nothing can be made of nothing,

recalls the answer of Cordelia that had so provoked Lear's wrath. And the Fool's retort, addressed to Kent,

> Prithee tell him, so much the rent of his land comes to. He will not believe a fool,

foretells the terrible irony of Lear's helpless position—because he has given all: "I had rather be any kind o' thing than a fool! And yet I would not be thee, nuncle. Thou has pared thy wit o' both sides and left nothing i' th' middle."

The proof follows immediately, with Goneril's entrance and her cold rebuke of her father. Lear's bewilderment, his gradual understanding of the situation, and his ungoverned fury retrace the pattern of his treatment of Cordelia, but in how different a context! Now Lear is the victim of a more frightening injustice; for he had rejected Cordelia in passion, in a fit of unaccountable rage, but Goneril (and later Regan) provoke Lear and reject him with calm and deliberate calculation. And it is too late for Lear to retaliate, save with impotent curses, too late to undo the wrong: "Woe that too late repents!"

We are shown the case of a great man who makes an appalling mistake and then must live out the consequences. Othello's tragedy culminates in the realization of his error; but Lear's tragedy begins with this realization, and, in its outcome, assumes grander and more terrible proportions. The father, who has divided his power and authority with his children, experiences the result of thus flouting the natural moral order of things: the children defy him and reject him; the king having relinquished his rulership, civil authority topples: the ungrateful daughters intrigue against each other, a foreign army invades Britain, the land is torn by civil war. And Lear is overwhelmed by these events, for a time loses his reason in the general chaos symbolized by the storm and rages madly against the universal disorder that has followed upon his single act of folly.

A terrible price to pay for a mistaken judgment! Yet Lear's was a mistake of the head rather than of the heart, and he remains a man more sinned against than sinning. If his division of his kingdom was touched with vanity and a little self-interest, it was also prompted by great-hearted and heedless generosity. He withheld nothing from his daughters, trusting that his open-handed munificence would meet with a generous return. He put himself utterly at their mercy. A foolish mistake, indeed! We cannot but be troubled about Lear's imperfection; it is so grossly, culpably human: generosity, imprudence, pride, anger, even a trace of sloth, are all discernible in his initial act, the inextricable intermixture of good and bad in human motives. Shakespeare has here embodied, most unforgettably, the fundamental faultiness of all human motives and all human acts, even the noblest. Lear is the grandest of all Shakespeare's tragic heroes, and his faults are on the scale of his grandeur. Yet if we find Lear's culpability at the centre of the tragedy, we surely miss the full compass of the tragedy itself. Lear's fault is the immediate cause of his suffering, and he pays a full price; but the ultimate effect of his fault is to enlarge the tragedy beyond the measure of justice, of *hybris* and *nemesis*, with the emergence of Lear's purified love.

We may look at the matter first in a negative light. Simply to insist upon Lear's folly and its consequences does not reckon with the wickedness of Goneril and Regan. It is not simply that Lear's sufferings are greater than he deserves: his sufferings transcend any question of justice or injustice; they relate to the deficiency of love, not in Lear, but in the daughters who should love him. Goneril and Regan do not attack Lear—it is Edmund who orders his death. They simply deprive him of that affection which would bear with his humours, which would smile good-naturedly at his follies and ease the burden of his old age. Even Cordelia has a share in this youthful intolerance of age; but she atones for her lapse with renewed love, and her fault ceases to matter or to exist. The elder daughters turn away from their father; they shut him out of their hearts, out into the storm; they are incapable of loving him, and so for them he simply ceases to exist. That is what makes their offence so terrible, more terrible even than if they had attacked him, for this would have been an act of passion which would have spent itself and led, perhaps, to remorse. But towards Lear they are loveless, passionless, and cold. They are unmoved by his tirades, by the most awful curses. "Hear, Nature, hear!" cries Lear, beside himself,

> dear goddess, hear!
> Suspend thy purpose, if thou didst intend
> To make this creature fruitful.
> Into her womb convey sterility;
> Dry up in her the organs of increase;
> And from her derogate body never spring
> A babe to honour her! If she must teem,
> Create her child of spleen, that it may live
> And be a thwart disnatur'd torment to her.
> Let it stamp wrinkles in her brow of youth,
> With cadent tears fret channels in her cheeks,
> Turn all her mother's pains and benefits
> To laughter and contempt, that she may feel
> How sharper than a serpent's tooth it is
> To have a thankless child. Away, away!

The horrified Albany turns to Goneril, and we may see her amused and scornful smile as she answers,

> Never afflict yourself to know the cause;
> But let his disposition have that scope
> That dotage gives it.

Lear turns to Regan, confident that she will receive him and his hundred knights; and she reasons with him, matter-of-factly, coldly, righteously,

> O, sir, you are old!
> Nature in you stands on the very verge
> Of her confine. You should be rul'd, and led
> By some discretion that discerns your state
> Better than you yourself.

Lear humbles himself to her, pleads with her; and, supported by Goneril, Regan drives him forth. She does not, indeed, think of her conduct in this way. More viciously petty than her sister

Goneril, she is the readier to excuse her behaviour. After Lear has rushed away from her hypocritical temporizing into the storm, she explains to Goneril that she would gladly receive Lear himself—but without a single follower; and to Gloucester, who enters with the account of Lear's desperate plight, as he wanders in fury through the stormy night, she speaks her real sentiments:

> O, sir, to wilful men
> The injuries that they themselves procure
> Must be their schoolmasters. Shut up your doors.
> He is attended with a desperate train,
> And what they may incense him to, being apt
> To have his ears abus'd, wisdom bids fear.

In the Lear of the great scenes that follow, we recognize the tragic nature of human love, as he passes from the pent-up agony of his frustration to hysteria, the mighty outburst of his mad raving in which he himself is the poet building, with the help of the Fool and Poor Tom, a tragic fantasia upon the central theme:

> Filial ingratitude!
> Is it not as this mouth should tear this hand
> For lifting food to't? But I will punish home!
> No, I will weep no more. In such a night
> To shut me out! Pour on; I will endure.
> In such a night as this! O Regan, Goneril!
> Your old kind father, whose frank heart gave all!
> O, that way madness lies; let me shun that!
> No more of that.

The love of parents for children is the purest form of human devotion, on the secular level, that we know. It is not anything that we learn; it is not anything that we attain through striving; the will to love is merely the assent to an instinctive law of human nature. Yet we know that it is good, when it is not possessive or otherwise perverted, that it is a duty, a sacred thing, part of a timeless mystery. Lear's love for his children has not, indeed, been perfectly disinterested; it has been mixed with a self-regarding taint in the beginning, though it becomes increasingly purified as it concentrates upon Cordelia in the end. But it has been essentially a generous motive from the beginning, as generous a motive as erring human nature admits of, and, as it is the most difficult of human virtues, so it is the greatest.

There is likewise a duty of children to parents that is not abrogated by time. It is the duty enjoined by the fifth commandment, the duty of honour, which is the child's form of love. It is this love that Goneril and Regan deny their father: the love that is obedience in childhood, forbearance and gentleness and respect in later years. This love, like that of parents for children, must be given freely, from the heart, or it is not given at all. It cannot reason or make conditions; it has nothing to do with justice or anyone's deserving; it is simply a law of human nature, the way things are.

This is the quality of the love Lear gives his children—unthinking, unconditional, and highly imprudent; and each of them denies him, in some measure, the due return. Cordelia later atones for her lack with the overflowing measure of love; but Regan and Goneril shut Lear from their hearts. The denial of love is inhuman and tragic, of universal human concern, recognizable in its essential elements in every time and in every place where men and women, parents and children, are to be found. It is an offence against nature, a sin against God and man; and our hearts swell with pity and indignation as we recognize it. It is one of the greatest of tragic themes, and Shakespeare has fixed it here with the unerring simplicity of genius.

In his recovery from his madness, Lear appears to us transformed and purified by suffering. His suffering has chastened him, made him humble, penitent, even, so that he seeks Cordelia's forgiveness; and in the storm he becomes mindful of the suffering of others:

> Poor naked wretches, wheresoe'er you are,
> That bide the pelting of this pitiless storm,
> How shall your houseless heads and unfed sides,
> Your loop'd and window'd raggedness, defend you
> From seasons such as these? O, I have ta'en
> Too little care of this! Take physic, pomp;
> Expose thyself to feel what wretches feel,
> That thou mayst shake the superflux to them
> And show the heavens more just.

Restored to sanity, rested and calm, Lear is all gentleness and love; and, in renewed misfortune, after he and Cordelia have been taken prisoner, he can jest, with mild irony that is almost gaiety, at their predicament:

> Come, let's away to prison.
> We two alone will sing like birds i' th' cage.
> When thou dost ask me blessing, I'll kneel down
> And ask of thee forgiveness. So we'll live,
> And pray, and sing, and tell old tales, and laugh
> At gilded butterflies, and hear poor rogues
> Talk of court news; and we'll talk with them too—
> Who loses and who wins; who's in, who's out—
> And take upon's the mystery of things,
> As if we were God's spies; and we'll wear out,
> In a wall'd prison, packs and sects of great ones
> That ebb and flow by th' moon.

These are the glimpses Shakespeare gives us—and he can afford only glimpses, with such a theme—of the transformation in Lear that his sufferings have wrought. He is immeasurably enhanced in dignity, purified in the fire and tempest of his suffering in the storm, transfigured to a symbol of human grandeur, like Sophocles' Oedipus in the *Oedipus at Colonus*, who moves us not so much to pity as to awe.

To consider the parallel theme of Gloucester and his two sons as we have considered the relationships of Lear and his three daughters is perhaps unnecessary; but there are certain significant variations that deserve attention.

Edmund owes allegiance to no man, as his soliloquy informs us (I, ii, 1 ff.). He is the "natural" man whose natural powers—his own strength and cunning—are his justification, his moral law. Since he is younger than his brother Edgar and since the custom of society brands him as base and illegitimate, he is doubly prevented from succeeding to the earldom of his father. He sees "custom," the law of nations, as his enemy (the distinction between "natural" right and man-made law, *νόμος* and *φύσις*, goes back to the time of the Greek Sophists, and earlier; we may read the arguments of Edmund expanded philosophically in the *Gorgias* of Plato and a hundred other sources) and he sets out to defeat the laws of society, to beguile his father and displace his brother with zest, with gaiety:

> Now, gods, stand up for bastards.

For Edmund, then, love does not exist; it has no claim. His opposition to Gloucester and Edgar is as impersonal as the natural force of the elements; they stand in his way and must yield to his triumphant course. There is no malice in his deception of them, only the delight of the artificer of his own fortune; and he plays off Regan against Goneril with the same cheerful relish: "Yet Edmund was beloved," he reminds himself with quiet satisfaction at the end,

> The one the other poison'd for my sake,
> And after slew herself.

He shows no interest in the fate of Gloucester, beyond the accomplishment of succeeding to his title; and Edgar he apparently forgets, after he has successfully disposed of him, as he thinks, until he learns that he was the knight who gave him his death wound. The changes which come over Edmund from this point onward are not to be accounted for by any study of his past behaviour. He assents to Edgar's frigid moralizing upon the situation:

> I am no less in blood than thou art, Edmund;
> If more, the more th' hast wrong'd me.
> My name is Edgar and thy father's son.
> The gods are just, and of our pleasant vices
> Make instruments to scourge us.
> The dark and vicious place where thee he got
> Cost him his eyes.

And he is apparently moved by Edgar's account of their father's death:

> This speech of yours hath mov'd me,
> And shall perchance do good; but speak you on;
> You look as you had something more to say.

Shakespeare does not always choose to avoid banality. Nor does he care very much about the plausibility of Edmund's conduct.

He is a minor figure in the great finale, and he is allowed to pass from our attention when he is carried off the stage, yielding place, as is proper, to the tragic spectacle of Lear's latest moments.

With Gloucester, Shakespeare takes more pains, for his case is carefully designed to parallel Lear's. He is represented as the easy-going man of the world, comfortably licentious, slyly priding himself on his spirit in having produced a presentable bastard in Edmund, and yet innocently gullible and superstitious, an ineffectual but well-intentioned libertine. Deceived by Edmund into condemning his good son and cherishing his bad one, he has nevertheless not been deceived about the motives of the others; unable to submit without protest when Lear is shut out into the storm, in his worried perplexity he reveals to Edmund his correspondence with the invading force of Cordelia. Thus betrayed into Edmund's hands, he suffers the torture of his blinding by Cornwall and Regan—a scene the violence of which is required, as Bradley notes, if we are not to experience anticlimax, since this scene punctuates the suspended power of Lear's mad wanderings. But there is a further point of contrast. As Gloucester's fibre is coarser and weaker than Lear's, as his mode of life is simpler, less imaginative, and more earth-bound, so his suffering, appropriately, is physically brutal, while Lear's is mainly of the spirit. It is as if body and soul of man are racked by the unkindness of children, in the stories of Lear and Gloucester. Gloucester's experience is mainly of the body, Lear's of the spirit; and we may observe this contrast all the way through the play. Gloucester is simply beguiled from his purpose of taking his own life, and while he is in his right wits, by Edgar's trick of describing his father's stumbling fall as prompted by a fiend and frustrated by divine intervention; but Lear's madness brooks no deception and wears itself out in imaginative fury. After Gloucester has encountered Lear near Dover and listened to his inspired raving, he himself comments:

> The King is mad. How stiff is my vile sense,
> That I stand up, and have ingenious feeling
> Of my huge sorrows! Better I were distract.
> So should my thoughts be sever'd from my griefs,
> And woes by wrong imaginations lose
> The knowledge of themselves.

And, in the end, Gloucester is merely a pathetic figure, in Edgar's account of his death:

> I ask'd his blessing, and from first to last
> Told him my pilgrimage. But his flaw'd heart
> (Alack, too weak the conflict to support!)
> 'Twixt two extremes of passion, joy and grief,
> Burst smilingly.

Gloucester has been cruelly betrayed by the son whom he has loved and benefited, protected and comforted by the son whom he has wronged; and the parallel holds, roughly, for Lear's relations with Goneril, Regan, and Cordelia. Lear learned to understand the difference between the hypocrisy of Goneril and Regan and the love of Cordelia at the cost of his reason; and Gloucester never truly "saw" the difference between his two sons until he had lost his eyes.[24] Yet we must guard against reading Lear's story in the light of Gloucester's. Lear is not another Gloucester; Edmund lacks the fiendishness of Goneril and Regan; and Cordelia, gentle and loving in the end, is far indeed from that severe young moralist Edgar:

> The gods are just, and of our pleasant vices
> Make instruments to scourge us.
> The dark and vicious place where thee he got
> Cost him his eyes.

Rather, we should take Gloucester's story as a transposing of the theme into a harsher and more strident key, an extension of its meaning to include not simply what is heroic and of the spirit of man but what is commoner and coarser and of the body as well.

Because the ending of *King Lear* is so patently and deliberately fashioned in a certain way, it offers the clearest and most impressive example of Shakespeare's final conception of tragedy. Having brought the action to the point where Lear and Cordelia have been led away to prison, under threat of death by Edmund's order but evidently not yet put to death; and then having represented the duel between Edmund and Edgar in which Edmund receives his death wound, Shakespeare could, at this point, do anything he liked with his story. At this highest reach of his poetic powers, too, he could have invested any sort of outcome with moving eloquence, and any sort of outcome would doubtless prove acceptable in this play which does not rely upon logic or very much upon probability for its effect. Certainly, Shakespeare could have given the action such an outcome as *Cymbeline* has—*Cymbeline*, indeed, in one aspect is the Lear story with a happy ending.[25] Goneril and Regan would have died, of course, but Edmund would have repented to more effect, Lear and Cordelia would have been restored, shaken and bruised, but still sound and triumphant over their enemies; and the King of France, being nowhere in evidence, could be reported dead and Cordelia married to Edgar; the good would be rewarded, and the penitent Edmund forgiven. And Shakespeare could have made all this beautiful and moving, at least as moving as *Cymbeline*, which has its lovely moments (as in the reconciliation of Posthumus and Imogen) despite the fact that it is something of a *tour de force*. We could even call a play with such an outcome "tragedy" according to Greek precedent, the precedent of the *Oresteia* or of Euripides' *Alcestis*. Shakespeare's editors, however, would probably have called it "comedy,"[26] and so, we may feel, would Shakespeare himself. That Shakespeare in *Lear* was not thinking of what a popular audience would like best, that *Lear* was intended as the most tragic of his plays, the one that should fix the audience's attention most uncompromisingly and poignantly upon the tragic outcome, there can be no doubt.

The entrance of Lear with the dead Cordelia in his arms is a calculated shock—so rude a shock that actors and audience from Nahum Tate's day to Charles Lamb's refused to have anything to do with it. Even Bradley, while expressing disdain for Tate's version or any other attempt to improve upon Shakespeare's designs, has nevertheless argued that though Shakespeare's ending of the play is no doubt imaginatively right it lacks "inevitability" and is too painful to be fully tragic.[27] What Bradley missed, we may think, is the symbolic appropriateness of this final scene. It is worth examining carefully.

The events preceding the last entrance of Lear mainly concern the fate of Gloucester, which is reported by Edgar, that it may not compete in interest with the approaching climax. The deaths of Regan and Goneril are even more briefly announced, and Edmund, after he has sent to reprieve Lear and Cordelia, is carried off dying. From the beginning of this final scene, the chief suspense concerns the fates of Lear and Cordelia. Edmund stated his intention of doing away with them, despite Albany's order to spare them, at the end of V, i; a little later, we see him instruct a captain to procure their instant death, and the captain agrees to carry out his commands (V, iii, 26–39). There has been the most explicit preparation for their destruction; still, we can hardly believe that Edmund's instructions will be fulfilled to the letter, if we are seasoned playgoers but seeing the play for the first time; that is not the way dramatic catastrophes are brought about. Some unforeseen development will occur: we hope it will somehow provide for the rescue of Cordelia and Lear. Shakespeare, we may suppose, deliberately counts upon this expectation.

When Lear enters carrying Cordelia, we are shocked and awed by the spectacle, and we begin to understand that there will be no happiness in the ending:

> Howl, howl, howl, howl! O, you are men of stone.
> Had I your tongues and eyes, I'ld use them so
> That heaven's vault should crack. She's gone for ever!
> I know when one is dead, and when one lives.
> She's dead as earth. Lend me a looking glass.
> If that her breath will mist or stain the stone,
> Why, then she lives.

The following comments of Kent, Edgar, and Albany are like a Greek chorus: "Is this the promis'd end?" asks Kent, with finely ironic ambiguity; and Edgar adds, "Or image of that horror?" and Albany, "Fall and cease!" But the dramatic interest centres upon Lear, as he tries to find signs of life in his beloved child. His eagerness is touching:

> This feather stirs; she lives! If it be so,
> It is a chance which does redeem all sorrows
> That ever I have felt;

so, too, is the compassionate attempt of Kent and Edgar to distract him from the further agony of disappointment: "O my good master!" Kent exclaims; and Edgar, " 'Tis noble Kent, your friend." But Lear's concentration upon his hope is single-minded, and he is fiercely impatient of interruption:

> A plague upon you, murderers, traitors all!
> I might have sav'd her; now she's gone forever!

There is the miraculous tenderness of the return of his illusion, in the same breath:

> Cordelia, Cordelia! stay a little. Ha!
> What is't thou say'st? Her voice was ever soft,
> Gentle and low—an excellent thing in woman;

and the savagery, again, of

> I kill'd the slave that was a-hanging thee.

The soberly admiring confirmation of Albany's captain who found Lear: " 'Tis true, my lords, he did," prompts Lear's chuckling reminiscence:

> Did I not, fellow?
> I have seen the day, with my good biting falchion
> I would have made them skip.

He has forgotten Cordelia and his sorrows, for the moment; he is vague and kindly, as he turns to Kent:

> I am old now,
> And these same crosses spoil me. Who are you?
> Mine eyes are not o' th' best. I'll tell you straight.

The recognition of Kent follows, though it is as in a dream:

> This' a dull sight. Are you not Kent?

and Kent attempts to remind Lear of his identity with Lear's servant who tripped up Oswald:

> KENT No, my good lord; I am the very man—
> LEAR I'll see that straight.
> KENT That from your first of difference and decay
> Have followed your sad steps.
> LEAR You're welcome hither.

Then the infinite sadness of Kent's reply:

> Nor no man else! All's cheerless, dark, and deadly.
> Your eldest daughters have foredone themselves,
> And desperately are dead.
>
> LEAR Ay, so I think.
>
> ALBANY He knows not what he says; and vain it is
> That we present us to him.
>
> EDGAR Very bootless.

A captain enters to report Edmund's death, and Albany ingenuously speaks of resigning his power to Lear:

> All friends shall taste
> The wages of their virtue, and all foes
> The cup of their deservings.

But Lear's restless eyes have found Cordelia again, and his sorrows:

> And my poor fool is hang'd. No, no, no life!
> Why should a dog, a horse, a rat, have life,
> And thou no breath at all? Thou'lt come no more,
> Never, never, never, never, never!
> Pray you undo this button. Thank you, sir.

The old fire of eagerness kindles again,

> Do you see this? Look on her! look! her lips!
> Look there, look there!

and he dies in the belief that Cordelia lives.

In his latest moments, Lear is freed of every motive but the love of his child. He has forgotten his wrongs, or any thought of retribution; and, as he joins Cordelia in death, his love has been made perfect through suffering. This is the "inevitability" of his end. This is the grandest, and, we may think, the necessary way of affirming that human goodness may triumph over the evils of this world—at a tragic cost.

This study has sought to show that *Antony and Cleopatra* and *King Lear* are the two most comprehensive of Shakespeare's tragic designs. *Antony and Cleopatra*, dealing with the themes of a man's love for a woman and the ambition of empire, mediates between the themes of *Julius Caesar* and *Troilus and Cressida*, comprehending and in some sense reconciling their moods, their conflicts, and their values; *King Lear*, dealing with the relations of the human family and of human ingratitude, similarly mediates between *Coriolanus* and *Timon of Athens*, comprehends and reconciles them. We have already considered *Antony and Cleopatra* in this light; it remains to speak of *King Lear* in the same way.

Coriolanus stands at the opposite pole from *Timon of Athens*, from one point of view; there are also some resemblances. Coriolanus is a good man, like Timon, frank, unselfish, single-hearted and uncompromising, the victim of his own generous qualities. His tragedy consists in this: his virtues set him in opposition to his native city; in the ensuing struggle, the claims of Rome are clearly superior to the claim of his own pride; through the ties of his love for his family Coriolanus is brought to recognize this superior duty to the state, and he pays the penalty of his rebellion with his life. In *Timon*, the individual is right and society is in the wrong; and the tragedy consists in the eclipse of the superior individual. The mood of *Coriolanus* is, relatively speaking, untroubled, quiet, thoughtful: we witness the emergence of a finer nobility in the just sacrifice of a great man to a duty that is greater than he; in *Timon*, all is bitterness, invective, loathing: Timon's indictment of the vileness of human society admits no qualification. *Coriolanus* shows us the strength and the virtue of family ties; Coriolanus's devotion to his mother and to his mother's teaching magnificently meets the crucial test of self-effacement; in his tragic fall, Coriolanus ennobles himself and vindicates the values to which he submits. *Timon* shows us that there are no ties of devotion or honour in a corrupt society, not even the respect of self; that in such a society sacrifices do not mean anything; all that a good man can do is to withdraw from it, to despise mankind and himself, to welcome death: *Timon* is the denial of the value of human life.

King Lear comprehends all of these motifs, evokes all of these moods, and unifies them in a larger coherent whole. Lear has all the virtues of Coriolanus and Timon—the frank, unqualified generosity, the heroic nobility, a grandeur that includes all their greatness and far surpasses it. His heart swells with raging madness at the cruelty of Goneril and Regan, he surpasses Timon in his curses, he sees mankind degraded below the level of beasts; but his passion purifies his own motives, there is humility and devotion in the reunion of Lear and Cordelia, and a tragic reconciliation of the forces of love and hatred in Lear. In the end he has forgotten the ingratitude of Goneril and Regan; all hatred has been transcended through his love. Yet the reconciliation does not issue in human happiness: it costs the life of Cordelia and breaks Lear's own heart. Lear becomes a supreme symbol of human love, but he is also the tragic victim of his love; and human life remains, as tragedy, a mystery, almost, one might say, an illusion, at the end of *Lear*—

> He knows not what he says; and vain it is
> That we present us to him.

But the reconciliation effects an ennoblement of human life, as represented in the great figure of Lear, an ennoblement of which we become aware through the effect of grandeur, the calm, solemn, serene mood in which the play ends for us, the mood of exaltation that is our response to the greatest art. As we witness the play, we see the worst of which human nature is capable, or so it seems; and gradually it is borne home to us that despite this wickedness—even, perhaps, because of it—human nature emerges finer, more heroic, so that its wickedness fades into insignificance. In his final suffering, Lear inspires us with reverence, with awe; in his tragic figure, the value of human life is vindicated, triumphantly and securely.

As the Oedipus of Sophocles' last great tragedy, the *Oedipus Coloneus*, passes beyond human sight in austere majesty towards the end of the play, he leaves with us impressions of awe and grandeur—though he has appeared, at the beginning, in a pitiable state, a blind and battered old man, an outcast from society, led in by his daughter to seek at Athens the refuge that he could not find in the city of Thebes which he once ruled. In the gradual emergence of the full tragic stature of Sophocles' hero, we see that

Oedipus' sufferings have not been the result of any wicked intent; he has ruled with piety towards the gods and justice towards men. His fault has simply been that he is human, that he cannot understand his position until it is too late, cannot foresee the tragic consequences of his acts. He is like Job in refusing to acknowledge that he has sinned, and he remains unbroken amid his afflictions. He is a terrible figure as he denounces his son Polyneices and repulses Creon who would forcibly drag him back to Thebes. And, in the end, he is accepted for what he is, a good man whose sufferings have invested him with such greatness that he becomes an object of veneration. He is so accepted by Theseus and the Athenians, to whom his shrine at Athens will bring blessing; and by the gods, who receive him as a hero, who recognize his human dignity and grandeur. As H. D. F. Kitto puts it, "In taking Oedipus to themselves as a hero the gods are but recognizing facts. By his stature as a man Oedipus imposes himself on the gods; it is not forgiveness, for there is no sin. The *Coloneus* is Sophocles' answer to the tragedy of life. He knows that he cannot justify God to man, but he can justify man to man."[28]

Oedipus Coloneus brings into a final reconciliation and harmony the tragic insights and values of the *Antigone* and *Oedipus Rex*. *Antigone* shows us the dilemma that may confront a guiltless person, the necessary choice between two duties—the duty to human law and to the divine—the result of which, inevitably, for the blameless protagonist, is destruction. What can we think of Antigone's plight, as she chooses to perform the religious rites for her brother in defiance of Creon's command, but that the gods punish the good and the bad, indifferently: it is the price we must pay for being human. In *Oedipus Rex*, the protagonist is a man of exceptional integrity; his only fault is that he is endowed with ordinary human passions as well. Oedipus' single aim, from the beginning of his story (as Sophocles tells it) to the end, is to act with piety towards his fellow men and towards the gods: with piety towards his parents (as he supposes them to be) when he leaves them lest he should fulfil the terrible prophecy; with justice towards the citizens of Thebes and towards the gods, as, like a good ruler, he tries his best to discover the offender against heaven and to purge the city of the guilt that afflicts it. It is all of no avail. The natural human passion that betrayed him into murdering his real father, the human blindness that betrayed him into marrying his mother and begetting children by her, can find no justification in the eyes of the inexorable gods; and he pays the penalty in the sacrifice of his eyes and of his kingdom, by becoming an outcast among men, a foul and polluted thing, a man accurst. It is one of the most pitiable spectacles the human imagination has ever conceived. There is grandeur in it, but there is also infinite sadness.

In the last, and, we may think, the crowning achievement of his genius, the *Oedipus Coloneus*, Sophocles reviewed the themes of his two previous Theban plays, and here he was able to see beyond the bitterness and the sadness of *Antigone* and *Oedipus Rex*. The basic insight, the tragic vision of an ordering of all things inexorably just, remained; but he added to this insight a great affirmation of the value and dignity of human life, an affirmation fully consonant with his unwavering view of the just rule of the gods, of the universality of law and order. Oedipus, in the epiphanic climax of the *Coloneus*, becomes an enduring symbol of human grandeur, the symbolic reconciliation of man with himself, even, in a paradoxical way, with the inexorable Powers that rule human life.

Such a reconciliation and harmony is likewise achieved in *King Lear*, a harmony of a different purport, in a later and very different context. Without raising the unanswerable question of the relative merits of Sophocles and Shakespeare as writers of tragedy, we may yet venture to bring the crowning masterpiece of the one dramatic genius into association with that of the other; for the two plays have this, at least, in common: that each represents a moment of supreme insight and exaltation achieved through the mediation of the same dramatic form. As Lear is revealed to us in the last scene of the play, sorrowing over Cordelia's death, protesting, refusing to accept this final bitterness as an end of all his torment, he represents for us the final affliction of suffering humanity; but he represents, too, the tenderness, the love of suffering humanity, and the dignity, the almost mystical dignity, with which that love is invested. It is a moment too solemn for tears. In his figure, as his great heart falters and dies, we recognize a supreme value that the ancients never knew, a value which surpasses—for us, at least—even the Sophoclean value of justice: the value of human love.

CONCLUSION

THE VALUE THAT EMERGES ULTIMATELY in both *Antony and Cleopatra* and *King Lear* is the value of human love. Shakespeare comprehends all of human love that matters to us (and in this we are different from the Greeks) in the love of Antony and Cleopatra, Cordelia and Lear. He represents it with such power, such tenderness, and such grandeur that all other values, even justice, seem to be transcended, or better, perhaps, merged in this governing conception and feeling. The ultimate sense of Shakespeare's tragic vision is that human love is the greatest good of human life, that without it life is barren, or trivial, or evil. He does not anywhere say so much; that is not his method; but he makes us understand it and feel it nonetheless.

The love of which Shakespeare treats in the two greatest of his tragedies is represented as a developing action, as the dramatic medium requires; and that action involves a conflict and resolution. In *Antony and Cleopatra*, the conflict is between human love and world empire and it occurs on two planes: in the opposition of Antony and Cleopatra to Octavius, and also as an element in the love of Antony *for* Cleopatra. The resolution of this latter conflict, as of the former, is that Antony sacrifices the world for his love; and in this sacrifice Cleopatra joins him, according to the comprehensive symbolism of the play, in a union which transcends material values, which scorns the world in all its power and magnificence (as represented by Octavius) and exists enduringly in the Elysium of true lovers. This enduring union is not attained without effort. The story of Antony and Cleopatra, as Shakespeare tells it, is the story of two very fallible mortals: of a man heroic and generous and loving, but also mistrustful, impulsive, easily betrayed into folly by his passions, and given to blaming his mistakes upon the woman he loves; of a woman who, as we all know, is no better than she should be. But these two lovers, in whom we can recognize something of ourselves—however far short of their heroic scale we may come, we may yet recognize ourselves in their failings—these two lovers are greater than their failings; their love is equal to the last sacrifice, more than equal to it. They triumph in their love; and, in so far as we may be capable of sharing in their experience vicariously, we triumph with them. For their story is a true one; it is all in Plutarch, though only Shakespeare could show us that it is there.

In *Lear*, we are in another world, the world of the primitive imagination rather than of Plutarch and the history books. Yet here the universal value of human love is even more plainly recognizable. The love of parents and children—and its opposite, the denial of love—is set forth in supreme poetic and dramatic form. The theme, too, emerges and grows stronger in the developing course of the action, triumphs overwhelmingly in the end: Lear suffers the purging of the storm; Goneril and Regan and Edmund perish, their petty ambitions and lusts and hatreds are forgotten; and all that remains finally is the love of Cordelia and Lear. In their love, we are reconciled to humanity, despite its passion, its blindness, its mistakes. The great figure of Lear, at the end of the play, is the type of human sorrow; but he is also the symbol of human love, of a love so great in its dignity and pathos that it makes us quiet and reverent.

In all of this, no Christian analogy is made explicit. According to the view of Shakespearian tragedy here afforded, it is because he avoids any issue involving specifically Christian doctrine —as distinct from issues the ethical solution of which reflects a Christian mode of feeling and belief—that Shakespeare is able to achieve the effects that have been ascribed to *Antony and Cleopatra* and *King Lear*. The final synthesis of Shakespearian tragedy is a reconciliation of other human values in the single value of human love, a value that reflects a Christian attitude but without any direct reference to Christian faith. The Shakespearian value of love is not the same as the Christian's love of God; there is precisely the difference between these two that Spenser deplored in the third of his *Fowre Hymnes* and so explicitly apologized for; the difference, too, that Sidney made the theme of his beautiful devotional sonnet, "Leave me, O love, that reachest but to dust. . . ." Of the "Heavenly Love," the theme of Spenser's third hymn, Shakespeare gives no account in his tragedies. Shakespeare's tragic matter, from beginning to end, is humanity, its passions, its blindness, its mistakes, its pathos; yet out of these very elements, he fashions a design that issues in a vision of humanity ennobled, that reconciles us to our human kind, with all its failings, that shows us an unmistakable human dignity emerging triumphant out of the tragic catastrophe itself.

The final synthesis of *Antony and Cleopatra* and *King Lear*, though not overtly Christian in its ethical scheme of reference, is nevertheless ultimately and distinctively Christian in the ethical attitude reflected. We may test the argument in this way. *Antony and Cleopatra* is a play which pays careful attention to its setting in pagan times, which scrupulously attributes to the actors only such beliefs and attitudes and sentiments as are vouched for in the historical accounts of Plutarch. Yet, if we agree that the dominant theme, the prevailing value of the play, is the triumphant vindication of the love of a man and a woman, then we must also reflect that only within Christian times could this value be treated as thematically central in so dignified a medium as tragedy. It could scarcely have occurred to an ancient that the love of Antony and Cleopatra could be considered in itself as particularly beautiful or exalted. The ancients did not customarily think of human love—and especially love between the sexes—in this way. The exaltation of human love as a value is of course a Christian conception, deriving ultimately from the greater and inclusive conception of God's love and the Christian's love of God. Similarly with *King Lear*. For all its careful avoidance of specifically Christian allusions, the centrality of the value of human love in the play reflects a distinctively Christian mode of thought and feeling—we need only recall the relationship between Oedipus and Antigone, as Sophocles represents it, in contrast with that of Lear and Cordelia, to see the difference. The value of human love in *Antony and Cleopatra* and *King Lear* is the normative value of natural ethics in a Christian view, and in these plays it is to be seen emerging as the supreme value of Shakespearian tragedy.

The tragedies are concerned throughout with *natural* ethics, with the behaviour of men and women in the natural order of this world. It is an interesting paradox that Christopher Marlowe, who was widely suspected of atheism in his day, wrote a great tragedy on a religious theme and from a specifically Christian point of view; whereas Shakespeare, whose Christian orthodoxy cannot be suspect, to judge by everything we know of him, never undertook to dramatize a specifically religious theme—if we take this latter statement to mean the dramatization of man's relation to God. The theme of *Dr. Faustus* is a man's defiance of the Christian God, his rejection of God's mercy, and his consequent damnation. But Shakespeare's *Macbeth*, while it may suggest such an interpretation of Macbeth's conduct and of his ultimate fate, does not actually dramatize this conception as the centre of Macbeth's tragedy; his tragedy, as Shakespeare prefers to study it, lies rather in the immediate, earthly consequences of his crime, his sufferings in this world. On the other hand—it may be said without elaboration, for it is obvious—the love that is thematically central in *Antony and Cleopatra* and *King Lear* does not raise any religious issue; this love is not the love of God but the earthly love of man and woman, parents and children.

We may perceive the emerging implication here ascribed to Shakespeare's tragedies, of the natural order seen in the light of Christian ethics, most clearly, perhaps, with reference to A. S. P. Woodhouse's lucid exposition of the orders of "nature" and "grace" as reflected in Milton's *Comus* and Spenser's *Faerie Queene*.[1] According to seventeenth-century testimony, which Woodhouse has cited at length, man's relation to God might be considered in the three following ways:

(1) In the state of nature man is governed by divinely instituted natural law, which operates not simply in man's nature but in all natures and is discoverable by the light of God-given natural reason. This natural order is as readily intelligible to reasonable pagans as to reasonable Christians, and thus it happens that Christian humanists of the Renaissance so often couple the moral authority of the ancients—of Socrates, Plato and Aristotle, Cicero, Seneca, and Plutarch—with the ethical teachings of the Bible and without any sense of incongruity or invidious contrast.[2]

(2) The natural order is subject to God's providential care and

overflowing love, vouchsafed independently of man's merits or his awareness of that love: the power which ordains and orders all things to ultimate good. This providential order will of course be more apparent to the instructed Christian, though even he is usually blind to its ways and apprehends its ordering presence—if he is aware of it at all—through loving faith (his proper response to God's love) rather than through reason.

(3) Transcending the natural order but also ratifying it and completing it is the order of grace to which man belongs as a supernatural being, the order which provides a remedy for man's fallen state when God's grace irresistibly turns the human will into the way of eternal salvation: a miraculous intervention—like Saint Paul's revelation on the road to Damascus—without which the utmost human merit would be of no avail. Divine grace is indeed but a particular application of God's over-ruling providence[3] —the application of that providence to man's fallen state—but it is of cardinal importance for man and distinguished in his apprehension as an immediate spiritual intuition affecting the will; whereas the other operations of divine providence are quite independent of man's will or of his knowledge.[4]

Of these three orders—really a single order, the divine love acting as an ordering principle in all things, but apprehended and distinguished by the Christian, according to his experience and insight, as threefold—Shakespeare in his tragedies deals only with the first two. With the third order, the order of grace which alone among the three concerns the specifically religious experience of the Christian, the tragedies have nothing to do. The triadic synthesis described as constituting an emerging pattern in the tragedies here considered may then be expressed in the following way.

Shakespeare projects a providential order of human experience, seen in the light of Christian faith, in *Romeo and Juliet*, *Hamlet*, *Othello*, and *Macbeth*, an order which is likewise the order of nature and in which the protagonists are but little aware of this ordering principle—only Hamlet becomes dimly aware of it as he approaches his tragic catastrophe. The unawareness of Hamlet himself throughout the greater part of his play, the blindness and ignorance—whether wilful or not—of all the others, might be called the Christian irony of these plays; for the reader or theatregoer, instructed in Christian doctrine as Shakespeare's audience was, becomes increasingly aware of the contrast between the ordering of events in the light of divine love and justice on the one hand, and the blind striving and frustration of the human agents on the other. It is not a paradox or an evasion to include the retribution of *Othello* and *Macbeth* under the order and power of providence, because human wickedness and its punishment, in the Christian view, is something negative, the wilful denial of love or the mere absence of goodness; so evil is always represented in the plays of Shakespeare in which Christian implications are evident. The wickedness of the Capulets and Montagues, of Claudius and Othello, Iago and Macbeth, is a rejection of love, and as the consequences of this rejection, the catastrophes of *Romeo and Juliet, Hamlet, Othello*, and *Macbeth* show us the providential goodness of the divine order through the eclipse, the punishment, the ceasing to exist, of all that we recognize as evil.

Shakespeare also wrote four tragedies—*Julius Caesar, Coriolanus, Troilus and Cressida, Timon of Athens*—in which no Christian implications whatsoever are apparent. These plays belong to the order of nature simply, as their subject-matter renders appropriate. The negative property common to all four is that nothing essential to a Christian conception of love anywhere figures in them; though it would not be proper to discuss the different themes of these plays simply with reference to such a negative criterion. We might indeed consider that the love of country manifested by Brutus and the love that Coriolanus feels for his family and above all for his mother are not incompatible with a Christian conception of love; and these we may feel to be the positive values in *Julius Caesar* and *Coriolanus* which chiefly warrant the classifying of these plays in the movement here called "thesis." But the virtues of Brutus and of Coriolanus flourish in all times without any necessary reference to a Christian scheme of ethics, and Plutarch valued these virtues as Shakespeare valued them, and as we value them when we read the plays Shakespeare based upon Plutarch's accounts.

The culminating synthesis of *Antony and Cleopatra* and *King Lear*, from the foregoing point of view, consists in the way in which the tragic feeling inherent in the natural order of things is rendered grander in its appeal to our sympathies through a shift in the focus of value which achieves a harmony between the natural and the providential orders. The operations of divine providence do not provide the fittest theme for tragedy. The reason is that the ways of providence are mostly beyond human comprehension: they are matter for wonder and for fear—but not for our fullest human sympathy precisely because they are beyond our human understanding. That is perhaps why *Hamlet* may seem to us like a fascinating paradox, a play that engages our deepest interest but not our deepest feelings. On the other hand, the theme of retribution—as we find it in *Othello* and *Macbeth*—from a Christian point of view, at least, seems incomplete: it implies but the negative aspect of the Christian order, as if we had the *Inferno* without the *Purgatorio* and *Paradiso*. The natural order, indeed, considered simply in the light of natural ethics, can never seem sufficient for those who have been reared in a Christian tradition. Natural ethics lacks grandeur because in this order man is the measure of all things. The greatness of a Caesar, a Brutus, or a Coriolanus inspires no awe and but moderate admiration; their virtues, like their limitations, are simply what we recognize in the best of men in any time; their virtues are self-contained and without any sanction or enlargement beyond what is typically and universally human. And it goes without saying that the dramatic presentment of the defect of human virtue in such plays as *Troilus and Cressida* and *Timon of Athens* leaves us unelated.

If, now, we consider the natural order, not with direct reference to a supernatural ordering power which we can apprehend only dimly, if at all, but indirectly with reference to the effect of that ordering power upon the natural order and upon natural ethics, we retain the human scope of the action while enlarging the limits of merely human virtue by means of a supernatural sanction. This is what happens in *Antony and Cleopatra* and *King Lear*. They achieve a harmony or synthesis, a transformation and refinement, of natural human ethics through the triumphant emergence of a supremely Christian value, the value of the new law of human love which takes precedence of the old law of justice.

Perhaps, then, on the basis of the foregoing argument, we may venture to propose an answer to the still disputed question of the part that Shakespeare's religious faith contributes to his plays. The answer is a simple one. No one, presumably, will dispute that there is a religious faith reflected in the plays and that this faith is Christian. To hesitate to call it Shakespeare's, as some would, is surely a misplaced scrupulosity; it seems only common sense to call it Shakespeare's, if it is there. The important critical questions concern the precise quality of that Christian faith and the way in which it becomes significant in the plays. If we answer the latter of these questions, we have sufficiently answered the former; and that endeavour has been a main preoccupation in the present study. But there is a simpler way of putting it, in terms of analogy. To state it is to labour the obvious; yet it needs to be said, if only because it is nowadays so easily forgotten or overlooked. The quality of Shakespeare's Christian faith, as it is reflected in his plays, is the quality of Edmund Spenser's faith as it is reflected in *The Faerie Queene*, or of Richard Hooker's faith as it is reflected in *The Laws of the Ecclesiastical Polity*—with the important difference that Shakespeare does not set forth the *whole* of that faith, as Spenser and Hooker in different ways each tried to do. Shakespeare writes as a layman for laymen, and the faith reflected in his plays is the basis of everyday Christian morality which he shared with his audiences, with the whole Christian community of his contemporaries. It is simple and unobtrusive, something taken for granted rather than insisted upon; hence it may be easily overlooked or neglected by those who do not wish to consider it. But that its presence in the plays should be questioned, or that it should be considered of less than fundamental importance in the effect of the plays themselves must surely have seemed incredible to Shakespeare and his contemporaries. When we today consider it as fundamental and central, we are, at the least, being historically minded. We may surely feel confident that we are studying the plays in the spirit in which they were intended.

APPENDIXES

APPENDIX I

Shakespearian Tragedy and the Aristotelian *Hamartia*

THE *hamartia* (ἁμαρτία) of Aristotle's *Poetics,*[1] the "error" on account of which the tragic hero suffers misfortune, is apparently not found by Aristotle himself to apply in every example of Greek tragedy but only in what he considered the *best* tragedy.[2] This criterion does not seem to belong in a critical judgment of the *Antigone* of Sophocles or the *Prometheus Bound* of Aeschylus, though it would be odd if Aristotle meant to exclude the *Antigone*, at least, from the category of the "best" tragedy. It has been cogently argued, however, that Aristotle's *hamartia* is generally irrelevant in the critical discussion of any of the surviving tragedies of Aeschylus or Euripides,[3] and, we might add, more than one of Sophocles as well.

The difficulty in attempting to apply this criterion to Shakespearian tragedy results especially from the doubtfulness and ambiguity of its meaning. The term seems to be intended, in the context of the *Poetics*, to indicate some measure of responsibility in the tragic hero for his downfall. But, as so often in this esoteric treatise, the context does not yield a sufficient indication of the precise sense of the word intended by Aristotle, a sense which Aristotle's hearers, as their teacher assumed, were already familiar with. In his thirteenth chapter, Aristotle is discussing the best kind of plot for tragedy. He rejects three kinds: a good man brought from prosperity to adversity, which is merely shocking; a bad man passing from adversity to prosperity, which is utterly alien to tragedy; and a bad man getting his deserts, which merely satisfies, without evoking pity and fear. "There remains, then, the character between these two extremes—that of a man who is not eminently good and just, yet whose misfortune is brought about not by vice or depravity, but by some error or frailty (ἁμαρτίαν τινά)."[4] And he adds, "He must be one who is highly renowned and prosperous—a personage like Oedipus, Thyestes, or other illustrious men of such families" (1453a, 10–11).

S. H. Butcher, in his chapter "The Ideal Tragic Hero,"[5] shows that it is not really feasible to limit the conception of *hamartia* to an "error of judgment," as Bywater renders it;[6] and, with Aristotle's example of Oedipus especially in mind, Butcher would interpret it (in an amplified version of the translation quoted above): "A single great error, whether morally culpable or not; a single great defect in a character otherwise noble"[7]—a definition which apparently amounts to saying that the tragic hero's downfall may be attributed to a human fault however accounted for, or simply to the fact that the hero is human and fallible and subject to the will of the gods. This is indeed an inclusive conception.

There are various possibilities of emphasis in this comprehensive definition; the student of Shakespeare may well hesitate to choose among them, or to attribute to Shakespeare a particular preference among the various nuances he may think of as coming within the terms of Butcher's conception; and he may doubt that Shakespeare, in any case, was much influenced by Aristotle's authority. We can, of course, always bring Shakespeare's tragedies within the range of Butcher's definition; each of his heroes is unmistakably human and therefore subject to *hamartia* in its broadest sense; and this is, truly, an important aspect of the tragic conception in Shakespeare. But this broadest use of the term, especially if it is rendered in English as a tragic "error" or "flaw," is extremely liable to suggest other more specific meanings—a fault of judgment or of will; the possibilities of ambiguity and confusion are enhanced by the unrecognized presence of the assumption, implicit especially in the use of the term "flaw," that the hero to whom the "flaw" is ascribed should have exemplified an impossible perfection; and there is the further curious consideration that though the ancients down to Aristotle's time and beyond did not recognize a conception of "will" in the sense we are likely to attach to it—a conception which we inherit mainly from the Roman jurists and from Christian thought—Shakespearian tragedy very often turns upon this non-Aristotelian conception. Since commentators upon Shakespeare have not always been sufficiently alert to these dangers, we may consider some of the difficulties that arise from applying Aristotle's criterion, without due safeguards against misunderstanding, to the tragedies discussed in this book.

A recent and in many ways distinguished study of Shakespeare's later tragedies offers a convenient illustration, Willard Farnham's *Shakespeare's Tragic Frontier*. Mr. Farnham associates Shakespeare's Timon with Macbeth, Antony, and Coriolanus, as a character "so deeply flawed that his faults reach to the very centre of his being and give a paradoxical quality to whatever is noble in his nature."[8] Now this description is certainly applicable in a clear, though probably non-Aristotelian, sense to Macbeth. He deliberately chooses to kill Duncan, recognizes that what he is doing is wrong, and persists in wrong-doing not only in killing Duncan but in the succession of crimes that Duncan's murder entails; and yet Macbeth is noble, too, as we cannot fail to recognize. His "fault," in an important sense, is inseparable from his best qualities; and we see the tragedy that results from this mixed nature of his.

But it seems more doubtful that there is any profit in looking at Antony in this way. His love for Cleopatra is not what we ordinarily mean by an act of choice. It is an irresistible attraction, an infatuation; it is an act of will and appetite (to use Shakespeare's terms), but not an experience in which the intellectual faculty is much involved. There remains the question of how much we are disposed to value this love; but we all presumably agree that Antony's love for Cleopatra is an essential part of him, of his whole being, that it is the man's very nature to love her, that—being the man he is—it is something he cannot help doing. He did not live to regret it, either. His love is impolitic, it loses him the world, it brings him to death; but he would do it all over again, if he had the chance; and the world he loses does not rate one of Cleopatra's tears. Shall we blame him for this? Then Octavius Caesar is surely the hero of the play and not Antony. Octavius does not permit himself to do anything so foolish; he wins the world; but then it is quite clear that he does not love anyone, and it would be very odd if anyone should love him.

This is to evade the issue, someone may object. Let us grant that Antony is noble, far nobler than Octavius, and that his love for Cleopatra is a worthy love. Yet the fact remains that Antony made a fatal mistake. He tried to gain the world (or at least to keep his third of it) and Cleopatra, too, and he lost; and it was his "flaw," his fatal susceptibility to Cleopatra's charms, that brought his downfall. Then Antony should have gained the world and Cleopatra? Or perhaps he should not have desired either of them? Or only one of them? Who, then, is at fault? The classroom chorus would answer, "Cleopatra!"; but here we may disregard such simplicity. Is it, then, the fault of the gods, perhaps? But this will never do as a way of putting it. Who are we to rearrange the universal nature of things, to call heaven to order? If we wish to say, here is a picture of the tragic limits of human life and human love; it is tragic because men and women are mortal, incapable of supporting their most heroic aims: this way of putting it will be helpful, but it is not necessarily a judgment of censure; and any talk about "errors" or "flaws" or—to guard against the betrayal of translations—the tragic *hamartia* in *Antony and Cleopatra* will probably give a misleading impression of the central conception of the play and of its effect.

Nor does the distinction help us much with Coriolanus. It seems an obvious course, at first glance, to apply the Aristotelian criterion to Coriolanus's pride; his pride, certainly, is a fault plain for everyone to see. It is a temptation to say that this fault brings about his downfall and let it go at that. Those who take this view are generally obliged to add that as tragedy the play is deficient in pity (the other great Aristotelian stumbling-block, pity and fear!) and to dismiss it as one of Shakespeare's least successful efforts in tragedy, a *tour de force* written when his tragic inspiration was petering out; or else we may regard it as an interesting but doubtful experiment with material that lies upon the "frontiers" of tragedy and hence misses the full tragic pathos. Such a conclusion hardly seems to do justice to Shakespeare or Aristotle.

Surely, again, this is not a fruitful way of looking at such a tragedy as *Coriolanus*. The chief point about this play seems to be that if Coriolanus has a fault of pride he overcomes that particular fault at the crucial moment of choice which the action affords; he unselfishly sacrifices his life and the very revenge and self-vindication he has striven for so passionately, and in the clear understanding of the consequence of his choice. The difficulty, if there is one, lies in understanding how a man could be as noble as this. It may still be urged that Coriolanus has a grave fault. So do we all; and we are all human. But this brings us to the ground already covered about *Antony and Cleopatra*. And while a great part of the effect of tragedy does indeed consist in bringing home to us our human limitations, it seems unduly paradoxical to keep insisting upon the "fault" of a character like Coriolanus when the main emphasis of the play falls upon his ultimate nobility.

But of all Shakespeare's tragedies, the one, perhaps, in which the criterion of the Aristotelian "flaw" is least helpful is *Timon of Athens*. Mr. Farnham writes: "The tragedy of Timon is that of a man who has an all-consuming love of humanity, but, when he finds that he himself is not loved, lets this love turn to all-consuming hate. His love is so little a true forgetfulness of self, and thus so grossly imperfect, that it can change into its very opposite."[10]

The first difficulty of this view lies in the interpretation of Timon's change of attitude. Mr. Farnham appears to equate Timon's change from love to hate with a fault of *self-love*. But Timon expressly includes *himself* in his detestation of man, in his equation of men with beasts. Shakespeare dwells particularly upon this point. It is the burden of Timon's great soliloquy in IV, iii:

> Who dares, who dares
> In purity of manhood stand upright
> And say "This man's a flatterer"? If one be,
> So are they all; for every grize of fortune
> Is smooth'd by that below. The learned pate
> Ducks to the golden fool. All's obloquy;
> There's nothing level in our cursed natures
> But direct villainy. Therefore be abhorr'd
> All feasts, societies, and throngs of men!
> His semblable, yea, himself, Timon disdains.
> Destruction fang mankind!

His answer to Alcibiades is in the same vein—"A beast, as thou art. . . . I am Misanthropos and hate mankind" (IV, iii, 49, 53); and there are many other suggestions to the same effect. Timon, at the outset, believes that men should love each other and share everything together. He discovers that no one else lives according to this principle; that most men, in fact, follow the plan of getting all they can for themselves, especially through flattery and hypocrisy; and in the shock of this realization, he doubtless recognizes something of the same motives in himself; at least, he understands these motives well enough, though he hates them, and he includes himself in his general loathing of mankind and all its ways. If he is still determined to follow the principle of generosity, even though he himself cannot live according to it in society because other men will not let him, his only resort is to flee from men as one would from a pack of dangerous beasts, and finally to flee from himself, even, in death. This is surely not self-love.

Has Timon, then, any other faults? He evidently had not heard of the principle that one should hate the sin but not the sinner. Mr. Farnham, we may suspect, blames him on this account. But this is to go outside the context of the play and seems contrary to Shakespeare's conception in *Timon of Athens*. It is, indeed, very interesting to observe, in the imaginative conception of *Timon of Athens*, the discrepancy between Timon's "natural" view of man in this world, and the Christian view of man in the light of the divine love; and this awareness may even contribute—and be meant to contribute—to our sense of the tragic quality of the play. But we should not judge the conception of the play by a standard that is external to the play itself. Timon, then, we may argue, has no "flaw," no tragic *hamartia* (unless in the sense that he is a human being); and the play *is* deficient in pity and fear. It is a good illustration of Aristotle's failure to anticipate the tragic genius of Shakespeare, though we really should not blame Aristotle for this, either.

Enough has been said, perhaps, to make further discussion of the "flaw" of Hamlet and Othello and the rest unnecessary. We can find a flaw in all of them, readily enough, even in Romeo and Juliet with their youthful precipitancy, if we are determined to. But the search for it is not very rewarding. Is Hamlet's melancholy at the root of his tragedy? How could he help feeling melancholy, in his situation? It is no use saying that Othello would not have put up with it. Doubtless he would have taken prompt action against Claudius; but then he would have been taking a leap in the dark, and he might have been as wrong about it, for all he knew, as he was about Desdemona. The chief trouble with this criterion of the "flaw" is that it too easily allows us to sit in censure upon the tragic hero, while we miss the deeper irony that Euripides has so memorably phrased in the concluding lines of several of his plays: "The ways of Heaven are manifold and past finding out. What we thought would happen is often not fulfilled, while the unlooked-for God brings to pass."[11]

All of this, of course, is not to say that the Aristotelian criterion of *hamartia* is not occasionally useful in the discussion of Shakespearian tragedy. This criterion, or something not unlike it, can be suitably applied to *Macbeth*, and it has here been invoked in speaking about Brutus and Julius Caesar. And even though we may disagree with some of Mr. Farnham's applications of this criterion, we may yet feel grateful to him for the fine penetration of many of his observations under this head. But it seems appropriate, nevertheless, to suggest that Aristotle's *Poetics* should be used with great caution in the discussion of Shakespeare, and that the criterion of the "flaw," in particular, is often so misleading as applied in a critical estimate of Shakespeare's tragic protagonists that, whenever we are in any doubt about the precise application of this criterion, it may be better not to use it at all.

APPENDIX II

"Imitation" and "Decorum" in Shakespeare's Plays

THE STUDENT OF A RELATED GROUP of Shakespeare's plays, such as the tragedies which have been considered in this book, may well be increasingly impressed, as he examines them, by the remarkable differences in dramatic technique from play to play, and thus be led to conclude that no one technical criterion is likely to prove very effective for critical purposes if uniformly applied even to so homogeneous a group as the tragedies—a point which the preceding appendix has tried to illustrate. If we consider the plays in the light of two critical principles universally admitted and invoked in Shakespeare's time, we may the better understand how it is that we should expect to find Shakespeare's dramatic methods varying greatly from play to play, especially in his latest work.

The two principles are those of "imitation" and "decorum," taught to every Elizabethan schoolboy and particularly to the young William Shakespeare, presumably at the Stratford-upon-Avon grammar school, as T. W. Baldwin has amply demonstrated in a series of learned volumes.[1] Shakespeare's developing dramatic technique illustrates and conforms with these two principles. The importance of the second of these principles, the principle of literary decorum, though it is well enough understood and indeed generally taken for granted by most Shakespearian commentators, has never, to this writer's knowledge, been clearly explained in one of its bearings upon his practice; and since the theoretical background—which must be recalled to explain it—is not a matter with which the general reader may be expected to be familiar, it may not be out of place to review that background briefly here.

The principle, in its application to Shakespeare's plays, may first be briefly stated, thus: the dramatist always undertakes to suit his dramatic method to the particular needs of his subject-matter—or, in a larger sense, his theme—as well as to the actors, the audience, and the other conditions of his presentation. It is well understood that Shakespeare always considered the capabilities and limitations of his acting company[2] and the physical properties of his theatre; and much attention has likewise been given to the kind of audience for which he wrote.[3] It has not always been borne so well in mind, perhaps, that his theme or subject was a variable of at least equal importance in determining his dramatic method; and it is this last point with which we are here especially concerned. The inclusive principle of "decorum," which, as Milton said, "is the grand masterpiece to observe,"[4] provides a fundamental criterion of Shakespeare's dramatic method in each play. In order to understand its increasingly important application in Shakespeare's dramatic development, we need to be aware of the way in which it was taught to him; and this in turn involves a preliminary consideration of the complementary principle of "imitation," a principle which is especially relevant in the study of Shakespeare's earliest plays.

In the theory and practice of eloquence as expounded by Cicero in his treatises on oratory and in his own letters and orations, Renaissance writers found the chief precedents and precepts by means of which they sought to train the young in the art of writing. The tradition of Roman rhetoric descends to the Renaissance in an unbroken line from Cicero through Quintilian—greatest of Roman educators who was Cicero's disciple and coadjutor in formulating and systematizing the tradition—St. Augustine and other fathers of the Church, the preachers and teachers who organized, exemplified, and taught the discipline of the "trivium" (grammar, rhetoric, dialectic) as the core of mediaeval education, until we come to the Renaissance humanists themselves—Petrarch, Poliziano, Erasmus, More, Elyot, Ascham and the rest. They continued the tradition of the trivium as they inherited it from their mediaeval predecessors, with the important difference that whereas the Schoolmen had commonly placed their major emphasis upon dialectical studies and exercises, the Renaissance humanists placed theirs upon rhetoric and returned enthusiastically to the sources of the rhetorical tradition, above all in the theory of Cicero and Quintilian and what they held to be the supreme example of eloquence, the practice of Cicero.[5] Cicero, accordingly, is the chief among the preceptors of the Renaissance in profane letters.

Cicero himself tells us that he derived his sytem of eloquence—in which he aimed to effect a practical union between philosophy and rhetoric—from Isocrates and Aristotle;[6] but since some, at least, of the writings of these authorities upon which Cicero drew have not survived, we must take the doctrine, as did the writers of the Renaissance, largely according to Cicero's formulation. The first principle he lays down is that of "imitation," by which he means that we should carefully choose only the best model to imitate and confine our imitation to the best traits of that model, sedulously practising to emulate the means he uses and the effects he achieves.[7] The model Cicero proposed was Demosthenes, whom he admired most among the Greek orators, and whose example he believed his own practice as an orator most closely resembled. Quintilian, writing in a later generation and in the light of Cicero's example, altered this injunction to take in a range of the best models, including Cicero himself.[8]

Hence it came about that Renaissance schoolboys commonly began their literary education by copying and imitating the easier passages from the letters of Cicero; then, a little later, laboriously analysed, memorized, and strove to reproduce the diction, figures, rhythms, and other stylistic effects of Cicero's orations by copying them over and over, or by the exercises of "double translation" recommended by John Sturm of Strasburg and Roger Ascham, or according to other and more complicated systems of literary imitation set forth in the long line of treatises entitled *Ciceronianus* which reflect the school practices.[9]

This discipline of imitation constituted the primary and earlier emphasis of Renaissance education in good writing. One must begin the practice of writing by scrupulously following a model, and that the best obtainable; and since the ancients were universally recognized as masters in this, as in other arts, one naturally learned to write in Latin according to the example of the best models. Imitation of models in one's own vernacular was not necessarily discouraged; still, the ancients provided the norm, and a thorough command of Ciceronian Latin was the first essential and *sine qua non* of Renaissance education—Latin was still the international medium of the educated. Such a grounding was undoubtedly a part of Shakespeare's early education. We may find evidences of

Shakespeare's command of Ciceronian turns of phrase throughout his plays, and especially in the earlier ones.

So the student was recommended to proceed in the practice of other literary kinds, using, of course, different models according to the kind he chose to imitate; in the drama, since Greek models would hardly be available to the schoolboy of Shakespeare's day, the principal model for tragedy would be the Roman Seneca, for comedy Plautus and Terence. Thus it was that Shakespeare inaugurated his practice as a dramatist with the imitation of Plautus in *The Comedy of Errors*, of Seneca and Renaissance Senecans in *Titus Andronicus*, as he had been taught to do in school and as his contemporaries were doing. It has sometimes mistakenly been thought that such imitative exercises tended to encourage slavish copies of models and even plagiarism; and it is indeed true that Renaissance ideas of literary property were not the same as ours. It was generally held that a writer was free to borrow material of any kind without acknowledgment if he could improve upon the original he borrowed in the use he made of it; and it was likewise held superfluous to acknowledge the use one made of the ancients, since such matter was common knowledge and common property. But Renaissance writers were not usually concerned about the degree to which they approximated the model or models they imitated[10] because the complementary principle of "decorum" which they aimed as sedulously to follow was a guarantee that their "imitation" would not be slavish.

Cicero had emphasized throughout his rhetorical writings that the orator's great aim in "imitating" Demosthenes should be to make himself equally a master of that literary tact with which Demosthenes had suited everything he said to his own character as a speaker, to the subject on which he spoke, and to the particular audience he addressed—in short, to all the varying circumstances under which each particular speech was made. This is the master principle of "decorum," of "what is fitting," the principle Cicero everywhere urges upon the would-be orator,[11] that is equally central in Quintilian's doctrine, and that became the crowning technical aim inculcated in the rhetorical tradition, embracing every literary genre, which the Renaissance inherited from antiquity. To those who reproached the great humanist of the court of Lorenzo the

Magnificent, Angelo Poliziano, because he was not sufficiently careful to conform his literary style to the example of Cicero, Poliziano replied, "What then? I am not Cicero. I express myself";[12] and Erasmus, in his *Ciceronianus*, shows that the whole point of imitating Cicero is that we should thus learn to write "appositely: that is to say, with particular regard to the subject on which we speak; the persons involved, both speakers and hearers; the place, the time, and all the remaining circumstances of our communication."[13] We cannot do this by imitating Cicero slavishly, Erasmus's spokesman in the dialogue declares; Cicero himself enjoins us to observe decorum of style above everything else; hence it is folly to try to be Cicero, or any other ancient, in the sixteenth century.

This is the doctrine on which Shakespeare was brought up; and we cannot doubt that, from the beginning of his practice as a dramatist, he was well aware of the need for fitting his dramatic method in each play he wrote to all the varying circumstances of its production. The evidence of this aim, and of its increasingly successful accomplishment, of the growing skill with which he mastered the finer points of decorum in stagecraft, everywhere confront us. He began with rather careful, almost academic imitation of the ancients, as befits a novice; and he proceeded to study and incorporate in his own practice everything of value that he could learn from his immediate predecessors and contemporaries—Marlowe, Lyly, Greene, Kyd, and the rest; but even in *The Comedy of Errors* and *Titus Andronicus*, we may be sure, Shakespeare was trying to attend to the requirements of his acting company, his theatre, and the tastes of his audience, as well as to the precedents of Plautus and Seneca.

The greatest technical improvement in the whole course of Shakespeare's development as a dramatist, perhaps, consists in the increasing tact with which he suits his dramatic method to his material. This is obvious enough in principle; nevertheless, we may consider one more short illustration—in addition to those which have been afforded in the foregoing study—to clinch the argument, from the latest group, chronologically speaking, of the tragedies.

Macbeth is a study of a man obsessed by fear. He is studied in two aspects: from within and from without. First we have the witches, who are to project Macbeth's ambition, his fear, and the nemesis that follows his crimes; then Macbeth as the outside world sees him, as Duncan receives the report of his bravery, resolves to create him Thane of Cawdor, and pays him the compliment of his visit. The scenes with Lady Macbeth then show us what is happening inside the man, and his soliloquies paint for us his inner conflict and the anguish that his ambition costs him. This balanced movement runs throughout the play—the inner struggles and suffering of Macbeth balanced against the sombre atmosphere of impending blood and destruction so powerfully informing the poetic imagery. As the Weird Sisters prophesy to the distraught Macbeth, as Birnam Wood approaches Dunsinane, we see the reflection of the nemesis Macbeth himself anticipates in his impassioned musings. Macbeth projects his own doom, describes it over and over, it fascinates his imagination; and the external action of the play is simply the fulfilment of what he describes.

Timon of Athens provides the most striking contrast with this method of projecting a character and what is happening to him on two planes. The play is primarily the lyrical presentment of an idea, the idea of generosity and what comes of it in this world. In the presentation of the theme, the psychology of the protagonist is hardly of any moment. Timon is not studied as an individual, as an actual human being: he is a sounding-board for Shakespeare's idea of man's ingratitude and greed, a symbol in the light of which we may consider what true generosity would be like if we met it in real life; but the point here is that we do not meet it—or if we do, that we try our best to exploit it out of existence, and succeed. In this kind of play, accordingly, it does not do to ask whether Timon is heroic. The criterion is irrelevant in this context, though it is highly relevant in *Macbeth*. But in *Timon of Athens*, the only action called for is Timon's withdrawal. There is nothing heroic about this; in Timon's situation, there can be neither heroism nor the lack of it: all there is room for is his denial of human society and his disgust.

Antony and Cleopatra is a dramatic interpretation of history.

In *Macbeth*, Shakespeare chooses his materials from various accounts in Holinshed and elsewhere, and supplies a good deal of it himself; it is perfectly plain that he does not consider himself to be presenting actual history but constructing an imaginative symbol of human guilt, an elaborate compliment to King James, a moral against tyrants; and his handling of his sources is suited to the legendary quality of his material, the interest in witchcraft and demonology of his auditory, the political and moral doctrine of his time. *Timon of Athens* takes scarcely more than a hint or two from Plutarch and Lucian; it is an entirely free creation of Shakespeare's imagination, intended for what audience no one knows—perhaps only for an audience of one. *Antony and Cleopatra*, however, *is* history, and Shakespeare has been at great pains to follow it faithfully (as in *Julius Caesar* and *Coriolanus*)—a point which has been already argued. Here are no evident anachronisms, no arbitrary contrivances of the plot. Save in a few necessary abridgments of the time scheme which help to make the motivations clearer and more logical than they are in Plutarch, as in the case of Antony's return to Cleopatra, there are no other tamperings with the evidence Plutarch supplied. The play is remarkable for its fidelity to history—so faithful that Shakespeare has been blamed for it by Dr. Johnson and Professor Hardin Craig!

Finally, we may recall the contrast afforded in the method of *King Lear*, which we have dwelt upon in chapter VI, above. It is the method of the romance and of the folktale, a method which we may also recognize, with many skilful variations, in Shakespeare's latest plays, those final exercises of his supreme technical virtuosity. It is of importance, in studying *King Lear*, as in studying the last plays, to recognize that all the arbitrariness of the contrivance is deliberate. Shakespeare knows what he is doing, far better than most of us do. The oddity of some of his devices and effects is not the result of carelessness, not the failing of the artist's hand, a foretaste of the "boredom" that Lytton Strachey suspected in the last plays,[14] but rather the latest refinement of Shakespeare's dramatic decorum which culminated in the technical masterpiece of *The Tempest*.

NOTES

CHAPTER I

1. See chapter V, note 4, below.

2. The distinction was first suggested to me by the fundamental study of A. S. P. Woodhouse, "Nature and Grace in *The Faerie Queene*," *ELH*, XVI (1949), 194–228.

3. George Lyman Kittredge, *Shakspere: An Address* (Cambridge, Mass., 1926), pp. 9–10.

4. A. C. Bradley, *Shakespearean Tragedy* (London, 1904; reprinted 1950), pp. 24–25.

5. This statement needs qualification, and the matter will be further discussed in chapter IV, below.

6. There are occasional, and casual, scriptural references in *Antony and Cleopatra*, for instance. Any references of this sort are designed for the sake of an immediate effect, e.g. of vividness, as in Antony's

> O that I were
> Upon the hill of Basan to outroar
> The horned herd!

Such references are never significant for the central thought or effect of the whole.

7. See S. L. Bethell, *The Winter's Tale: A Study* (New York, 1947).

8. See T. M. Parrott, " 'God's' or 'Gods' in *King Lear*," *Shakespeare Quarterly*, IV (1953), 427 ff.

9. *Romeo and Juliet*, V, iii, 153.

10. *Hamlet*, V, ii, 10.

11. The Christian view of the universal order divinely imposed is comprehended in the words of the Almighty in *Paradise Lost*, III, 132–34:

> In Mercy and Justice both,
> Through Heav'n and Earth, so shall my glorie excel,
> But Mercy first and last shall brightest shine.

Shakespeare deals only with that aspect of "mercy," according to the Christian conception, which is divine providence conceived as a just and beneficent order. This point will be resumed in the concluding chapter.

12. Bradley, *Shakespearean Tragedy*, pp. 5–39.

13. It will be understood that the order of faith includes the order of nature. The order of faith signifies the natural order viewed in the light of Christian faith and with particular reference to the supernatural ordering power. See chapter VII, below.

CHAPTER II

1. The first prologue describes the action of the whole play. The sonnet-prologue of Act II describes only what happens in that act, and in a very general way, though it emphasizes for the audience an important point: that Romeo's love for Rosaline (which, Friar Laurence later tells us, was but "doting," II, iii, 82) comes to nothing; his real love is for Juliet. The authenticity of this second prologue has been doubted; it seems, indeed, to interrupt the forward movement of the action unnecessarily. See Granville Barker's discussion, *Prefaces to Shakespeare*, II (Princeton, 1951), 323–27.

2. The title of a Shakespearian play is not always a sufficient clue to its central conception or even to its central figure, witness *Cymbeline*. It is hard to discover a consistent principle in the naming of Shakespeare's plays. The title selected was doubtless calculated for box-office appeal, and the piquant and non-committal titles of so many of the comedies are obviously intended to stimulate curiosity. The "name" titles of plays appeal to the commonest ground of interest, the interest in characters, especially eminent and familiar ones. In *Romeo and Juliet*, the title points to the centre of emotional interest as distinct from the governing theme, as is argued in the following discussion.

3. The structural parallelism of *Romeo and Juliet* has been noted by R. A. Law, "On Shakespeare's Changes of his Source in *Romeo and Juliet*," *University of Texas Studies in English*, IX (1929), 86–102, to which I am here indebted; see also the same author's "Belleforest, Shakespeare, and Kyd," *Joseph Quincy Adams Memorial Studies* (Washington, D.C., 1948), pp. 282 ff.

4. In this paralleling of the two scenes in which each lover turns from something like despair to a pathetic hope for the continuance of their love (III, ii, iii), it is Juliet who shows the greater strength: when the Nurse offers her the chance to repudiate Romeo and she is left without comfort from the Nurse, with no one else to turn to, and unswervingly loyal to her love; here too the parallel with the Nurse's earlier manner of breaking the news of Romeo's arrangements for their marriage reiterates the Nurse's utter incapability to act as a guide or support for the inexperienced Juliet and prepares us to appreciate the courage of Juliet's repudiation of her. Romeo, in much the same situation as Juliet, more nearly yields to despair and is with difficulty comforted by Friar Laurence. It is further

ironic that Romeo, in his despair, relies wholly upon the guidance of Friar Laurence, who, in his unworldliness, is but ill fitted to extricate the young lovers from their plight.

5. Friar Laurence's exit-line ("Come, go, good Juliet. I dare no longer stay") might have been made the occasion of exonerating him completely from responsibility for Juliet's death, had he actually made his exit at this point. But he is intended to hear Juliet's answer as he is leaving: "Go, get thee hence, for I will not away." Friar Laurence's timidity is an essential part of Shakespeare's characterization of him.

6. Arthur Brooke, *Romeus and Juliet*, edited by P. A. Daniel for the New Shakespeare Society, Series III, no. 1, 1875, p. 89.

7. Granville Barker, *Prefaces to Shakespeare*, II (Princeton, 1951), 330. The technique of balanced contrasts runs throughout the play, contrasts between scene and scene, between character and character, even between the greater lyrical ornateness of the earlier part of the action and the swifter and more sober rhythm and diction of the catastrophe; and there are contrasting effects equally in the imagery, especially of darkness and light. Correspondingly, the emotional pitch varies, from the broad mirth of the Nurse's encounter with Benvolio, Mercutio, and Romeo, to the following lyricism of Juliet (II, iv, v); from the antiphonal lamentations for Juliet's death to Peter's jesting with the musicians—here apparently for the sake of avoiding a false climax (IV, v); from the ironic optimism of Romeo's opening speech in Act V to his following tight-lipped resolve.

8. See Olin H. Moore, *The Legend of Romeo and Juliet* (Columbus, Ohio, 1950). In a separate preface reflecting his Protestant bias Brooke blames the lovers and their Catholic upbringing, but this view scarcely colours his retelling of the story he takes from Pierre Boaistuau's version. An interesting earlier study of the literary ancestry of the Romeo and Juliet story is contained in Henri Hauvette, *La "Morte Vivante": Etude de littérature comparée* (Paris, 1933).

9. Granville Barker, *Prefaces to Shakespeare*, II, 312 n.

10. E. K. Chambers, *Shakespeare: A Survey* (London, 1925), p. 76.

11. *Hamlet and Orestes: A Study in Traditional Types*, The British Academy Annual Shakespeare Lecture (London, 1914). On the ritual heritage of drama in general, see the recent highly stimulating study of Theodor H. Gaster, *Thespis* (New York, 1950).

12. Francis Fergusson, *The Idea of a Theater* (Princeton, 1949), pp. 98–142.

13. *Hamlet*, by William Shakespeare, with a psycho-analytical study by Ernest Jones (New York, 1948); Ernest Jones, *Hamlet and Oedipus* (London, 1949); F. L. Lucas, *Literature and Psychology* (London, 1951), pp. 15 ff.

14. See E. R. Dodds, *The Greeks and the Irrational* (Berkeley & Los Angeles, 1951), p. 46.

15. Caroline F. E. Spurgeon, *Shakespeare's Imagery and What It Tells Us* (New York and Cambridge, 1935), pp. 318–19.

16. Among recent interpretations of the play that I have consulted with interest and profit may be mentioned Roy Walker, *The Time is out of Joint* (London, 1948); G. R. Elliott, *Scourge and Minister: A Study of Hamlet as Tragedy of Revengefulness and Justice* (Durham, N.C., 1951); H. C. Goddard, *The Meaning of Shakespeare* (Chicago, 1951); G. B. Harrison, *Shakespeare's Tragedies* (London, 1951). See also P. S. Conklin, *A History of Hamlet Criticism* (New York, 1947).

17. Robert Bridges, "The Influence of the Audience on Shakespeare's Drama," in *Collected Essays* (London, 1927), pp. 21, 25 ff.

18. J. Dover Wilson, *What Happens in Hamlet* (3rd ed., Cambridge, 1951), pp. 220–23.

19. *Ibid.*, p. 229.

20. *Ibid.*, p. 225.

21. *Ibid.*, pp. 137 ff.

22. Lily B. Campbell, *Shakespeare's Tragic Heroes: Slaves of Passion* (Cambridge, 1930), pp. 120–47; "Theories of Revenge in Renaissance England," *Modern Philology*, XXVIII (1931), 281–96. See also F. W. Moorman, "The Pre-Shakespearean Ghost," and "Shakespeare's Ghosts," *Modern Language Review*, I (1906), 85–95, 192–201; Fredson Bowers, *Elizabethan Revenge Tragedy, 1587-1642* (Princeton, 1940), especially chapter VI, "The Disapproval of Revenge."

23. Dover Wilson, *What Happens in Hamlet*, pp. 51 ff.

24. Lewes Lavater, *Of Ghostes and Spirites Walking by Nyght*, ed. J. Dover Wilson and May Yardley (Oxford, 1929).

25. It is difficult to suppose that even the most thoughtful Elizabethan, while in the grip of the dramatic situation here, or even later on, would reflect, as Roy Battenhouse suggests he might (*Studies in Philology*, XLVIII, 161 ff.) that this shifting back and forth between suggestions of hell and purgatory means that the Ghost must belong not in a Christian conception of an after-life but in a pagan conception of Hades.

26. Shakespeare expresses the Christian view of revenge explicitly in *Richard III*, I, iv, 220–24:

> If God will be avenged for the deed,
> O, know you yet he doth it publicly!
> Take not the quarrel from his pow'rful arm.
> He needs no indirect or lawless course
> To cut off those that have offended him.

See also *Richard II*, I, ii, 6–8.

27. A. C. Bradley, *Shakespearean Tragedy* (London, 1904; reprinted 1950), pp. 23, 27.

28. Hamlet's age is a matter of "make-up," as Dover Wilson has aptly put it. Most of us probably think of him, despite the reckoning of his thirty years in the scene with the gravediggers, as a young man of university age (that is, under twenty), contemporary with Rosencrantz and Guildenstern, Horatio, and Laertes.

CHAPTER III

1. Clifford Leech, *Shakespeare's Tragedies and Other Studies in Seventeenth Century Drama* (London, 1950), pp. 18, 103 ff.

2. See Caroline F. E. Spurgeon, *Shakespeare's Imagery and What It Tells Us* (New York and Cambridge, 1935), pp. 159 ff., for the support which the study of the imagery of the play brings to this view of it; and, more recently, S. L. Bethell, "Shakespeare's Imagery: The Diabolic Images in *Othello*," *Shakespeare Survey*, 5 (1952), 62–80 and Paul N. Siegel, "The Damnation of Othello," *Publications of the Modern Language Association of America*, LXVIII (1953), 1068–78; though I cannot agree with the contention of Mr. Bethell and Mr. Siegel that Shakespeare's use of imagery in this play warrants us in concluding that Othello is damned.

3. To suppose that the slight Iago feels at Cassio's being preferred before him is anything more than the immediate pretext of his conduct in the play is surely to underestimate the man and to miss the subtlety of Shakespeare's study of the effects of egotism. Shakespeare postulates Iago's egotism and shows us its effects, one of which is that he cannot, or will not, recognize clearly the source of his behaviour.

4. E. E. Stoll, *Art and Artifice in Shakespeare* (Cambridge, 1933), pp. 6 ff.

5. T. S. Eliot, *Selected Essays, 1917–1932* (New York, 1932), p. 111.

6. See chapter IV, below.

7. Both Iago and the Duke likewise serve as commentators upon the action which they direct in their respective plays, for the benefit of the audience; and in each play, the other characters are unaware how they are being directed until the denouement is reached. For a further consideration of this dramatic method, see a study by the present writer, "Action and Symbol in *Measure for Measure* and *The Tempest*," *Shakespeare Quarterly*, IV (1953), 375 ff.

8. A. C. Bradley, *Shakespearean Tragedy* (London, 1904; reprinted 1950), pp. 181–82.

9. Yet we must notice, also, that Roderigo, Cassio, Emilia are all equally

deceived. Roderigo and Emilia are not supposed to be clever, but Cassio shows every sign of being as easily deluded as Othello.

10. Stoll, *Art and Artifice in Shakespeare*; see also his chapter, "Literature and Life," in *Shakespeare Studies* (New York, 1927), pp. 39 ff.

11. See note 2, above.

12. G. Wilson Knight, *The Wheel of Fire* (4th ed., London, 1949), pp. 114–15.

13. *Macbeth*, ed. Kenneth Muir; the (new) Arden Shakespeare (London, 1951), p. li.

14. *Ibid.*, pp. lviii-lx.

15. Another kind of irrelevance is typified in the odd and now celebrated question proposed by L. C. Knights concerning Lady Macbeth's children. On the other hand, there are relevant questions for which the text provides no answer. When Macduff says, "He has no children" (IV, iii, 216), in the theatre we take this as referring to Macbeth or to Malcolm according to how or where Macduff looks, and his tone as he says it. There is no criterion of psychological probability here; it would be impressive either way, and there is no sufficient indication of which reference Shakespeare intended.

16. R. G. Moulton, *Shakespeare as a Dramatic Artist* (3rd ed., Oxford, 1901), pp. 151 ff.

17. The defiance of the consequences in an after-life is reiterated in III, ii, 16; V, viii, 34. We may contrast the reflections of Richard III (*Richard III*, V, iii, 178 ff.). Indeed, the more or less close parallel between the two tyrants underlines for us the absence of any sign of religious penitence in Macbeth.

18. In the interval between I, v and I, vii, Lady Macbeth has apparently told Macbeth that she is willing to murder Duncan if Macbeth fears the actual deed (cf. II, ii, 13–14: "Had he not resembled My father as he slept, I had done't"), as Macbeth's words in I, vii, 31 ff. imply. Macbeth has then protested that *he* would do it. They have left it at that, until Macbeth tries to back out of his promise. It is a fine irony that Lady Macbeth, more ruthless in intention, is yet less able to act, when brought to the test, than her more imaginative husband.

19. I have not found the observation in the notes to Kittredge's edition of *Macbeth*.

20. The lore of this matter has been recently reviewed by Willard Farnham, *Shakespeare's Tragic Frontier* (Berkeley and Los Angeles, 1950), pp. 99 ff. See also T. N. Parrott in *Shakespeare Quarterly*, I (1950), 281–85.

21. Henry N. Paul, *The Royal Play of Macbeth* (New York, 1950).

22. See especially Roy Walker, *The Time is Free: A Study of Macbeth* (London, 1949), in which the author presses the Christian implications of the play a good deal further than I should care to but which contains many valuable insights.

23. Bradley, *Shakespearean Tragedy*, p. 180.

CHAPTER IV

1. On the different materials of ancient Scottish history amalgamated to make *Macbeth*, see E. K. Chambers, *William Shakespeare: A Study of Facts and Problems* (London, 1930), I, 475–76; the New Variorum *Macbeth*, ed. H. H. Furness, Jr. (Philadelphia, 1903), pp. 379 ff.; W. Farnham, *Shakespeare's Tragic Frontier* (Berkeley and Los Angeles, 1950), pp. 79 ff.

2. An interesting reflection of the veneration felt for ancient historical authorities in Shakespeare's age occurs in a marginal Latin note (here translated) of Gabriel Harvey in his folio copy of Livy (Basel, 1555): "We have no historians nowadays of the stature of Livy and Tacitus. Grafton, Stow, and Holinshed are mere asses compared with them. These writers lack a sound historical method and any comprehensive view of history. Better things may be expected of Camden and Hakluyt."

3. See M. W. MacCallum, *Shakespeare's Roman Plays and their Background* (London, 1910).

4. Brutus's appeal to "honour" (I, ii, 85–89) curiously recalls Hotspur's more extravagant boast (*1 Henry IV*, I, iii, 201 ff.); and the portents of *Julius Caesar* are somewhat reminiscent of Glendower's account of the upheaval of nature at his birth, the one account perhaps a smiling parody of the other. Cf. also Hotspur's interview with Lady Percy (*1 Henry IV*, II, iii, 39 ff.) and Brutus's with Portia (*Julius Caesar*, II, i, 233 ff.).

5. F. G. Fleay, *A Chronicle History of the Life and Work of William Shakespeare* (London, 1886), pp. 215, 252; J. M. Robertson, *The Shakespeare Canon*, I (London, 1922), 66 ff.; see the judicious summing-up of E. K. Chambers, *William Shakespeare*, I, 398–99.

6. A recent example is Willard Farnham, *Shakespeare's Tragic Frontier*, pp. 3–4.

7. Dover Wilson, introduction to the New Cambridge edition of *Julius Caesar* (Cambridge, 1949), p. xxi.

8. *The Tragedy of Julius Caesar*, ed. G. L. Kittredge (Boston, etc., 1939), p. xiii.

9. H. M. Ayres, "Shakespeare's *Julius Caesar* in the Light of Some Other Versions," *Publications of the Modern Language Association of America*, XXV (1910), 183–227.

10. Granville Barker, *Prefaces to Shakespeare*, II (Princeton, 1951), 373.

11. Antony's role in this play will be considered in comparison with his role in *Antony and Cleopatra* in chapter VI, below.

12. For example, the rant of

> Danger knows full well
> That Caesar is more dangerous than he.
> We are two lions litter'd in one day,
> And I the elder and more terrible.

And yet, in real life such absurdity is not incompatible with greatness. We cannot doubt Shakespeare's just estimate of Caesar's greatness; but he had a lively sense of the ridiculousness of his more extravagant pretensions, and, doubtless, of the more extravagant worship of his memory, as his casual allusions elsewhere than in *Julius Caesar* suggest—"The hook-nos'd fellow of Rome," *2 Henry IV*, IV, iii, 45; "Caesar's thrasonical brag of 'I came, saw, and overcame,'" *As You Like It*, V, ii, 34. We may likewise recall that Polonius did once enact Julius Caesar (*Hamlet*, III, ii, 105 ff.).

13. Cassius understands Brutus best, as his masterful handling of him in I, ii shows. We might say that Cassius here flatters Brutus; and yet it is not so much that Brutus is subject to flattery as that he sincerely believes himself to be the model of virtue that Cassius describes—and with some justification; and Cassius really believes all that he says in compliment to Brutus, too.

14. See Pindar, *Isthm.* V, 16; Paul Elmer More, "Nemesis, or the Divine Envy," *Shelburne Essays, Second Series* (New York and London, 1905), pp. 219 ff.; E. R. Dodds, *The Greeks and the Irrational* (Berkeley and Los Angeles, 1951), pp. 29 ff.

15. Montaigne, "Apologie de Raimond Sebond," *Essais*, II, xii, *ad fin.*

16. "The Life of Marcus Brutus," in *Shakespeare's Plutarch*, ed. C. F. Tucker Brooke (London, 1909), I, 133–34; cf. II, 20.

17. Such reiterated or parallel episodes (II, i, 155 ff.; IV, iii, 196 ff.), already noticed as part of the technique of *Romeo and Juliet*, are an occasional feature of the technique of *Julius Caesar*. Cf. Cassius's flattery of Brutus (I, ii, 55 ff) with Decius's flattery of Caesar (II, ii, 92 ff); Cassius's interpretation of the portents of the storm to Casca (I, iii, 57 ff.) with Decius's interpretation of Calphurnia's dream (II, ii, 83 ff.); and the passages between (*a*) Brutus and Portia, (*b*) Brutus and his servant Lucius, which reiterate the point of Brutus's sensibility as the necessary qualification of his otherwise inflexible temper to make him recognizably human.

18. Aristotle, *Poetics*, 1453a, 10, 16. See Appendix I, below.

19. Granville Barker, *Prefaces to Shakespeare*, II, 390.

20. The cavil against the great quarrel scene of Act IV, which Bradley thought failed to advance the action, has been shown to be an unwarranted objection by a number of commentators, notably Kittredge, *The Tragedy of Julius Caesar*, notes to IV, iii; and Dover Wilson, *Julius Caesar*, New Cambridge ed., p. xx.

21. It is not to be supposed that Shakespeare's care to think himself into the historical milieu of the Roman plays extended to the unnecessary exactitude of avoiding any suggestions of the contemporaneous. Such suggestions are of course often calculated expressly for the sake of Shakespeare's contemporary audience. In his variation from the authentically ancient to the situation and

outlook of his own time, to suit his dramatic purposes, Shakespeare everywhere exercises a sovereign freedom and tact.

22. See, e.g., Stopford Brooke, *On Ten Plays of Shakespeare* (New York, 1905), p. 226; George Brandes, *William Shakespeare: A Critical Study*, trans. Wm. Archer and others (New York, 1935), pp. 537 ff.

23. J. E. Phillips, Jr., *The State in Shakespeare's Greek and Roman Plays* (New York, 1940).

24. A. C. Swinburne, *Shakespeare* (London and New York, 1909), p. 187; A. C. Bradley, "*Coriolanus*," in *A Miscellany* (London, 1931), pp. 73–104 (British Academy Shakespeare Lecture, 1912).

25. "The Life of Caius Martius Coriolanus," *Shakespeare's Plutarch*, ed. C. F. Tucker Brooke, II, 137, 142.

26. Her procedure here repeats the tactics of her appeal to Coriolanus in III, ii. The finally effective stroke is a speech of withering scorn (III, ii, 123–30; cf. V, iii, 178–82) which, from any man, would have cost his life.

27. A. C. Bradley, *Shakespearean Tragedy*, p. 84; cf. Bradley, *A Miscellany*, pp. 75, 93.

28. Granville Barker, *Prefaces to Shakespeare*, II, 152.

29. Sir Arthur Eddington, *The Nature of the Physical World* (Cambridge, 1948), p. 74.

CHAPTER V

1. It has also, at various times, been regarded as a comedy, as a "problem play," a "comicall satyre," and a political allegory. The preface to the 1609 quarto describes the play as a comedy; but this preface is a publisher's advertisement, of distinctly less authority than the opinion of the editors of the First Folio.

2. J. S. P. Tatlock, "The Chief Problem in Shakespeare," *Sewanee Review*, XXIV (1916), 129–47, a shorter version of his thorough study, "The Siege of Troy in Elizabethan Literature, especially in Shakespeare and Heywood," *Publications of the Modern Language Association of America*, XXX (1915), 673–770.

3. Peter Alexander, "*Troilus and Cressida*, 1609," *The Library*, 4th series, IX (December, 1928), 267.

4. Sir Walter Greg, "The Printing of Shakespeare's *Troilus and Cressida* in the First Folio," *Papers of the Bibliographical Society of America*, XLV (1951), 273–82. See also the same author's *The Shakespeare First Folio* (Oxford, 1955), pp. 338 ff.

5. In the following discussion, I am much indebted to the findings of Tatlock cited in note 2, above.

6. See Hyder E. Rollins, "The Troilus-Cressida Story from Chaucer to Shakespeare," *Publications of the Modern Language Association of America*, XXXII (1917), 383–429.

7. Tatlock, pp. 676 ff.; Rollins, pp. 388 ff.

8. The five plays are printed together in the third volume of the Pearson imprint of Heywood's dramatic works (London, 1874).

9. Tatlock, pp. 709 ff.; see also Allan Holaday, "Heywood's *Troia Britannica* and the Ages," *Journal of English and Germanic Philology*, XLV (1946), 430–39.

10. Pearson impr., III, 264.

11. This episode parallels in situation the council of *Troilus and Cressida*, II, ii. The council at Troy, either before or after the rape of Helen, is a feature of all the versions examined by Tatlock (p. 698, note 4).

12. The First Player's lines read somewhat like a Senecan messenger's account of the scene in Heywood. It is usual, however, to compare the First Player's Pyrrhus speech with the corresponding passage in Marlowe's *Dido* (II, i), and, in style, with that of the Bleeding Sergeant in *Macbeth* (I, ii).

13. *1 Iron Age* goes on to represent the deaths of Troilus and Achilles, the quarrel over Achilles' armour, and Ajax' suicide. For a tabulation of parallels, see Tatlock, pp. 744–46.

14. These instances are cited in detail by Tatlock, pp. 747 ff.

15. Pearson impr., pp. 299–300.

16. *Ibid.*, p. 351.

17 All of these points are closely parallel in *Troilus and Cressida* and *1 Iron Age*.

18. See the study of this tradition in Willard Farnham, *The Medieval Heritage of Elizabethan Tragedy* (Berkeley, 1936).

19. An important corrective of this view is contained in F. P. Wilson's recent argument that Shakespeare virtually led the way for the development of the chronicle history play with *2* and *3 Henry VI*; see his Clark Lectures, *Marlowe and the Early Shakespeare* (Oxford, 1953); see also a paper by the present writer, "*Philaster* and *Cymbeline*," *English Institute Essays*, 1951 (New York, 1952), pp. 146 ff.

20. See Tatlock, p. 737; and R. A. Small, *The Stage-Quarrel between Ben Jonson and the so-called Poetasters* (Breslau, 1899).

21. We may recall the famous triple pun in Aeschylus, ἑλέναυς, ἕλανδρος, ἑλέπτολις (*Agamemnon*, 692), which has been aptly rendered "Hell-to-ships, Hell-to-men, Hell-to-cities." Cf. *Troilus and Cressida*, II, ii, 110-12.

22. *Johnson on Shakespeare*, ed. Walter Raleigh (London, 1946), p. 21: "It may be observed, that in many of his plays the latter part is evidently neglected. When he found himself near the end of his work, and, in view of his reward, he

shortened the labour to snatch the profit. He therefore remits his efforts where he should most vigorously exert them, and his catastrophe is improbably produced or imperfectly represented." Though this is a generalization in Dr. Johnson's *Preface*, it is interesting to note how closely his opinion follows Dryden's strictures upon the plot of Shakespeare's *Troilus and Cressida* in the preface to Dryden's own version of the Troilus and Cressida story.

23. See especially R. A. Small, *Stage-Quarrel*, pp. 147 ff.

24. R. K. Presson has recently argued that the 1598 version of Chapman's translation did importantly influence Shakespeare's treatment of the war theme in *Troilus and Cressida* (see *Shakespeare's Troilus and Cressida & the Legends of Troy*, Madison, Wisc., 1953). Many of his citations of parallel passages doubtless are relevant. It seems likely that Shakespeare would be interested in Chapman's translation when the first instalment of it appeared in print, if not before, and that he may have taken some useful hints from it for his play. But the spirit of Shakespeare's *Troilus and Cressida* is far indeed from the spirit of Homer's *Iliad*, or of any part of Chapman's translation of it. The fact of critical importance is that Shakespeare's play belongs in the mediaeval tradition of the Trojan War story.

25. G. Wilson Knight, *The Wheel of Fire* (4th ed., London, 1949), pp. 207–39.

26. For example, in the opinion that "Timon is the archetype and norm of all tragedy."

27. E. K. Chambers, *William Shakespeare: A Study of Facts and Problems* (London, 1930), I, 442, 480–81.

28. *Ibid.*, I, 480 ff., and *Shakespeare: A Survey* (London, 1925), pp. 268–76; see also Una Ellis-Fermor in *Review of English Studies*, XVIII (1942), 270 ff.

29. The production of the play at the Old Vic in 1952, further discussed below, skilfully emphasized the theme of the play by producing a sumptuous "golden" atmosphere, in the splendid costume of Timon—later to become sadly tarnished—and corresponding effects of stage properties, lighting, etc.

30. An evidence of the tentative and unrevised state of the text has been shrewdly pointed out by Terence Spencer, who calculates that Shakespeare, when he began the play, did not know the value of a Greek talent, learned it before he finished the surviving draft, but did not correct his inconsistencies with reference to it; see "Shakespeare Learns the Value of Money: The Dramatist at Work on *Timon of Athens*," *Shakespeare Survey*, 6 (1953), 75–90.

31. See William Empson, "Timon's Dog," in *The Structure of Complex Words* (London, 1951), pp. 175–84.

32. Both versions of the contradictory epitaphs reported from Timon's tomb, in one of which he names himself and in the other wishes to be anonymous (V, iv, 70–73) seem to be prepared for earlier, in IV, iii, 379–81 and V, i, 218–21.

33. There is no available evidence for dating the play precisely. It appears to belong to the period 1605–8. Willard Farnham, *Shakespeare's Tragic Frontier* (Berkeley and Los Angeles, 1950), p. 7, regards it as preceding *King Lear*. A. C. Bradley, E. K. Chambers, and others would place it after *King Lear*.

34. The suggestion that *Troilus and Cressida* may have been designed to please a particularly sophisticated audience at one of the Inns of Court has been widely regarded as plausible; but there is no dependable evidence to support such a conjecture, and it has been emphatically rejected in some recent discussions of the play; see especially *Troilus and Cressida*, New Variorum edition, ed. H. N. Hillebrand and T. W. Baldwin (Philadelphia, 1953), p. 356. That the play was not a popular success is sufficiently indicated by the preface to the 1609 quarto.

CHAPTER VI

1. *The Imperial Theme* (3rd ed., London, 1951), pp. 210 ff.
2. *Shakespeare's Plutarch*, ed. C. F. Tucker Brooke (London, 1909), II, 35–36.
3. *Ibid.*, II, 16.
4. *Julius Caesar*, II, i, 188–89.
5. *Shakespeare's Plutarch*, II, 47–55.
6. *Ibid.*, II, 55: "Then began this pestilent plague and mischief of Cleopatra's love (which had slept a long time, and seemed to have been utterly forgotten, and that Antonius had given place to better counsel) again to kindle, and to be in force, as soon as Antonius came near Syria."
7. *Shakespeare's Plutarch*, II, 97, 101.
8. Kittredge (*Antony and Cleopatra*, Boston, etc., 1941, p. 188) points out that, in Plutarch's Greek, Octavius's reply means that many ways of death are open to *Antony*; but North rendered the ambiguity of Amyot's French, "Caesar luy feit response, qu'il auoit beaucoup d'autres moyens de mourir que celuy-là," and thus made available for Shakespeare a much finer irony than the original contained.
9. *Shakespeare's Plutarch*, II, 98, 118–19.
10. One of the notable contrasts of the play is that of the degrees of "honour": in Antony, whose honour is extravagant and unthinking but generous and heroic; in Pompey, whose honour is naïve and hypocritical; and in Octavius, who has no sense of honour but rather a sense of expediency. We may be reminded of *1 Henry IV* where degrees of honour—though not quite of the same "kinds"—are illustrated by Hotspur, Prince Hal, and Falstaff.

11. A good recent discussion of the relation of Shakespeare's play to Daniel's tragedy, and also, possibly, to Daniel's *Letter from Octavia to Marcus Antonius*, and to the Countess of Pembroke's *Antonius* (translated from the French of Robert Garnier) is contained in Willard Farnham, *Shakespeare's Tragic Frontier*, (Berkeley and Los Angeles, 1950), pp. 148 ff.

12. Samuel Daniel, *Delia and Rosamond augmented; Cleopatra* (London, 1594), sigs. 12r-15r. The remainder of the play follows the pattern of events in Plutarch's account of Cleopatra's last days and has little or no bearing on Shakespeare's play.

13. A. C. Bradley, "Shakespeare's *Antony and Cleopatra*," in *Oxford Lectures on Poetry* (2nd ed., London, 1950).

14. *Three Plays for Puritans* (London, 1901), pp. xxvii-xxviii.

15. Hardin Craig, *Shakespeare: A Historical and Critical Study with Annotated Texts of Twenty-one Plays* (Chicago, etc., 1931), p. 726. Cf. the recent discussion of the text in W. W. Greg, *The Shakespeare First Folio* (Oxford, 1955), especially the opinion (p. 398) that behind the Folio text "lies a very carefully written copy, elaborately prepared by the author for the stage with directions respecting the manner of production."

16. *Johnson on Shakespeare*, ed. Walter Raleigh (London, 1946), p. 180: "The events, of which the principal are described according to history, are produced without any art of connection or care of disposition."

17. Granville Barker, *Prefaces to Shakespeare*, I (Princeton, 1947), 371 ff.

18. Bradley, *Oxford Lectures on Poetry*, p. 292.

19. E. M. W. Tillyard, *Shakespeare's History Plays* (London, 1948).

20. Perhaps *Othello* would be considered by some to fall under this heading as well. Yet it is not the love of Othello and Desdemona that brings tragedy, but the distrust, the jealousy—or, more precisely, the malice of Iago and the blindness of Othello.

21. See Wilfrid Perrett, *The Story of King Lear* (*Palaestra*, no. XXXV; Berlin, 1904), which traces the story from the simple and universally disseminated folk-tale of the daughter who told the old king, her father, that she loved him like salt, to the many versions extant among Shakespeare's immediate predecessors and contemporaries, including the contemporary drama of *King Leir*, by an unknown author, which is thought to have provided an important part of Shakespeare's material—see *The History of King Leir*, in the Malone Society Reprints (London, 1908). See also Madeleine Doran, "Elements in the Composition of *King Lear*," *Studies in Philology*, XXX (1933), 34–58; R. A. Law, "Holinshed's Leir Story and Shakespeare's," *ibid.*, XLVII (1950), 42–50.

22. For all the doubts about whether Horatio is a native of Denmark or not (see G. F. Bradby, *Short Studies in Shakespeare*, London, 1929, pp. 145–50), he

lives in the contrast he affords with Hamlet, and above all in Hamlet's famous tribute to him (III, ii, 59 ff.). So too Enobarbus underlines for us, by his commentary, Antony's imprudence, his disregard of the course of reason, and, finally, his generosity; and Enobarbus seems thus to possess something of the qualities he desires in Antony. Kent, to be sure, warns Lear of his folly with a vehement insistence that sufficiently individualizes him in the earlier part of the action, and he is similarly blunt with Oswald, with Regan and Cornwall. But this trait fades as he supports Lear in the storm; and, in the final scene, his symbolic role is plainly marked.

23. A. C. Bradley, *Shakespearean Tragedy* (London, 1904, 1950), pp. 443 ff.

24. See R. B. Heilman, *This Great Stage* (Baton Rouge, 1948), pp. 41 ff., 173 ff.

25. The same symbolic contrast between court and country is suggested in both plays, though this motif is not peculiar to any particular period of Shakespeare's writing and it figures most notably throughout the comedies. In *Lear* and *Cymbeline* this contrast is part of the larger, pervasive contrast on the familiar commonplaces of "nature" and "art," likewise observable in other plays, notably *The Winter's Tale*. On this theme in *Lear,* see John F. Danby, *Shakespeare's Doctrine of Nature* (London, 1949). For the intellectual background, see especially A. O. Lovejoy and George Boas, *Primitivism and Related Ideas in Antiquity* (Baltimore, 1935).

26. How *Cymbeline* came to be included among the tragedies in the First Folio has never been explained. Probably it was through an accident or oversight of some kind.

27. Bradley, *Shakespearean Tragedy,* pp. 252 ff.

28. *Greek Tragedy* (2nd ed., London, 1950), p. 401.

CHAPTER VII

1. "The Argument of Milton's *Comus,*" *University of Toronto Quarterly*, XI (1941), 46–71; "Nature and Grace in *The Faerie Queene,*" *ELH*, XVI (1949), 194–228.

2. See especially Douglas Bush, *The Renaissance and English Humanism* (Toronto, 1939, 1956).

3. Hence the frequent Elizabethan use of "grace" in the sense of God's providence; see Woodhouse, *ELH*, XVI (1949), 207.

4. The fullest explanation of these orders, of the utmost importance as a background for Shakespeare's plays, is contained in Richard Hooker, *Of the Laws of Ecclesiastical Polity*; see especially I, iii, 2–3; V, App. i.

APPENDIX I

1. *Poetics*, 1453a, 10, 16.

2. See S. H. Butcher, *Aristotle's Theory of Poetry and Fine Art* (4th ed., London, 1932), p. 329.

3. H. D. F. Kitto, *Greek Tragedy*, pp. 111 ff.

4. *Poetics*, 1453a, 7–10; trans. S. H. Butcher, p. 45. 1453a, 16 repeats the reference as "a great error" (ἁμαρτίαν μεγάλην).

5. Butcher, *Aristotle's Theory*, pp. 302–33.

6. *Aristotle on the Art of Poetry*, ed. Ingram Bywater (Oxford, 1909), p. 215.

7. Butcher, *Aristotle's Theory*, p. 321.

8. I do not choose Mr. Farnham's argument about the Aristotelian "flaw" (if I may so describe it) with any invidious intention, but rather because it affords a systematic appeal to a criterion which is often invoked by other Shakespearian commentators but more casually and with less regard for definition. Though I think the argument about the "flaw" as applied to Shakespeare's characters a doubtful argument, I have a high regard for Professor Farnham's study and I have frequently profited from it in these pages.

9. Farnham, *Shakespeare's Tragic Frontier* (Berkeley and Los Angeles, 1950), p. 44.

10. *Ibid.*

11. *Bacchae*, 1388–92; etc.

APPENDIX II

1. T. W. Baldwin, *Shakspere's Petty School* (Urbana, Ill, 1943); *William Shakspere's Small Latine & Lesse Greeke* (Urbana, Ill, 1944); *William Shakspere's Five-Act Structure* (Urbana, Ill, 1947).

2. See T. W. Baldwin, *The Organization and Personnel of the Shakespearean Company* (Princeton, 1927); Alfred Harbage, "Elizabethan Acting," *Publications of the Modern Language Association of America*, LIV (1939), 685–708; A. C. Sprague, *Shakespeare and the Actors* (New York, 1941); B. L. Joseph, *Elizabethan Acting* (Oxford, 1951).

3. See especially Alfred Harbage, *Shakespeare's Audience* (New York, 1941); *Shakespeare and the Rival Traditions* (New York, 1952).

4. "Of Education," in John Milton, *Prose Selections*, ed. Merritt Y. Hughes (New York, 1947), p. 45.

5. This brief statement greatly over-simplifies the actual process of development in the Middle Ages, a process which has been learnedly studied in a series

of articles by Richard McKeon: "Literary Criticism and the Concept of Imitation in Antiquity"; "Rhetoric in the Middle Ages"; "Poetry and Philosophy in the Twelfth Century: The Renaissance of Rhetoric," in *Critics and Criticism Ancient and Modern*, ed. R. S. Crane (Chicago, 1952). See also an informative study by P. O. Kristeller, "Humanism and Scholasticism in the Italian Renaissance," *Byzantion*, XVII (1944–45), 346–74.

6. *Ep. ad Fam.*, I, ix, 23, in R. Y. Tyrell, *The Correspondence of M. Tullius Cicero* (Dublin and London, 1879 et seq.), II, 178–79.

7. *De Oratore*, II, 90–92.

8. *Inst. Orat.*, X, ii, 24–26.

9. These exercises have been explained at length in T. W. Baldwin, *Small Latine*; see also Donald L. Clark, *Milton at St. Paul's School* (New York, 1948); Rosemond Tuve, *Elizabethan and Metaphysical Imagery* (Chicago, 1947); Madeleine Doran, *Endeavors of Art* (Madison, Wis., 1954). The example of Demosthenes and other Greek classics was not commonly available to the Renaissance schoolboy because of the comparatively undeveloped state of Greek studies, though heroic efforts were made to study Greek even by those who had no adequate lexicons, grammars, or other such tools at their disposal.

10. When one deliberately imitated ancient models such as Cicero, Plautus, Terence, or Seneca, it was a high compliment to be thought to approximate closely to one's model. The highest trope of literary compliment in the age of Petrarch and Coluccio Salutati was to call a writer "the ape of Cicero." Later, the increasing emphasis upon "decorum" modified this view; yet it remained more or less characteristic of the Renaissance humanists.

11. Many citations from Cicero and other ancient authorities could be given; but it is probably enough to note that the principle is central and constantly reiterated in Cicero's *De Oratore* and *Orator*.

12. Poliziano, *Opera* (Lyons, 1550), I, 240.

13. *Opera* (Leyden, 1703–6), I, 991b.

14. Lytton Strachey, *Books and Characters* (London, 1922), p. 60.

INDEX